*The 1864 field party of the California Geological Survey.*
*From left: James T. Gardner, Richard D. Cotter, William H. Brewer,*
*and Clarence King.*

# THE EXPLORER KING

*Adventure, Science, and the Great Diamond Hoax—*
*Clarence King in the Old West*

## ROBERT WILSON

SCRIBNER
New York   London   Toronto   Sydney

SCRIBNER
1230 Avenue of the Americas
New York, NY 10020

SCRIBNER and design are trademarks of Macmillan Library Reference USA, Inc.,
used under license by Simon & Schuster, the publisher of this work.

Maps by Doug Stern

DESIGNED BY ERICH HOBBING

Set in Caslon

For information about special discounts for bulk purchases,
please contact Simon & Schuster Special Sales at
1-800-456-6798 or business@simonandschuster.com

Manufactured in the United States of America

1   3   5   7   9   10   8   6   4   2

Library of Congress Cataloging-in-Publication Data

Wilson, Robert, [date].
The explorer King : adventure, science, and the great diamond hoax,
Clarence King in the Old West / Robert Wilson.
p. cm.
1. King, Clarence, 1842–1901. 2. Geologists—United States—Biography. 3. West (U.S.)—
Intellectual life. I. Title.

QE22.K5W55 2006
551.092—dc22
[B]
2005053598

ISBN-13: 978-0-7432-6025-1
ISBN-10: 0-7432-6025-2

*To Martha*

# CONTENTS

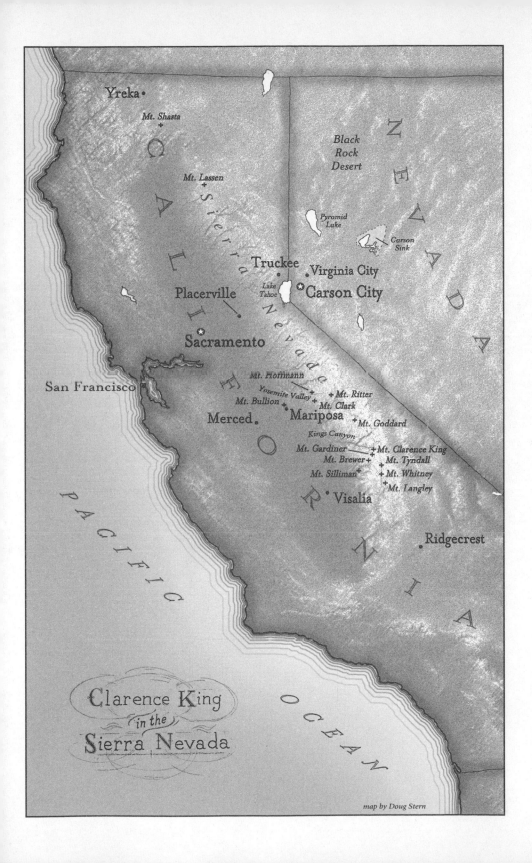

Clarence King
in the
Sierra Nevada

map by Doug Stern

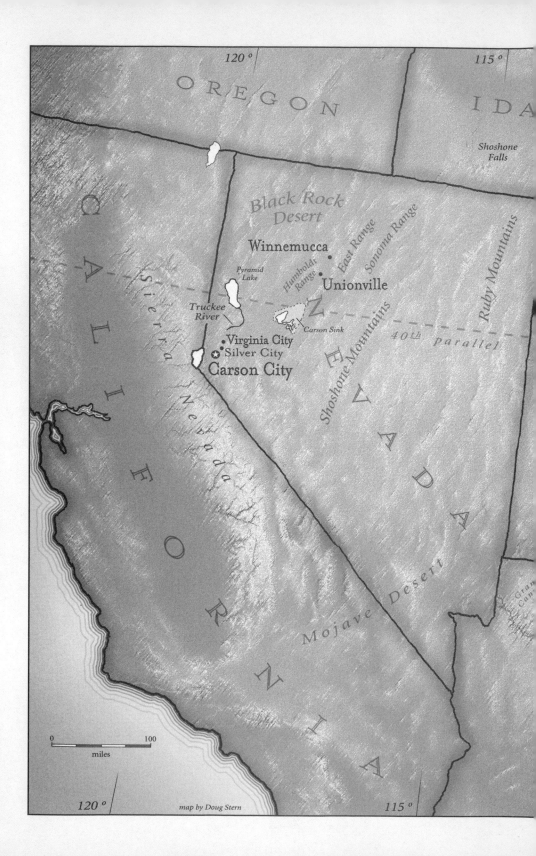

110°

105°

ROCKY

WYOMING

South Pass

Great
Salt
Lake

Green River

Black Butte Station

Ft. Bridger

Cheyenne

Salt
Lake City

Kings Peak

Mt. Agassiz

Browns Park

Uinta
Mountains

Estes Park

site of
Diamond Hoax

Longs Peak

Denver

UTAH

COLORADO

Colorado River

Grand
Canyon

MOUNTAINS

HUMBOLDT

N

the
Fortieth
Parallel
Exploration

W

E

ARIZONA

NEW

S

MEXICO

110°

105°

# THE
# EXPLORER
# KING

# The Little White House

*Clarence King at about forty.*

In the early months of 1881, in a boxy three-story mansion on Lafayette Square in Washington, D.C., a small group of friends fell into the rhythm of meeting nearly every day at teatime for witty, often scathing conversation about the city that churned along around them. The Greek Revival structure where they met, white with a modest portico supported by Ionic columns, was known in the neighborhood as the little White House, and it faced that other more imposing White House just across the square. The smaller residence was rented by Henry Adams, whose grandfather and great-grandfather had inhabited the larger one, and by Henry's wife, Clover. The couple had just returned to Washington after eighteen months in Europe while Henry researched a history of the United States in the years when Jefferson and Madison were president. During the two winters of an earlier residence in the city, when Henry was working on a biography and a novel at a yellow house draped in wisteria a block east on H Street, Clover and Henry had stood back from Washington society, which then as now was all about job seeking and job keeping. They favored a smaller circle of friends selected for their ability to engage and amuse them. This exclusivity had caused their social stock, already fairly high given Henry's lineage, to rise; an invitation to either of the H Street houses was valued in proportion to the difficulty of achieving it. Even senators were sometimes snubbed, although Henry James probably goes too far when in his story "Pandora" he has a character based on Henry Adams say, "Hang it . . . let us be vulgar and have some fun—let us invite the President." Adams himself said, "Socially speaking, we are very near most of the powerful people, either as enemies or friends."

The inner circle within this wider group of friends consisted of one other couple, John and Clara Hay, and one bachelor, Clarence King. When they could, the five of them met each day at five o'clock during the winter of 1881, and would often share dinner and then talk well into the evening. John Hay was ending a brief term as assistant secretary of state, and Clara, the daughter of a rich businessman from Cleveland, was living in town with him that winter. Hay had first come to Washington two decades earlier as a young man, employed as personal secretary to the new president, Abraham Lincoln, and had resided in the White House until the assassination. In the intervening years he had worked in the diplomatic corps in Europe, written editorials for the *New York Tribune*, published several books, including a popular collection of poems, and begun a massive biography of Lincoln that would occupy him for a decade. After his marriage to Clara in 1874 he moved with her to Cleveland to help her father tend to his millions. When Hay went to Washington for the State Department job in 1879, he left

Clara and their young children behind, and took a room at Wormley's, a comfortable hotel on 15th and H streets.

There Hay fell in with another resident who was an acquaintance from New York, a brilliant scientist, explorer, and writer who at the age of thirty-seven had already done enough living to fill several lifetimes. This was Clarence King. He was in Washington serving as the first director of the United States Geological Survey, which had been established by Congress in 1879 after intense lobbying by King and his friend John Wesley Powell. Hay and King were soon together all the time, meeting for breakfast and attending social functions in the evenings. Before long the two of them and a third man, General Francis A. Walker, the superintendent of the tenth national census then under way, rented a house at 1400 Massachusetts Avenue, which Hay referred to as the "bachelor castle." They kept a private dining room at Wormley's, where the food was much better than at home and where, according to one man who sometimes joined them for lunch, "I doubt whether there ever was table-talk more brilliant than that to which we listened in that room."

King basked in the admiration of the other four members of the group that gathered at the Adamses' house that winter, who were drawn not only to his table talk but to his charm, wit, and intelligence. "No one is as good company," Clover wrote to her father. Henry, who had known King for a decade, had also taken a serious interest in his scientific pursuits, and through King was drawn into what Adams's biographer Ernest Samuels calls the "scientific renaissance" taking place in Washington at the time. Even Clara, the one member of the group who was not dazzlingly verbal, must have admired King, given his admiration for her. He was not often drawn to women of his own class, but he found the handsome Clara "calm and grand," a person who represented "the best of the 19th century." So close did the five of them become that winter that they began to call themselves the Five of Hearts, a little joke but also an acknowledgment of their mutual affection and of the exclusivity of their club. The name evoked some jealousy and even a nasty rumor or two among the other residents of Lafayette Square. But within the group the name was a bit of harmless whimsy, soon reinforced by notepaper with the five of hearts engraved on it. King took the joke to its extreme when in 1885 he gave Henry and Clover a china tea set, complete with heart-shape cups, teapot, and a double-heart sugar bowl. Each piece carried the face of a clock whose hands showed five, teatime, the hour when the gossip would begin.

Both King and Hay served as emissaries to the other three from the world that their salon held at bay, the daily give-and-take of Washington politics. King, especially, as the head of a government bureau, had to keep up his contacts with members of Congress, whose yearly appropriations, and the meddling in his affairs that went with them, were necessary to his success. Because Wormley's, owned and run by the black son of a former slave, was considered to be the best hotel in Washington, congressmen and cabinet officers often lived there; it was a place where backroom deals were made, including the compromise in 1877 that made Rutherford B. Hayes the winner of that contested presidential election. All of the five friends knew important cabinet officers, foreign diplomats, and the more interesting sort of congressman, and for all their aloofness they were familiar with the inside of the other White House. As Ernest Samuels puts it, "President Hayes was the first of a long line of Presidents with whom Adams was to endure an intimacy of sorts." King would go regularly to Mrs. Hayes's Saturday receptions at the White House, where the Marine Band played, and at the insistence of the First Lady, known as "Lemonade Lucy," no alcohol, not even wine, was offered. But the guests would include a slew of legislators King needed to see, or such potentates as Treasury Secretary John Sherman or Interior Secretary Carl Schurz, who had helped King get his job and was now his boss as well as his friend. It would all make entertaining chatter for the others at 1607 H Street, the little White House across the square.

For much of the summer and fall of 1880, King had been out west, mixing public and private business while trying to recover from a wicked combination of illnesses of the body and the spirit—

fatigue and depression on top of a recurring malaria mixed with dysentery that caused him to drop thirty pounds, at least temporarily. When he returned to Washington in early 1881, he had given up the bachelor's castle, and there were no rooms available at Wormley's. Rather than share a room at the hotel, he moved in with the Adamses at 1607, where there were six bedrooms and two baths on the second floor, and where six servants looked after the three of them.

Downstairs, the house was a model of Victorian elegance. Carpenters had built bookshelves for Henry's library, and plumbers, painters, paperhangers, and other workmen had spent two months in the fall preparing the house for the Adamses' fifteen wagonloads of furniture, objets d'art, paintings, and Oriental rugs. (The preparations included one highly unsettling event. One of the painters, a German whom Adams scolded for not doing a better job, "lost his temper with Henry," Clover wrote, "saying he 'couldn't please him.'" Both of the Adamses tried to calm him down and thought they'd succeeded. But later that day he went home and cut his wife's throat with a putty knife.) But the rest of the workmen proved sane enough to finish the job, and the walls were hung with drawings by Rembrandt, Michelangelo, Raphael, and others. In the library, beneath the thirteen-foot ceilings, were an oil painting by Constable, a Turner watercolor of the Rhône River Valley, two Joshua Reynolds portraits, and forty-four other watercolors. Two Turners were among the oils in the dining room, and thirty-two prints graced Henry's study. There were Japanese vases on display, as well as Oriental bronzes and porcelains, and rugs from Shiraz, Kashmir, Kurdistan, Bokhara, and elsewhere. Potted palms added another touch of Victorian exoticism.

King held court in the drawing room, where dark red leather armchairs, small enough to be comfortable for the diminutive Henry and Clover, were arrayed. At five feet six, King was the tallest of the five. He was a handsome man who had been a beautiful boy, and in spite of his recent illnesses his hazel eyes held the liveliness and confidence of one who had always been adored by those around him. His short-cropped blond hair was receding and he had a beard trimmed low off his sun-darkened cheeks. Although he retained much of the physical strength that had made him a famous mountaineer in his youth, he had lost his athletic build. Now he was gaunt from his recent illnesses, but generally he carried extra weight that even good tailoring could not hide, a girth which in that age gave King the look of a prosperity he could not always claim. Too many nights of sleeping on the ground out west had begun to make his joints creaky with arthritis. When he spoke, his voice was soft, but his talk could make a room go silent around him.

Like any other form of performance in those days, conversation was an art that died at birth, and unlike a concert or a play it left no score or script to hint at what the experience of hearing it must have been like. The few snatches of his talk that friends wrote down consisted mainly of puns, for which King had a propensity. None of these witticisms travels the years very successfully, but then not many puns succeed on the page as well as they can in conversation. One of the better surviving examples of King's spontaneous wit comes from the summer of 1883, when he was in England visiting one of his literary heroes, the art critic John Ruskin, who happened to be selling off his famous collection of Turner paintings. Because King had charmed Ruskin so thoroughly, the older man took "King to his heart and poured lyric toffy all over him," according to John Hay. Ruskin offered King the chance to buy either of the two best Turners remaining in his collection. King bought them both, saying, "One good Turner deserves another."

Perhaps the closest thing to hearing the rhythm and tenor of King's speech comes in Henry Adams's novel *Esther*, in which the character George Strong is closely patterned on King. In it, Esther has decided to marry a clergyman, although she suffers from the religious doubt of that post-Darwinian time. Strong is a scientist, a professor of paleontology who, like King, has spent years in the field as a "practical geologist." He represents the new religion of science. Esther begins a crucial exchange between them:

"Will you answer me a question? Say yes or no!"

"That depends on the question, Mistress Esther! Old birds are not to be caught in old traps. State your question, as we say in the lecture-room."

"Is religion true?"

"I thought so! Cousin Esther, I love you as much as I love any one in this cold world, but I can't answer your question. I can tell you all about the mound-builders or cave-men, so far as is known, but I could not tell you the difference between the bones of a saint and those of a heathen. Ask me something easier! Ask me whether science is true!"

"Is science true?"

"No!"

"Then why do you believe in it?"

"I don't believe in it."

"Then why do you belong to it?"

"Because I want to help in making it truer. Now, Esther, just take this matter coolly! You are bothered, I suppose, by the idea that you can't possibly believe in miracles and mysteries, and therefore can't make a good wife for Hazard. You might just as well make yourself unhappy by doubting whether you would make a good wife to me because you can't believe the first axiom in Euclid. There is no science that does not begin by requiring you to believe the incredible."

"Are you telling me the truth?"

"I tell you the solemn truth that the doctrine of the Trinity is not so difficult to accept for a working proposition as any of the axioms of physics."

*Esther* is a novel of ideas, and those ideas, like its dialogue, belong of course to its author. But it is also a roman à clef, and many of the characters in it are closely drawn from people Adams knew, including Esther herself, who in her religious doubt resembles his wife, Clover. When Adams describes Strong as "an intelligent man, with a figure made for action, an eye that hated rest, and a manner naturally sympathetic," we can take it as a description of King. If a novel of ideas is to succeed, as *Esther* does, its characters can't just be cartoons of the ideas themselves. In this sense, King was a good model for Strong, a man whose science fills him with doubts rather than with certainties. King himself was fervently religious as a boy and young man, but after his education at the Sheffield Scientific School at Yale and his entry into the country's intellectual elite in the years after Darwin's *On the Origin of Species* had seeded religious doubt in the minds of thinking people, King's religious beliefs became less dogmatic. In the novel, Esther asks Strong if he believes in God. "Not in a personal one" was Strong's reply. "Or in future rewards or punishments?" Esther continues. "Old women's nursery tales!" he says. King himself continued to make references to God throughout his life, as in an important speech he gave at the Sheffield School in 1877, when he speaks of "He who brought to bear that mysterious energy we call life upon primeval matter." As King's principal biographer, Thurman Wilkins, puts it, "King's final theology, whatever it was . . . enabled him to face death calmly and without fear."

Given his promise, his courage, his intelligence, his energy, and his optimism, King was for many of the people who knew him an exemplar of the best aspects of America after the Civil War. John Hay would call him "the best and brightest man of his generation," and Adams said of King that "men worshipped not so much their friend, as the ideal American they all wanted to be." King crossed the continent for the first time at the age of twenty-one, in 1863, and after the war the nation itself followed him, pouring into the West, especially after the transcontinental railroad was completed in 1869. When he arrived in California, King went to work for a major geological survey of the state then under way. In his several years with the survey he was, as far as history knew, the first man to climb some of the highest peaks in the Sierra Nevada, and he named several of them. On these climbs, King and a companion would scale sheer cliffs of rock or ice, leap across precipices, lower one another down level by level with ropes, sleep through freezing nights without so much as a blanket—holed up under outcroppings or in small caves or clinging to bare rock that held a bit of the sun's heat. They would often go for several days, expending tremendous amounts of energy to climb, with only a few biscuits in their pockets for nourishment. King also crossed deserts, survived a killer snowstorm, swam a raging, rain-swollen river, and viewed stupendous sites of natural beauty, from Yosemite, which he was the first person to survey, to the Shoshone Falls of the Snake River, to the Pacific as seen from mountaintops a hundred miles inland. He was a close and at times bemused observer of the people who were establishing California in the decades after the Gold Rush, and of the rough, often deadly communities in which they lived.

Much of this King wrote about in the early 1870s in articles for the *Atlantic Monthly*, which were collected in 1872 in a book called *Mountaineering in the Sierra Nevada*. The book tells one of the last adventure stories of America's own youth, the final chapter of its exploration; it was popular in its time on both sides of the Atlantic and is still considered to be a classic work of nature writing. But during the decade of 1863 to 1873, King did more than wander the Sierra Nevada and write well about it. Soon after reaching the West, King conceived the idea of leading an important scientific expedition of his own. By 1867, when he was only twenty-five, he had convinced Congress to fund what would grow into one of the great scientific projects of the nineteenth century, the Fortieth Parallel Survey, and to put him in charge. King assembled a team of leading scientists to study the geography, geology, paleontology, biology, and meteorology of the Great Basin, focusing on a hundred-mile-wide swath along the path of the transcontinental railroad from the eastern half of Wyoming across the Rockies to the eastern slope of the Sierra Nevada, more than eighty thousand square miles in all. The survey took five years to complete, and the seven volumes reporting on its findings appeared throughout the 1870s, culminating in King's own important scientific work, *Systematic Geology*, which used his observations for the survey to explain the whole subject of geology as understood at the time. This work helped establish a new paradigm of the western adventurer in the second half of the nineteenth century—the scientist-explorer, who seeks knowledge rather than territory or riches. In 1872, King became a national hero for exposing a scam involving the faked discovery of a diamond field in northwest Colorado, within the parameters of the Fortieth Parallel Survey. The exact location was secret, but King found it and proved that the land there had been salted with diamonds—that uncut stones had been buried with the intention to deceive. If not for King, thousands of people could have lost millions of dollars by buying stock in the venture, and his exposé made his name familiar to newspaper readers across the country and in London.

King was cast again as a representative figure—the objective man of science standing up against the forces of greed. But his story would turn out to be much more complicated than that. In the years after the diamond swindle exposé, King would, as Adams puts it in his famous autobiography, *The Education of Henry Adams,* begin "to seek his private fortune in the west." King started in ranching and ended in banking, but for most of the second half of his life he was as avid as those drawn in by the diamond hoax for riches dug from the earth. Even while serving as the director of the U.S. Geological Survey he made trips to Mexico in search of gold and silver mines that could be bought and exploited with new mining methods. As Adams puts it late in *The Education,* King "had played for many millions . . . but the result was still in doubt, and meanwhile he was passing the best years of his life underground." King was not literally down in the mines much, of course. But he was often on the back of a burro looking for the next mine—the one that would make him rich. Or he was in Boston, New York, or London raising more investment money from his increasingly skeptical friends.

One way of looking at the whole course of King's life is to see it as divided between the two things that replaced religious certainty in America after Darwin, those two new secular religions of the second half of the nineteenth century: science and greed. Before the diamond hoax, King devoted his life to science; after it, he increasingly devoted himself to wealth. But the two halves were not neatly divided, because King tried to exploit his scientific achievements and reputation to make a fortune. In the country at large, science and greed were also joining forces, not only in extracting the mineral wealth of the West, but in crisscrossing the continent with railroads and telegraph lines and building cities overnight where dusty settlements had stood. The forces of science and greed struggled within King, who had an aristocratic disdain for commerce even as he pursued it. If he didn't lose his soul as a result, then he certainly put it at risk.

In his biography of John Wesley Powell, *Beyond the Hundredth Meridian,* Wallace Stegner refers contemptuously to King's willingness "to go whoring after Mexican gold mines." When King quit the U.S. Geological Survey in March of 1881, he told President Garfield that he was leaving to resume his scientific career. Stegner writes, "His scientific work after 1880 is negligible, even trivial, and his days and nights after the survey were obviously not spent over scientific books. He quit the Geological Survey because he frankly wanted to be rich." But Stegner overstates the case, wishing to make his man Powell look better at King's expense. Stegner's view comes out of his own time and place, that of a twentieth-century western environmentalist who quite rightly deplored what the combination of science and greed had done to too many of the magnificent landscapes of the West—as well as to the people who had first inhabited them. But King lived in what Mark Twain helped name the Gilded Age, and most of King's contemporaries felt as Adams did, that there was nothing wrong in King's aspiring to enrich himself, and even something admirable about it. In *The Education,* Adams writes (in the third-person voice of that great book), "Hay and Adams had risked nothing and never played for high stakes. King had followed the ambitious course."

What King achieved as an explorer-scientist and a writer in the first half of his life ought to have made his name as well known today as that of John Wesley Powell or Bret Harte. But his achievements have mostly been forgotten, and to the extent that he is remembered at all it is as the friend of Henry Adams, and for the extravagant way that Adams and Hay praise him in *The Education.* Is it because he turned from science to the pursuit of wealth that King has been forgotten, or because he did not succeed in becoming rich? Another way of breaking down the two halves of King's life is to say that he succeeded in the first half and failed in the second. After leaving his job in Washington, King lived another twenty years. He traveled the world and knew almost everyone worth knowing in Europe and the United States. He had as much raw energy for business as he had had for science, but as the months grew into years and the mines either failed or produced only modest profits, it became obvious that King had all the credentials to make a fortune but lacked something else. Some people called that something luck, but the problem almost certainly arose from within King himself. As he lived more and more for fine food and wine, for collecting works of art and famous friends (among them the Prince of Wales, who would become Edward VII, and Henry James), he talked about producing new scientific or literary works. But all he did was talk.

The distractions that kept him from serious intellectual undertakings must have contributed to his inability to succeed in mining and later in banking. Friends like Adams and Hay said King lacked the ruthlessness for business, and blamed the age, but others, including those friends whose investments King had solicited and helped lose, felt that the problem was inattentiveness. Years later, the critic Van Wyck Brooks would blame King's failures on a lack of mental toughness to match the physical toughness he had demonstrated in the West in his youth: "For sensitive intellectuals, like Clarence King . . . the reckless life which the West implied, its hardships and fever of speculation, meant ruined health and broken souls and madness."

One other aspect of King's later years might have contributed to his undeserved obscurity today. Throughout his life King was drawn to women of other classes and races than his own, and along with Adams believed that dark-skinned women represented a primitive female ideal. Sometime around the beginning of 1888, King fell in love with an African-American nursemaid he met at a friend's house in lower Manhattan. Her name was Ada Copeland. Now in his midforties, King had never been married before, and had been engaged only once. But in a matter of months he married Ada in a ceremony that included all of the matrimonial traditions except a license. He kept the marriage secret from his family and friends, even as he and Ada produced five children together, and he supported her in a house in Brooklyn where he only occasionally lived. But he was so worried that the relationship and then the marriage would be discovered, by his mother and by society at large, that he even hid his identity from Ada, telling her that his name was James Todd. At the ceremony she became Ada Todd. She learned his real identity only as he was dying, in 1901, after they'd been married for thirteen years. King's letters to Ada suggest that he loved her and their children unreservedly, but the pressure of keeping his secret even from Adams and Hay seems to have affected his physical and mental health. After his death, when the truth came out, the common-law marriage scandalized the world in which King had lived publicly. The Century Club in New York, where he had been a member, refused to hang his portrait despite the urgings of Adams and Hay, and his family and friends destroyed letters that alluded to the relationship. Did King's glittering reputation begin to tarnish with this revelation? Did racism contribute to his tumble from the highest peaks of renown?

Another way to look at the parts of Clarence King's life is to say that he spent the first half of it achieving things and the second half talking about those achievements. The doing/talking divide might be as deflating as the science/greed or success/failure ones except for this: King was a brilliant talker, a man who was able to turn the facts of his life into wonderful stories. Like memoirists in any age, King felt free while shaping the tales of his own past to ignore the limitations of fact. In the clubs of Manhattan or London and in such drawing rooms as the one at 1607 H Street, King tirelessly held forth on his youthful exploits in the West, both real and imagined. There was the time he shot a buffalo with a handgun and was almost stomped to death in the stampede that followed; the time he followed a bear into a cave, a rope around his feet so that a soldier could drag him out if the bear attacked; the time he was pursued by bandits on horseback for two days and nights—a tale that appears in *Mountaineering in the Sierra Nevada*. Several of the sketches in *Mountaineering* fall into the category of tall tales, such as Bret Harte or Mark Twain were writing at just about the same time. King, like many a hero and would-be hero before him, was an active participant in the making of his own myth, and like all myths his begins in fact and ends in fiction. The myth made others wish to emulate him, including a young Theodore Roosevelt, who retold the buffalo stampede tale in his book *The Wilderness Hunter*. But if the fictions delight us, the facts make King someone worth remembering.

It's worth remembering, too, that, beyond his family, the friends who loved King best had the most cause to be disappointed by him. But when he died alone and in debt in a small brick house in Phoenix in 1901, those friends came out for his funeral in Manhattan and later contributed to an evening of fond and glowing memoirs of him. These tributes were collected in a book, and alongside *The Education of Henry Adams*, also written after King's death, they give evidence that his friends forgave him the sins of his later years by remembering the accomplishments that came before them. More than a century later, that still seems to be a good way to think about him.

Imagine the well-tailored Clarence King, then, standing in the high-ceilinged Washington drawing room, with its Oriental rug and potted palms, his friends Henry and Clover, John and Clara seated in their leather armchairs, expectant looks on their faces. They called him "our Byron," this sunburned man of action, with his tales of distant and dangerous places. Henry James called him a charmer, "the most delightful man in the world." William Dean Howells lamented that, in drawing rooms such as this one, King had talked away novels that he might have written. The voice is soft, cultured, and oozing with charm, as he regales his friends with the stories of his youth.

# PART ONE

# GOING WEST

※

*When Jim and I went west in '63, we met a friend named Willie Hyde at Niagara and set off there by rail, to Chicago and then south to Hannibal. The line from Hannibal to St. Joe's ran on a new road, built so fast that it was still bone-jarringly rough, and I amused myself as the train rattled along by distracting the children of a family in our car. Between my silly stories we learned that the pater was a mule-and-horse trader from St. Louis named Speers, leaving like us from St. Joe's by emigrant train, heading for California with his family and his stock. Would we join their party? he asked, and swap our extensive experience as drovers for free victuals along the way. We agreed, not knowing that their cook would be about as accomplished at cooking as we were at droving horses and mules, and that the stock would feed better on new prairie grasses than we would from cook's pot.*

*Willie was from out West, his father being a foundryman in Nevada Territory. I've always tried to dress for any part, so when we reached St. Joe's we urged Willie to outfit us for our journey, and soon he had us looking like stage cowboys in leather hats and coats and chaps, along with the holstered Colts we needed to guard the mules and horses and indeed ourselves against bandits and aborigines. Each of us also bought a sturdy plains pony and comfortable saddle. We joined the procession as it headed out and had barely crossed the Missouri into the lush Kansas bottomland when the skies opened up, a black thunderstorm in early May such as you would not see even in August in Hartford or New Haven. Overnight the road turned to deep mud and the wagons went ploddingly for the next two weeks, as the storms continued in diluvian profusion.*

*We'd barely begun to acquire the authentic look, and smell, of cowboys when a band of Kansas zealots captured Jim and Willie and me and accused us of being "nigger thieves." They led us into what could only be called a town because it had a name, Troy, where they were ready to try us before a judge in a muddy little shanty when Speers showed up. He explained that we were not even remotely the criminals we were suspected of being—men who kidnapped free Kansas negroes and sold them back into slavery in Missouri. The judge let us go with a crestfallen look and we did not wait around to exchange pleasantries.*

*Our wagons slogged through the northeast corner of Kansas and into Nebraska, where the landscape turned more sere after we reached the Platte and went westward along its southern bank. The natives were not a problem this far east in that year, although the next year there would be attacks on emigrant parties in Nebraska. We saw small groups of Potawatomis in the distance but none drew near. In truth the journey's boredom unnerved us much more than its dangers, at least in those first days and weeks of slow going across a landscape that was beautiful but unvarying. The food grew ever more monotonous—cornbread, beans, and fatback day in and day out. Even in my youth—I was only twenty-one—I had a finicky palate, and I longed for something fresh to eat. We began to hear from other travelers rumors of buffalo in the vicinity and then at Fort Kearney we received a definite report of a vast herd to the southwest of the fort drifting north to feed on the year's new grasses. I conceived the idea of shooting a buffalo to see what cook might do with its choicest cuts, and engaged a guide and an experienced hunting pony.*

*Next morning early the guide and I set off and before long we could see the beasts in the distance, ambling in clumps that, as we came upon the herd's edge, stretched as far as the eye could see. To estimate its size we rode partway into the herd and concluded that the animals covered an area thirty miles wide and more than twice that distance long, although I was too green to know for myself and the guide might only have been trying to give me my money's worth. We rode back to the edge of the herd and, on his advice, I picked out a young bull for my quarry and drove him away from his fellows. He moved faster than you would expect given his size and I rode alongside him for some two miles across the prairie—until he stopped in a small basin of land and turned on my pony and me. I fired my Colt at him twice and red blotches burst out on his dark shaggy hide. In the silence that followed the shots I could hear the sounds of some other buffalo that had followed us. I turned my pony to see how close the beasts were, and at that instant the bull charged and struck us just behind the saddle, breaking the pony's back and knocking him, and me, to the ground. The charging buffalo somersaulted over us and died where he landed, while the pony, crying out in agony, fell on my left leg, pinning me. I was in no little pain myself. The buffalo from the herd panicked upon hearing the pistol reports and as they approached us their panic increased to the point of full stampede. They forked past me, jumping into and even over each other to avoid the three of us piled together in the basin. To say that the sound was like thunder hardly describes its thrumming depth, and soon the air grew thick with dust stirred up by their hooves. The pony continued to shriek in pain until I put a bullet in its head. Who can know how many beasts passed by, each one big as a buggy but moving faster than any buggy safely could. Clearly they wished to step on me as little as I wished to be stepped upon, but the result would have gone much better for one of them than for me. I judged that a mile and a half's worth of the herd rushed around me as I lay there. The guide came to my rescue soon enough, I suppose, since, as you can plainly see, I did survive. But at the time it seemed he might have saved me a little more promptly . . .*

Note: The preceding passage, as well as italicized passages at the beginning of Parts Three and Four, are fictional re-creations of anecdotes that King often told his friends. These passages are based on their memories of his stories, but are in no sense literal retellings. The italicized passage at the beginning of Part Two is quoted verbatim from King in the memoir of a friend.

CHAPTER ONE

# Alone Together

*Newport, Rhode Island, in the nineteenth century:
a view of Thames at Church Street.*

When Clarence King was born in 1842, the field of geology
had a glamour quotient that might be compared to that of
space exploration in our own time. In the nineteenth century, the
subject promised to unlock many of the fundamental mysteries
about the earth and its history, and it was at the heart of one of the
most significant scientific questions of the time, the age of the planet
and the ramifications of its age for the literal truth of the Bible.
Since the seventeenth century, biblical scholars had agreed that the

earth had been created by God only about four thousand years before the birth of Christ and that Creation had been achieved in the literal six days the Bible describes. But even a rudimentary understanding of geology showed that gradual processes such as erosion could not have worked fast enough to explain such dramatic changes in the earth's surface as the rerouting of rivers or the wearing away of mountains.

This problem led to a theory called catastrophism, which said that dramatic forces of short endurance such as volcanic eruptions had altered the planet within the prescribed six millennia since it was created. A decade before King's birth, the English geologist Charles Lyell had published the first volume of his book *Principles of Geology* just in time for Charles Darwin to take it along on the voyage of the *Beagle*. Lyell held that geological processes had not been catastrophic but both gradual and continuous since the earth began, which meant that the earth had to be far older than the Bible suggested. Lyell's principles, known as uniformitarianism, provided a basis for Darwin's theories. Because the six-thousand-year age limit also precluded the gradual development of species (which, in any case, had all been developed on a single day, according to the Bible, and had not been increased or diminished in number since then), its elimination made the idea of natural selection possible. The publication of Darwin's *On the Origin of Species* in 1859 applied geological uniformitarianism to biology (as Lyell had also done in the second book of *Principles of Geology*) and changed forever the relationship of man to God.

Both Lyell and Darwin remind us that in King's time the degree of academic specialization we know today did not exist. Many students including Darwin himself came to science by way of natural history, the study of all of nature's aspects, the earth and everything on it, an interest that often grew out of a life lived in or near the woods or, for city dwellers, from outings in the country. Darwin did a lot of what was called geologizing on his *Beagle* journey, and afterward published an important treatise on volcanoes, coral reefs, erosion, and the formation of continents. He always spoke of geology as his first love. In the same way, the geologist Lyell wrote about flora and fauna. Natural historians who developed into geologists, as King would, were not just interested in rocks but also embraced geography, paleontology, archaeology, and cartography, as well as botany and zoology. As a result of this breadth of pursuits, geologists in the nineteenth century often led or participated in explorations. For example, James Dwight Dana, who would be one of King's geology professors at Yale, set off with Captain Charles Wilkes on the United States Exploring Expedition three and a half years before King's birth, and helped discover Antarctica and chart many South Pacific islands and the coasts of South and North America.

George Washington had been a surveyor, and Thomas Jefferson and the other Founding Fathers considered the mapping of the new American territories to be a crucial step in the establishment of the nation. Jefferson's *Notes on the State of Virginia* (1787), with its typically eighteenth-century cataloguing of the geographical features and resources of the state, was a forerunner of a spate of official state surveys to come. Beginning in 1830 with Massachusetts, the states of the East, South, and Midwest began to commission geological surveys to map the land within their boundaries and to catalogue their natural resources. As William H. Goetzmann writes in his Pulitzer Prize–winning history, *Exploration and Empire*, the spread of state surveys became a sort of competition, with a survey becoming "a hallmark of enlightened state administration, a source of local cultural pride, and the means whereby exploitable natural resources might be cheaply located and advertised to would-be investors." The surveys followed the country westward, culminating in the first comprehensive geological survey of California, which began in 1860. Not only was California one of the most geologically diverse of the states, with its vertiginous mountains, fecund valleys, appalling deserts, and variable coastline, but a significant amount of it had still not been explored at all. So the state geological survey would also be an adventure of discovery.

Nineteenth-century European Romanticism was deeply enchanted by nature, of course, by its beauty and sublimity and mystery. Whether nature drew one closer to God by giving evidence of his works or whether it elevated one's view of humankind because of man's unique ability to perceive and appreciate the natural world of which man is a part, the nineteenth century's prevailing mode of thought was defined by the human connection to the physical world. Writers from Wordsworth at the beginning of the century to Proust at the end pondered the inexpressible feelings that nature evokes. One writer in particular, from the middle of the century, John Ruskin, influenced King and a raft of others of King's generation and the generation after him. King would be especially inflamed by Ruskin's odes in prose to the Swiss Alps in *Modern Painters,* where the critic lingered over the structure and shape and color of mountains—an aesthetic appreciation in terms that aspired to the scientific:

> I find the increase in the calculable sum of elements of beauty to be steadily in proportion to the increase of mountainous character; and that the best image which the world can give of Paradise is in the slope of the meadows, orchards, and corn-fields on the sides of a great Alp, with its purple rocks and eternal snows above; this excellence not being in any wise a matter referable to feeling, or individual preferences, but demonstrable by calm enumeration of the number of lovely colours on the rocks, the varied grouping of the trees, and quantity of noble incidents in the stream, crag, or cloud, presented to the eye at any given moment.

To explore mountains as King would, to be the first to walk among some of the most majestic peaks of the Sierra Nevada, a range that rivaled and many thought exceeded the Alps in beauty, took him to the far romantic extreme of science. Geology would be for him and for others of his time anything but the dusty study of rocks.

◆ ◆ ◆

When Clarence King's father, James Rivers King, began to court Clarence's mother, Florence Little, he gave her a copy of one of his favorite books. A romantic volume of Petrarch's sonnets, you might guess, or perhaps a collection of sermons, since he knew that Florence was raised in a strict Moravian household. No, it was a book of science, and not just any branch. "I was very young when I became engaged to James King," Florence would write more than six decades after the fact. "One of his first tributes to me was to bring me 'Buckland's Geology' to read and waken my mind to the subject." The two had known each other in Newport, Rhode Island, since childhood. Perhaps he had first noticed her as she emerged from the old church where her family worshipped, just across the street from the gambrel-roofed, dormered house that James's great-grandfather Benjamin had built, and where generations of Kings through Clarence would live. When James married Florence in 1840 she was still a child, just shy of fifteen. He was twenty-one and had aspired to be a scientist himself, or perhaps a doctor. Science was in the family gene pool: Benjamin had made quadrants, compasses, and other ships' instruments, and was said to have helped Benjamin Franklin with his electrical experiments. One of Benjamin King's instruments was used to establish the latitudinal line separating Massachusetts and Rhode Island. But Benjamin's grandson, Samuel, who was James's father, had gone to work for an East India company that made port in Canton and had prospered in the China trade, becoming one of its merchant princes. That was the family business now, and each of Samuel's sons, like it or not, would be raised in it.

James was sent to New York City to work in a successful counting house, Olyphant, Talbot, and Company, a part of the same firm in which his older brother Charles was rising to become a partner in Canton. When the Opium War began in China in 1839, Charles was among the foreign merchants trapped in their hongs until a six-weeks' blockade was lifted and he was permitted to leave. By the time he returned home his health was compromised, and it had not improved by early 1841, when the British Royal Navy forced the reopening of Canton, also winning Hong Kong for the crown for its trouble. The family business needed a King watching its interests in China, so James would go until his brother's health improved. By the time a ship was readied for the journey and James sailed, he had left his sixteen-year-old wife pregnant with their first child. As she whiled away the lonely months at the King house on the corner of Church and High streets in Newport, "a house bright with the rich fabrics, grim with weird carvings and porcelains and fragrant with the strange scents of the Far East," as a friend remembered it some years later, she began to teach herself Greek, Latin, and French, so that she might herself tutor the child who was growing within her. Clarence Rivers King was born on January 6, 1842, named by the mother who was less than a generation older than he. King's biographer Thurman Wilkins suggests that she picked the name Clarence "because it suggested the lilt of her own name," and the Rivers came from his father.

They lived with James's sister, Caroline; Florence's mother, Sophia Little, and grandfather, retired U.S. Senator Asher Robbins, lived nearby in the already old little town of Newport. But like many children who have children, Florence affixed herself to her baby with a single-mindedness that would never leave her, even after that baby had died sixty years later. Once James received news of his son's birth he almost certainly began to urge Florence to join him in Canton, where the political situation had calmed for a time and where wealthy foreigners lived quite well. She and Clarence nearly went in 1843 on a large new company ship called the *Huntress,* but in the end she decided to stay in Newport with her son and wait for her husband to come home. In 1845 he did, once Charles felt well enough to return to China and relieve him. But James had not been home for long when he learned that Charles had again fallen ill and as his ship crossed the Indian Ocean on the way home, had died and was buried at sea. James knew that his brother's death meant that his own days in Newport were numbered, that at some point he would have to ship out again for the other side of the world.

James managed to delay his return to Canton for something less than two years, and this was all the time that Clarence would have in the presence of his father. During that interlude a sister, also named Florence, was born and died, and when James sailed again to China in the first part of 1847, Florence was pregnant with what would be a second daughter, Grace, who was born in the fall. Florence never heard directly from James again. No letters from him had reached her in the more than a year since he'd left home, when, as Clarence would tell the story years later, one morning in early June of 1848 Florence awoke with the knowledge that James was dead. When confirmation of her fear arrived several months later, on her twenty-second birthday, she learned that he had died, probably of a fever, on June 2, the exact day of her premonition.

After the Chinese and the British signed the Treaty of Nanjing in 1842 and a separate treaty between the Chinese and the United States followed—negotiated by a Massachusetts congressman named Caleb Cushing, who was a King family friend—business in Canton and the other four established treaty ports was expected to be stronger than it had been before the Opium War. But there was so much antiforeign feeling in Canton that business had been an ongoing disappointment. James had sailed up the coast of China to Amoy, now Xiamen, to ply the camphor trade—the island of Formosa, which Amoy faced, was rich in the trees from which camphor comes, and camphor was valuable medicinally and as an ingredient in explosives. James had apparently died on a camphor packet to or from Formosa, and was buried in Amoy. As if this news was not terrible enough, it was only half the blow that Florence and her six-year-old son had to absorb. As she wrote years later, "My youngest child lay dead while I heard of her father's death." Little Grace had not reached her first birthday. In their bewildering grief, Florence and Clarence would face the world alone, and together.

Newport was already two hundred years old when Clarence King was a child there in the 1840s. Its most prosperous era as a seafaring town ended with the Revolutionary War, when the British captured and occupied it and Providence became the more important trading port. The China trade and whaling continued to sustain the town in the first part of the nineteenth century, but by the time Clarence came along both of those enterprises were on the decline, as merchants turned to shorter, more profitable shipping runs and as the whaling business on the East Coast began to play out, killed finally by the Gold Rush when whalers hauled prospectors to the West Coast and stayed to ply the more abundant waters of the Pacific. Newport's fame as a summer resort began to grow in the 1830s when it became more accessible because of improvements in transportation, but its era as the playground of America's robber barons with their great cottages was still in the future.

Old Town Newport, where the Kings lived, was characterized, as Henry James wrote in an essay called "The Sense of Newport," by "little very old streets" that resembled, in James's attenuated view, "little very old ladies." How so? The streets seemed to James to have "the same suggestion of present timidity and frugality of life, the same implication in their few folds of drab, of mourning, of muslin still mysteriously starched, the implication of no adventure at any time, however far back, that mightn't have been suitable to a lady." If this had been literally true it would make Newport unique among port towns, and one might well ask whether, if there had been unladylike activities in the town, James would be the one to have discovered them. But James is writing only of the impression the cobbled streets created in this between times of Newport prosperity; in another essay he refers to Newport as having been "remarkably quaint," with an "antique shabbiness that amounts almost to squalor."

Newport was a place, then, where a young boy, even one living with an overprotective mother and a maiden aunt, might have the freedom to roam about in safety. Clarence would have had access not only to the quiet narrow streets and relatively lively docks but to the natural world. James refers to Newport's "thousand delicate secret places, dear to the disinterested rambler, small mild 'points' and promontories, far away little lonely, sandy coves, rock-set, lily-sheeted ponds, almost hidden, and shallow Arcadian summer-haunted valleys, with the sea just over some stony shoulder." Everyone who knew Clarence and his mother agrees that his interest in nature developed early, and that she encouraged him in this passion even as she taught him the languages she had learned to become his tutor. One of King's biographers, Harry H. Crosby, suggests that Florence developed in him a love of water as much as of landscape, and as Henry James writes, there was water at every turn in Newport. "She spent many hours swimming and boating with him," Crosby writes, "until, though smaller than most boys his age, he became better coordinated and quicker than any of his friends." Certainly by the time he went to Yale he had developed the preternatural strength that he would have all the rest of his life, and in addition to boxing, skating, and playing Boston baseball (an older variant of New York baseball, which became the national pastime) and cricket, he was stroke oar while rowing crew and a fleet captain in the Yale Navy, as the rowing club was called. "It's funny how the fellows take me as a boating oracle," he would write from Yale to one of his boyhood friends.

James King's two surviving brothers, Frederick and David, had taken over the family business, and proceeds from James's interest in the company continued to flow to Florence after his death. She had the means, then, to enroll Clarence in a good school away from Newport and the sadness that lingered there. He would attend Christ Church Hall in Pomfret, Connecticut, only ten miles from the Rhode Island line but far enough away that he and his mother would live in a boardinghouse there during the months that classes were held. The headmaster, the Reverend Dr. Roswell Park, had gone to West Point and served in the army and then been ordained. He had been a professor of natural philosophy at the University of Pennsylvania before coming to Christ Church, and published poetry as well as volumes of his sermons. A strict, dour teacher, he is known to history primarily, perhaps, as the first person (of many who would want to do so throughout his lifetime) to have the pleasure of caning James McNeill Whistler, who was also a student at the school when Clarence attended. Perhaps most important for King's intellectual development, Park was a man who could balance his interest in natural history with his theology, believing that the two could be reconciled. As he would write in a book modestly called *Pantology; or, a Systematic Survey of Human Knowledge,* "the book of nature and the book of revelations, when fully understood," would "agree entirely, both being the work of the same infinitely wise and omnipotent Author."

For a boy already used to wandering about in the country, Pomfret provided plenty of nearby natural wonders. One cold January day, his mother would recall, Clarence "came to see me . . . and asked if I could go a little way over the frozen snow to see something. . . . The 'little way' proved to be about a mile, and the something was a remarkably distinct fossil fern in a stone wall. He asked me to explain how it came there. I promptly confessed my ignorance." But Florence, who apparently had not studied the book of geology that James had given her years before, was anxious to know more if only for Clarence's sake. She helped him look up fossils in Hitchcock's *Geology,* and encouraged him to collect specimens on his nature walks. "From that time on," she would report with a combination of pride and ruefulness, "my rooms became a veritable museum." Florence would supplement Clarence's opportunities to explore the natural world in Pomfret and Newport by taking him to the Green Mountains for "long summer vacations, spent in fishing, hunting and botanizing," according to a longtime friend.

Mother and son continued this routine until Clarence was ten years old, when Rev. Park left Christ Church and Florence enrolled Clarence briefly in a Latin school near Boston. Florence had always lived close enough to the sea to enjoy its moderating effects on New England winters, and she found Boston to be far too cold. By 1853, she had moved with Clarence to New Haven, where her brother, Robbins Little, was doing graduate work at Yale. Little had just returned from an adventure aboard a clipper ship, *Wild Pigeon,* owned by the King family firm, now called King and Co. The clipper had raced three other ships around the Horn of Africa to California, reaching it in the losing time of 118 days. Then the ship had recrossed the Pacific with Little, making Hong Kong in thirty-eight days, and soon enough he was back home and ready to return to his studies.

New Haven would be an auspicious place for King to live. As he wrote later in notes for a friend who was preparing a biographical sketch of him, his familiarity during this time "with the birds, fishes and plant life of New Haven was something remarkable" and "undoubtedly had much to do with the development of [my] powers of observation." The city was considered to be a center of scientific studies in the United States, due partly to the publication there of *Silliman's Journal*, still published to this day in New Haven as the *American Journal of Science*. Benjamin Silliman had been the first person appointed to teach science at Yale, when he became professor of chemistry and natural history in 1802. He started the journal in 1818, virtually assuring that it would be known familiarly by his name when he gave it the jaw breaking title of "The American Journal of Science more especially of Mineralogy, Geology, and the Other Branches of Natural History, including also Agriculture and the Ornamental as well as Useful Arts." Silliman had early fallen under the influence of the rising tide of British geologists, and geology was and remains one of the journal's principal subjects. The professor stepped down at Yale in 1853, the same year that Florence and Clarence moved to New Haven, and his son-in-law, James Dwight Dana, who had returned from the Wilkes South Seas expedition a decade earlier, succeeded him as professor of natural history. Although Yale now proudly claims that the teaching of geology began in the United States with Silliman, the college remained hostile to science and committed to a traditional classical education until well beyond Silliman's time. But Silliman and his son, Benjamin Jr., had established their own independent scientific school that would later become associated with the college, if not exactly embraced by it. By the end of the decade, King would be enrolled in the Yale Scientific School himself.

As they had in Newport, Florence and Clarence were again living on Church Street, in rented rooms across from the residence of the Yale president, Theodore Dwight Woolsey. The Yale librarian Daniel Coit Gilman (who would later found Johns Hopkins) remembered King as a schoolboy in New Haven from the distance of half a century. "His appearance at that time I recall distinctly. He had the same bright face, winning smile, agile movement, that we knew in later life." Clarence must have thrived at school and under his mother's continued tutelage, because when he turned thirteen he passed an examination for one of the best public secondary schools in the Northeast, Hartford Public High. The school had merged with the private Hopkins Grammar, which had been known for its classical education as the "Rugby of Connecticut." Its excellence alone would have been reason enough for Florence to move with Clarence to Hartford, but finances might also have played a part in her decision. At the public high school, Clarence could get a private school education for free.

By this time King and Company had opened an office in Shanghai, which among the five treaty ports established after the Opium War was the only one to thrive. Business was good and the company's prospects bright when James's brother Frederick's coastal steamer disappeared in the South China Sea and was never found. The last surviving brother, David, took charge of the company and managed, at about the same time that Florence and Clarence were moving to Hartford, to have himself appointed the exclusive agent to the king of Siam. Florence could not have known this yet, but she would have known that the family interest now depended on only one brother, and that the life expectancy for a King of his generation was not long. As it would turn out, Florence was wise to brace herself for future financial disaster, although David did not have to die to precipitate it.

Florence and Clarence lived in Hartford not far from the high school with a retired judge, named John M. Niles, in his house on Main Street. Niles had been a friend of Florence's late grandfather, Asher Robbins. Clarence started classes in October 1855, one of about thirty-five students of the classics master, a Yale graduate named Samuel Capron. The course of study included Latin gram-

mar and composition in the first year, Greek grammar and composition in the second year, and ancient history, geography, and myth
in the third. Clarence was also able to take math, English, and
modern history, which was probably a relief, because during his
high school years he developed a lifelong enmity for classical ped-
agogy. In one essay written later in life he referred to classics students as having to learn how to "successfully receive the determined
and bitter charge of attacking tutors" (with "attacking" as an adjec-
tive, not a verb) while in another he referred to classics teachers as
a "corps of badgering grammarians." As an only child and what one
of his friends would later call a mother's boy, who had been raised
on a steady diet of adoration and encouragement, Clarence did not
respond well to the stern discipline of memorization and rote
translation that characterized the teaching of the classics. Rev.
Park at Christ Church had employed the same sort of discipline as
Master Capron did, but much of King's education before high
school had been autodidactic, either learning alongside his ambitious young mother or through the soles of his feet, as he made his
own natural history investigations. His independent-mindedness as
a scholar would be both a virtue and a curse as his life progressed,
giving him the imagination to do some things that others would
not have attempted, but leaving him without the measure of discipline that can push imagination forward when the energy of youth
begins to wane.

But King was always a good student, and thrived in English
under a young teacher who "still had the sweetness of natural
womanhood," as King would remember later. Her name was Mary
Dodge, and she would become well known for her abolitionist
writings under the pen name Gail Hamilton. She undoubtedly
deserves some credit for King's facility in English prose, although as
a friend who knew him at Hartford later wrote, "Already at fifteen,
he wrote beautifully, having been trained in literary judgment and
skill by his mother, who possessed in high degree both the faculty
of expression and power to inspire enthusiasm."

This same friend, Jim Gardner, also remembered that King's

own natural history studies continued while he was in high school, and gives an insight into how King would accomplish so much in his life without the rigorous self-discipline he might have developed. "On Saturday," Gardner said, "we usually spent the whole day walking in the country. If any question arose as to any object seen during the day, whether we had particularly noticed it or not, King could always describe it from memory with great minuteness. He seemed to photograph unconsciously everything that passed before his eyes, and to be able to recall the picture at will. He studied enthusiastically the botany, the bird and animal life, and the rocks, of the regions over which we rambled."

One of King's most essential and appealing qualities emerged for the first time that anyone noted when he moved to Hartford. Until he turned fifteen Clarence seems, perhaps only because there is no evidence to the contrary, to have been a solitary child though not an unhappy one, moving about New England with his mother from one school to another and, once settled, exploring the nearby countryside in contented isolation. But when he met Jim Gardner soon after moving to Hartford, he not only established a lifelong friendship but a lifelong capacity for friendship that was commented upon by almost everyone who knew him. Gardner said later in life that King's gift for friendship was as "marked in him at fifteen as at fifty," and that he and Clarence had been from the start "on terms of intimacy closer than those of most brothers." Soon there was a third member of the group, another schoolboy named Dan Dewey. The three considered themselves to be a brotherhood, and would write long letters to one another, often exploring their growing enthusiasm for religion and referring to themselves as "brothers in Christ." On the Saturday nature rambles they would sometimes build a fire and cook trout that they had caught, and when the weather got too cold for such outings the three boys would go sledding or ice skating. As Dan wrote, "We have had a strangely happy boyhood together." One day, according to a memoir by a friend named Edgar Beecher Bronson, Clarence and Jim "were returning to Hartford from a trout-fishing excursion, both attired in costumes, gotten up for the occasion, which were far more picturesque than conventional, when, in passing a country school-house where a lot of big girls were at play, the appearance of the boys excited shouts of laughter. Instantly King turned, struck a pose of severity, and gravely remarked: 'Always remember, young ladies, that modesty is the best policy.'" Such high-spirited good fun, from the getups to the mock seriousness, would characterize King throughout his life.

But at about the age when boyish happiness often turns into something else, whether it is a need to untie maternal apron strings or the beginnings of an adult search for meaning, events on the other side of the world came together in a way that would break the pattern of Florence and Clarence's life since James's death. Throughout the nineteenth century, China's Qing dynasty faced more and more challenges to its increasingly corrupt and bureaucratic rule, and these uprisings reached a crisis point in the 1850s with the Taiping Rebellion. As the Qing were weakened and distracted by the Taiping, the British pushed to renegotiate the Treaty of Nanjing on far more favorable terms for them and the other foreign traders. The British again began to back their demands with military force, and the long-simmering xenophobia in Canton boiled over in riots at the end of 1856. All of the foreign-owned buildings in the city, from the hongs to consulates, were burned. King and Company sued for reparations for its severe losses, but the Qing authorities blamed the fires on the British, and the company was forced to decamp to Hong Kong. Then a steamer carrying a large amount of the firm's money disappeared on the way to Shanghai. The third and final blow came when the company could not afford to pay accumulated duty on opium imports. King and Company went broke, making James's interest worthless. Florence now had no income at a time when the United States at large was enduring the depression of 1857.

However few financial resources remained at her disposal, Florence still had her youth, her intelligence, and her good looks. As Harry Crosby wrote of Florence in his unpublished biography of

King, "Friends of her son remembered years later how all conversations in her presence followed her lead, how all eyes were turned to her diminutive figure, her erect head, her dark eyes, and her jet-black hair." Soon she permitted herself to be courted by an older widower, a Brooklyn factory owner who had lost, in addition to his wife, three of his four children. He was looking for a younger woman to provide him more progeny. His name was George S. Howland.

A decade had passed since the death of Florence's husband and Clarence's father, and in that time the mother and son had formed an inseparable alliance against a world that could take so much from them. Samuel Franklin Emmons, a Boston geologist who knew both Clarence and Florence well later in their lives, wrote that they had always enjoyed "a close intellectual companionship." Florence herself would say of their relationship, "I have never known a more perfect human tie than that which bound my son and myself. We were one in heart and mind and soul." Somewhat less believably she would also say, "No clouded look or hasty word ever marred the sweetness of our relation." Given their closeness in age, their lively emotional and intellectual connection, and the lifelong effects that his feelings for his mother would have on his relationships with other women, it's tempting to think of their relationship as being nearly marital, if it's possible to propose such a thing without also suggesting a whiff of incest. In any case, Clarence did not react well to the sudden appearance in their lives of George Howland, although Howland seems to have been a generous and sympathetic man. Clarence went into what was at the very least a deep funk, and at worst the first episode of a real mental instability that would touch him once or twice later in life. He withdrew from Hartford Public High School in April 1859, just weeks before he would have graduated, and never did receive a high school degree. The school records reported that he had withdrawn "because of illness." He retreated into a self-pitying sort of religious mania, writing to Jim Gardner months later that "my only comfort is that God who overrules all will be the father of the fatherless." But however depressed he felt, however much he believed that his mother had deserted or disappointed him, he was still a physically healthy young male of seventeen, with the libidinous urges that the age stirs up. "Oh, Jim," he would write his close friend, "my hot nature must need a great deal of checking. I am sure my trying troubles must be sent for the purpose of teaching me to govern myself."

Nothing suggests that Clarence was bedridden or hospitalized during this period, when he remained in Hartford with his mother as her courtship with Howland progressed. Judge Niles had died and they had moved in with the family of an insurance executive named James Bowles. Clarence spent a lot of time in the surrounding countryside in these months, on foot or on the back of one of Bowles's mares, like any good young Romantic finding solace in the natural world. Toward the end of 1859, Clarence felt well enough to look for work in Manhattan, perhaps with the idea of following in his father's footsteps in business. He quickly found a clerk's job in the office of a flour merchant, not realizing that George Howland was silently pulling a string on his behalf. It's clear that Clarence hadn't really gotten over the hurt he felt because of his mother's relationship with Howland when he wrote to Jim in early January, two days before his eighteenth birthday, that "My old enemy Pride is laughing in its sleeve at my scorning assistance, both in carrying on my education and in procuring me a place. I feel I am my own man, dependent on no one, and if I fail no one but myself is to blame."

Still, his mother soon moved in with him in an apartment in Brooklyn, where he took the two-cent ferry to Manhattan each day but Sunday. It could not have made Clarence happy that Florence and George Howland were in the same city now, and on top of that Clarence, the free-spirited roamer, predictably hated the drudgery of clerkdom, which left him feeling overwhelmed and by week's end "perfectly fagged out." His father had also suffered at the drudgery of business. Even in the exotic environs of Canton, as Thurman Wilkins writes, James "grew to hate clerking, to hate keeping books, or preparing manifests for tea and silks, rhubarb, canes, and camphor." Clarence tried to salve his spirit by reading the Psalms and attending church services, but he was also overwhelmed by his continuing problems with the temptations of the flesh:

> It was very nice to talk about moral purity in a little city, but Great Jones!, Jim—how many more seductive, wicked, beautiful, fascinating, jolly, voluptuous, apparently modest, artful women there are to one poor chicken here; they show you their necks and bosoms without intending to, and all the abominable wiles they practice on a fellow . . . are mighty inflaming.

In April, Florence announced her engagement to George Howland and by May, Clarence was already looking for an escape from office life. He had continued to seek "heavenly aid in eradicating the melancholy" he felt, but more drastic steps would be required, it seemed. "What is to become of me is uncertain," he wrote to Jim. "Probably I shall remain where I am, but the scientific school or a farming life is not impossible." The scientific school at Yale required only entrance exams (in math, physics, and chemistry) for admittance, so his failure to get a high school diploma would not be a drawback, as it would have been at most colleges, including Yale proper. Florence and George were married in July. By that time Clarence was reconciled enough to the new situation at home, or so little reconciled to the situation at work, or probably a combination of the two, to swallow his pride and take his stepfather's offer to pay his way to college. He passed the entrance tests and in September 1860 signed up for a three-year course in applied chemistry. The tuition would be two hundred dollars a year, but George Howland could afford it.

College is always a turning point in a young person's life, but King's choice of the scientific school, which carried with it an almost risky commitment to modernity and the future, suited his nature especially well. He would not be a lawyer like Florence's father or a politician like her grandfather, and to be a businessman like so many of the Kings now definitely seemed out of the question. A restlessness had begun to stir in Clarence alongside the hormone-driven lusts of youth. An education in science would seem to be even less palliative than religion for the problems of the flesh, but it would address his problems of the spirit for many years to come.

## CHAPTER TWO

# A Scientific Education

*The campus of Yale University in the nineteenth century.*

W e can barely imagine, in this era when the status of scientific truth has long since outstripped that of religious truth, and when science is popularly accepted to be the only legitimate path to truths of any sort, that in 1860 science could have been less than completely respectable not only in the public mind but also in the academic world. At the time that Clarence King enrolled at Yale, very few colleges in America offered special programs in science. Two of them were Harvard, which had made the Swiss naturalist Louis Agassiz a professor of natural science in 1847 and founded the Lawrence Scientific School to accommodate him, and Yale. Although the scientific tradition at Yale stretched back to Benjamin Silliman's appointment in 1802, the Yale Scientific School evolved from classes that Silliman's son and namesake offered outside the purview of the college, beginning in the early 1840s, to students who wanted more science than Yale would give them, and to the public at large.

When this informal program was absorbed by Yale in 1854, it might seem in retrospect to have been an acknowledgment of the growing centrality of science to all human intellectual endeavor. But it is also possible, given the way Yale regarded the school for years afterward, that there were less noble motives involved. Perhaps now that Harvard had a scientific school Yale simply felt that it must have one, too, and perhaps the creation of the new school gave the college an opportunity to evict unwanted courses from the general academic program. In the 1853–54 academic catalogue at Yale, the science and engineering courses were lumped together under "the aegis of a nonexistent institution," the better to distance the college from these disciplines, with their odor of actual work, even before the nonexistent new institution could exist. Once it did exist, the Yale Scientific School limped along for a few years on sporadic gifts until 1858. In that year the railroad baron Joseph E. Sheffield paid $165,000 for the old Medical Institution building at the corner of Grove and Prospect streets, which backed up to his own mansion on Hillhouse Avenue. Sheffield added two wings to the stone structure, which had been built as a hotel in 1814, fitted it out with the latest scientific equipment, and gave it to Yale, along with a fifty-thousand-dollar endowment for professorships in engineering, metallurgy, and chemistry. The building was ready for occupancy in the summer of 1860, just before King became a student there. The next year Yale showed its gratitude by renaming the science program as the Sheffield Scientific School of Yale College.

But it was only barely of Yale College. The students in the academic program could not be expected to miss an opportunity to express their intellectual and social condescension toward the students in the new program. As one academic student later said, "I regarded the studies of my contemporaries at the Sheffield Scientific School with a sort of contempt—with wonder that human beings possessed of immortal souls should waste their time in work with blow pipes and test tubes." The snobbery extended to the faculty as well, with the professors of Greek and Latin sniffing that Sheffield was offering only a vocational education. Even in the late 1860s, Sheffield's governing board wrote, with that whining tone we associate with academic affairs in our own day, "A year does not pass without our seeing that the work which we are trying to perform is quite imperfectly understood by the graduates and friends of Yale College, by many writers on the higher education, and by parents and teachers who are called upon to select for young men their advanced courses of study." As Loomis Havemeyer, an early twentieth-century student and later an administrator at Shef, summed it up, "During the second half of the 19th century, Yale College and Sheffield Scientific School, separated by only a few streets, were two separate countries on the same planet."

King certainly noticed the divide. Years later he wrote that classics professors "felt entitled . . . to look down upon a teacher of natural science, and by the same quaint sort of logic the Yale academic students excluded the 'scientifics.'" But it did not seem to bother him at the time. He had signed up for the three-year general course at the school, which consisted of natural sciences and modern languages, but would finish it in two years while also throwing himself at sports and continuing his nature rambles in the countryside outside New Haven. Because his specialty was applied chemistry, he took chemistry courses ranging from organic and agricultural to experimental and analytic. He also studied physics and geology, and took German with a new faculty member, William D. Whitney, "whose stories of student life on the Rhine and walking excursions in Switzerland" inflamed his imagination, as King told his friend Jim Gardner in a letter.

Joseph Sheffield had outfitted the science building with two modern laboratories, and much of the instruction involved the students—there were fewer than two dozen at the time— conducting laboratory experiments under the supervision of two faculty members, George J. Brush, who was a professor of metallurgy, and Samuel W. Johnson, a professor of theoretical and agricultural chemistry, both of whom had themselves studied under Silliman at Yale. In 1861, Johnson would publish a paper called "Soil Analyses: Notice of the Agricultural Chemistry of the Geological Surveys of Kentucky and Arkansas," so it's a pretty good bet that testing southern dirt was one of the things King did during his first year. Unlike the regular Yale students, the scientifics did not have to live in a dormitory on campus or attend chapel. The laboratories opened at eight each morning, and the students worked at their own speed on the experiments. They had occasional lectures to attend but for the most part learned by doing, a philosophy that dovetailed nicely with the approach to natural history that King had been taking since childhood. After a year he wrote to Gardner, "I am happy in my studies," and even before that he had begun to encourage Jim to transfer to Yale. King had been disappointed when Jim had moved to Troy, New York, and enrolled at Rensselaer Institute, but by the spring of 1862 King had talked his friend into joining him in New Haven.

In high school, Gardner had shared King's enthusiasms for religion and natural history. He had considered becoming a minister, but a problem with his voice persuaded him to study science instead. His family had moved from Hartford to Troy, and since Rensselaer had been founded in 1824 "for the purpose of instructing persons . . . in the application of science to the common purposes of life," it made sense for him to enroll there. Jim and Clare, as he called his friend, seemed to evolve together from being brothers in Christ to being acolytes of the new religion, science. Harry Crosby speaks in his unpublished biography of King's "conversion" from the one to the other. In June 1861, King told Gardner that his science studies had calmed his spirit as religion had failed to do. "I have undergone a revolution," King wrote, or overwrote, "and the tumult of it seems to have gone from my soul as a black storm cloud sweeps away on the eddying winds and leaves the face of nature fresh and full of sunshine." By the next winter, not long before Gardner's transfer, King wrote to him that "Science is almost a revelation. I don't love the practical minutiae of the lower details of science although I work at those for discipline, but the lofty laws of creation, the connection of the material with the human, the esthetic, and the eternal, and the cosmic relations of God's earthly planes all are clearer to me now."

Despite the low regard in which the badgering grammarians held them, the faculty members at the Sheffield School were an important force in American science for the rest of the nineteenth century, through their own research and writing and through the accomplishments of many of their students. George Brush, who was Shef's director from 1872 to 1898, was "the life of the school," according to Daniel Gilman. But James Dwight Dana, who was generally considered to be the most important American geologist of his time, was clearly its star. Born in 1813, Dana studied under Silliman at Yale and after graduation sailed the Mediterranean as a mathematics instructor on a U.S. Navy ship (a common practice before the U.S. Naval Academy was founded in 1845). Although his own studies on the trip were of insects, Dana watched Vesuvius erupt and wrote about it for *Silliman's Journal,* the start of an interest in volcanology that would last for more than half a century, culminating in a major study of volcanoes that he published at the age of seventy-seven. Back in New Haven in 1834, he created a new system for classifying minerals, based on chemistry and crystallography, publishing his first book, *System of Mineralogy,* in 1837 at the age of twenty-four. The next year he became the geologist and mineralogist for Charles Wilkes's United States Exploring Expedition, an ambitious and important undertaking funded by Congress and carried out by the navy. Dana joined a team of scientists and naval officers with scientific backgrounds, setting off from Norfolk on six ships to explore the South Atlantic and South Pacific, the Sandwich Islands (as Hawaii was then known), and the west coasts of South and North America. One of their accomplishments, according to William Goetzmann in *Exploration and Empire,* was that "they had mapped the broad Pacific so accurately that nearly a hundred years later their charts could be used by marine divisions landing at Makin and bloody Tarawa."

Parts of the four-year voyage paralleled the later legs of the *Beagle* expedition, which had ended in 1836, and Dana carried Darwin's *Journal of Researches* (now known as *Voyage of the Beagle*) along with him after it was published in 1839, just as Darwin himself had carried Lyell's *Principles of Geology.* Like Darwin, Dana was interested in how volcanic islands and coral reefs were formed, and he independently reached similar conclusions about them. Also like Darwin, Dana was, as one scientist put it in a recent biographical sketch, "adept at grand geological synthesis," which would surely inspire King in his most important scientific work, *Systematic Geology.*

It took Dana most of a decade to write up his geological findings from the Wilkes expedition, and he spent much of the rest of his life drawing upon them. But it was the tales of his adventures on the trip that made him, along with his raven-haired good looks, appeal to Silliman's nineteen-year-old daughter Henrietta, to whom he would become engaged soon after his return. The same tales—of a deadly storm in the Straits of Magellan, of establishing the existence of Antarctica as a continent (which Wilkes did, having dropped the scientists off in Australia), of cannibalistic Fijians, of the beautiful bubbling crater of Kilauea in Hawaii (into which Dana had descended 1,300 feet), of losing his samples when his ship, the frigate *Peacock,* foundered on a bar in the mouth of the Columbia River and was wrecked—charmed Clarence King and Jim Gardner when they took Dana's "long course of lectures in geology" at Yale in the spring of 1862. It was the first course Dana had taught in three years, a period of recovery from mental exhaustion during which he traveled with Henrietta to Europe and then "did nothing" at home in New Haven. Still, he had revived enough to be an energetic teacher. As Jim wrote to his mother that June, "Dana has the most vivid powers of description, setting before us . . . scenes from his travels." Among the things that Dana had seen was "the Shasty Peak" in California, which he had written about in 1849 in *Silliman's Journal.* The allure of Mount Shasta, then thought to be the highest mountain in North America, would soon figure importantly in the lives of both King and Gardner.

Another student at the school, James D. Hague, met King in 1862. Although Hague was six years older and the two were not close at the time, Hague would work with King on the Fortieth Parallel Survey and on many other projects, becoming one of his closest companions. After King's death, Hague collected the tributes of his friends, which were published as *Clarence King Memoirs*. In one of these, Hague himself describes King in 1862:

> I well remember him as he was then, an active, sprightly youth, quick to observe and apprehend, full of joyous animation and lively energy, which always made him a leader of the front rank, whether in the daily exercises of the classroom and laboratory or in an impromptu raid by night on Hillhouse Avenue front fences, with the mischievous purpose of lifting off and swapping around in neighborly exchange the door-yard gates of lawns and gardens. "Off fences must come," he sometimes said of the gates, "but woe unto him by whom they come—if found out."

The woe unto the students and the school might have been especially great had one obvious target of these pranks, Joseph Sheffield himself—with his Hillhouse Avenue mansion invitingly situated right behind the school building—found out. Sheffield would go on to construct a second classroom building for the school that bore his name, and would leave Yale his mansion and a nice chunk of his fortune when he died in 1882.

So King's dark night of the soul was followed by a two-year idyll at Yale. He would graduate "with honor" with a Ph.B. in July 1862, having been invited to join the Berzelius Society, a science fraternity started at the college in 1848. Some quality or set of qualities—his intelligence, his good looks, his appealing energy—had drawn professors such as Brush and Whitney to take a special interest in him. He was admired by his fellow scientifics as an athlete who could excel at almost any sport he attempted, and he was prized as a companion for his wit and high spirits. His strength of personality made him an instinctive leader, and his ability to work his will on others had paid off in an especially gratifying way when his friend Jim Gardner had joined him in New Haven.

But however normal King's life might have seemed on the surface, however typically that of a college boy of any era, the years 1861 and 1862 cast a dark, dark shadow over the lives of almost every American, and especially every young American male. The election of Lincoln two months after King enrolled at Yale soon led to the secession of seven southern states, and after Lincoln's inauguration in March came the shelling of Fort Sumter on April 12 and 13 and the war's beginning. Four more states would then join the Confederacy. Because of the growing bad feelings between North and South during the decade of the 1850s, there were only thirty-three southerners left at Yale in 1860, a dramatic decrease from the seventy-two enrolled in 1850. On the night of January 19, 1861, a group of southern students broke into Alumni Hall on the college's Old Campus and ran up a secessionist flag—white with a red cross, and in one quadrant a crescent moon and palmetto tree symbolizing the first state to secede, South Carolina. The southerners filled the locks to the building's doors with nails and removed the door-knobs, slowing the northern students who the next morning rushed the building to remove the flag. After Fort Sumter many Ivy League schools expelled their southern students, and although Yale did not, most of them immediately made their way home. Only a handful of the northern boys answered Lincoln's first calls for troops. Eventually about 25 percent of the eight hundred men from the north who attended Yale in the years 1861 to 1865 would join the Union effort, but at first the war did not go smoothly for the Yankees, and there was no great rush of northern Yale students to join, as there had been on the more confident Confederate side.

King's grandmother, Sophia Little, had been an ardent abolitionist at least as far back as the 1830s, when she had been part of a group threatened by a Boston mob that had also nearly strung up the antislavery newspaperman William Lloyd Garrison. She had helped fugitive slaves through the underground railroad, and when the Fugitive Slave Act was passed in 1850 she had written a novel meant to undercut it. In it the narrator, a runaway slave girl named Gibby, asks with a rhetorical flourish that perhaps explains why *Uncle Tom's Cabin*, which was published at about the same time, was the more effective work: "Oh, Slavery, where is there a fiercer fury than thou art?" Both Florence and Clarence called themselves abolitionists in the 1850s, and in 1860 Clarence had written to Jim from New York that "I am more than ever a Wendell Phillips man, heart and soul with the philanthropic radicals." Phillips, the so-called "knight-errant of unfriended truth," was a Boston Brahmin who was uncompromising on the subject of slavery, a man who helped return John Brown's body from Virginia to New York after his execution and gave the eulogy at his graveside. But Sophia Little's Moravian faith had made her both an abolitionist and a pacifist, someone who took the biblical injunction against killing without exception.

As Louis Menand writes in *The Metaphysical Club*, many abolitionists who had also been against civil war, like Wendell Phillips, who argued that the South should be allowed to secede from the union, "switched from pacifism to militarism overnight" after Fort Sumter. Menand points out that even Emerson, "once almost the incarnation of post-Christian nonviolence," said after Fort Sumter, "Sometimes gunpowder smells good." King was similarly torn between an abolitionism that might seem to make him eager to enter a fight that was at least partially against slavery, and the pacifist sentiments of his grandmother. "God knows . . . I would not quail before death for my land," he wrote to Jim, "but the act [of killing] would crucify in me many of my noblest impulses. It is like tearing my soul in two." On a less exalted plane, he was torn between the visceral need to answer a call to arms that seems built into the genes of young men (although natural selection would suggest otherwise), and the realization that, at the Sheffield School, he had found a place where he belonged. At Harvard, a good many students dropped out in response to Lincoln's call with the intention of enlisting, but most of them returned to school within a matter of weeks when the college allowed them back. Similarly, at Yale, the students formed companies and marched on the green after Fort Sumter but soon lost their enthusiasm for military drills.

At Trinity College in Hartford, where Clarence and Jim's friend Dan Dewey was going to school, the students also took to the parade ground. In a letter to King, Dan wrote, "I suppose we are to go south and fight for *States rights*. I've become a regular fire-eater, and practice swallowing a few coals before breakfast every morning, just to keep in trim." But Dewey's nervous joking covered a serious intention to volunteer once his mother could be persuaded to agree to it. Clarence wrote Jim that he might volunteer, too, but then wrote again to recant, saying that he should not have wanted "to push the bayonet. I was hot with passion . . . excited by the outrage at one of my pet ideas—'freedom.'" Clarence's indecision about volunteering, and the guilt he felt over finally not doing it, were far from rare among men of his class and generation. William and Henry James did not fight, although two of their brothers did. Henry Adams sat out the war in Britain, working for his ambassador father, although his brother Charles saw action as a cavalry officer. John Muir objected to the war on moral grounds, and took off for Canada. Of the 75 percent of the northern students at Yale who did not go during the war years, many could afford to buy their way out of service, and not a single student from the Sheffield School died in the fighting. Still, the decision ate at King, and he worried that it would be taken as a sign of cowardice or of a reluctance to become a leader of men.

When Clarence graduated in July, he had no clear idea what he would do next. However seriously he took the war and his possible obligations to it, he was still enough of a college student to take a long-planned graduation trip with Jim and Dan that would combine weeks of living in the outdoors, as a way to decompress after his studies, with training for the Yale regatta, in which King intended to compete in the fall. He borrowed a lightweight rowboat called the *Undine* from the Yale Navy and had it transported to Whitehall, New York, at the southernmost end of Lake Champlain. The three friends and a fourth, another student named Sam Parsons, launched the boat there and began to row north to Fort Ticonderoga, covering a little more than twenty miles in five hours. Over the next week or two they fished and camped and rowed along the shore of Lake Champlain toward Canada, enjoying the warm days and cool nights of late July and early August. The troubles of the world must have seemed very far away.

But however distant, the troubles were great, and they would soon create trouble enough for the four carefree boatsmen. The Union army had begun to turn the tide by the spring and summer of 1862, and the only person who didn't know it was the army's commander, George B. McClellan. The general simply could not accept victory. He continued to slink away from battles and call for more troops, even while his army killed twenty thousand Confederates during the engagements north and east of Richmond known as the Seven Days. On August 8, after Lincoln had at last replaced McClellan, Secretary of War Edwin M. Stanton signed an order forbidding men of draft age from leaving the country, in an attempt to discourage the growing tendency of young men to light out for Canada to avoid service. A bounty of five dollars a head had been placed on those caught crossing the border illegally, and U.S. marshals watching Lake Champlain "apprehended and detained" King and his friends, who were unaware of Stanton's order, before they reached the Canadian border. Jim wrote to his mother on August 14 that "We were obliged . . . to go up to the U.S. office and make affidavit that we were students and therefore exempt from the draft," which was not strictly the truth in King's case, since he had graduated the month before. But the boys were allowed to continue their journey, and eventually made their way down the Richelieu and the St. Lawrence to Quebec. If they followed the plans that King had proposed in a letter to Jim the previous fall, they went farther down the St. Lawrence and took a left at the Saguenay River, where they could fish for salmon. In any case, they eventually shipped the boat back to New Haven, took a steamer to Montreal, and went on foot back to New York State.

Returning to the United States undoubtedly caused the reality of the war to crash back in on them. Being suspected as draft dodgers must also have had its effect. As soon as Dan returned to Hartford, he volunteered and was mustered into the Twenty-fifth Regiment. Sam Parsons was a Quaker, so his decision not to fight must have been as certain as Dan's to fight. But Clare and Jim were torn, especially so, one can imagine, when news reached them of Antietam, the battle in the middle of September in which twenty-five thousand soldiers from both sides were either killed or wounded, making it the grimmest day in American history, worse even than D-day would be. The newspaper accounts must have been shocking enough, but then at the end of September Mathew Brady opened a show at his studio in New York of photographs taken of the Antietam battlefields by his associates Alexander Gardner and James F. Gibson. For one of the first times in history those who had not fought in a war saw its terrible price, the bodies of young men strewn like oak leaves in the lanes and fields. The relatively new medium of photography had never before stirred a nation's revulsion as these photographs did. Whether King saw the show or not we don't know, but he almost certainly felt its effects. The images did not send him off to war or even back to Canada, but he did absorb one lesson they had to teach, about the documentary power of the photographic image. Later King would hire a member of Alexander Gardner's Civil War corps of photographers, Timothy H. O'Sullivan, for the Fortieth Parallel Survey, establishing for the first time the value of photography to a large-scale scientific inquiry.

Given the war news, the fall regatta at Yale must have been a subdued affair. Yale and Harvard were among the few colleges that did not suspend their rowing programs during the war, but the two schools didn't meet in 1862, and the Yale Navy itself, which had had upward of three hundred members in the 1850s, had dwindled dramatically in the early 1860s. We don't know who participated in this regatta, then, nor how Clarence King fared. But it was significant in King's life because it kept him around New Haven long enough to hear a letter read aloud that would help him decide what direction his life would take.

In October 1862, King dropped by the New Haven house of Professor Brush one day and found him holding a letter that had just arrived from his friend and former classmate at Sheffield, William H. Brewer, in California. Brush read aloud to his eager young protégé from Brewer's account of an ascent of Mount Shasta, the peak in northern California then believed to be the tallest mountain in the country. Brewer described the scene at the base of the mountain, where reddish-purple insect-eating *Darlingtonia californica,* or cobra lilies, proliferated. From their camp at the base they could see the huge snow-covered cone of the mountain and its pinkish alpenglow as it loomed above them in the evening light.

"And then the moon rose," Brush read, "and we sat around our cheerful campfire (for it was cold) and gazed still. And I got up from my blankets late in the night, when the moon's illumination was finer, to look at it by that light." The letter told how the party, led by his boss, the director of the California Geological Survey, Josiah Dwight Whitney, set out before dawn and after a hard climb reached the peak by noon, where they took their measurements to determine Shasta's height. Brewer described the 360-degree view from the summit, how off to the west lay one mountain range after another all the way to the Pacific and how to the south, seventy-five miles away, rising from a valley white with haze, the top of Lassen's Butte showed, "an isolated peak of black rock and white snow rising from this sea of smoke."

At this the bedazzled King looked at his former professor, allowed himself to breathe once again, and said, simply, "That settles it."

What that settled was not, immediately, that King would go off to California to climb the stirringly beautiful peaks of the Sierra Nevada. The letter settled King on an intellectual course before he would set himself a geographical one. He began to read more geology, using as a guide Dana's new book, *Manual of Geology* (which Dana would revise throughout his lifetime, and which would become a standard text for the late nineteenth century), and by the end of January 1863, he would write to Brush that he had "pretty much made up my mind to be a geologist if I can get work in that direction." In addition to his reading, he had attended a lecture by the renowned Harvard naturalist Louis Agassiz sometime in the late fall of 1862. Agassiz, who was credited with creating the idea of the Ice Age, was lecturing on glaciology, a subject that would be of particular interest to King when he did begin to explore the Sierra Nevada in a matter of months. William James, who was a student at Harvard at the time, had written to his family that he had attended a series of Agassiz's lectures called "Methods of Study in Natural History." "He is evidently a great favorite with his audience and feels so himself," he wrote. "But he is an admirable, earnest lecturer, clear as day and his accent is most fascinating. I should like to study under him."

Agassiz's interest in glaciology went back to 1836, when his investigations of glaciers in the Swiss Alps convinced him that a thick sheet of ice had been a more important mover and shaper of the earth's surface than, for instance, water and icebergs bumping around, as Charles Lyell believed. The evidence Agassiz found was so widespread that by the next year he suggested in a lecture that "Siberian winter established itself for a time over a world previously covered with rich vegetation and peopled with large mammalia. . . . Death enveloped all nature in a shroud, and the cold, having reached its highest degree, gave to this mass of ice, at the maximum of tension, the greatest possible hardness." He reinforced his theory of an Ice Age with two studies published in the 1840s, before he moved to the United States and through the popular success of his public lectures became America's best-known scientist.

Agassiz was perhaps the last significant scientist whose views were unshaken by Darwin. As Louis Menand points out in *The Metaphysical Club*, "The purpose of *On the Origin of Species* was not to introduce the concept of evolution; it was to debunk the concept of supernatural intelligence—the idea that the universe is the result of an idea." Evolution was a theory that had been around for half a century by 1859, when *On the Origin of Species* came out. The new thing that Darwin's natural selection proved was that changes occur in nature with utter randomness. They don't occur to make a species more perfect; they simply occur, and the changes that make a species less perfect are selected out. This insight argues against a grand design created either by God, by Nature, or by some other force with an outcome in mind. As a scientist, Agassiz had dealt enough with observable geological facts to know that a literal interpretation of the Bible's creation story could not be true. He believed with the catastrophists that large natural events had wiped the slate of the earth clean periodically—the Ice Age being a prime example. After each such event, Agassiz believed, new and more perfect species were created.

The species themselves were "categories of thought embodied in individual living forms," as Agassiz put it, and so catastrophe was God's way of starting over whenever he had new and better ideas for his creation. Darwinian randomness was, to say the least, antithetical to such an idea. As Menand puts it, Agassiz "was unable to see how chance could be a cause of order, and he was unable to imagine order that was not the product of a mind." To Agassiz, Darwin had made "a scientific mistake." But by the time William James and Clarence King attended Agassiz's lectures, Darwinism was already taking hold, and Agassiz's unwillingness to accept it was turning him into a figure of the past rather than the future. For King, though, Agassiz was a man who bridged his own religious past and his dedication to a life in science. Only months later, when King was first exploring the Sierra Nevada, he would parrot Agassiz in a journal entry in which he said that God "scented all with design . . . that lessons were taught in Nature which were not elsewhere." King also believed in catastrophism and would hang on to a version of the idea throughout his useful scientific life, giving a commencement address called "Catastrophism and the Evolution of Environment" when he was invited back to Sheffield in 1877. The speech was much talked about at the time he gave it, but it would not help his long-term reputation as a geologist. And yet the theory that the late

Stephen Jay Gould helped propound a century later, of "punctuated equilibria," in which geological and biological changes occur in cycles where periods of very little change are followed by brief periods of dramatic change, resembles what King called "modified catastrophism" in his Sheffield graduation speech.

Besides Dana and Agassiz, King found one more influence in the fall of 1862 and the winter of 1863. That was John Ruskin, the English art critic whose five-volume *Modern Painters* (published from 1843 to 1860) argued that art must find its truth in nature, that the contemplation of nature was a source of emotional energy for the artist, and that the natural world is not a passive, orderly creation but is chaotic, ever changing, and deeply alive. Mountains, especially the Alps, about which Ruskin wrote in *Modern Painters* with a singular passion, were for him anything but set in stone:

> Mountains are, to the rest of the body of the earth, what violent muscular action is to the body of man. The muscles and tendons of its anatomy are, in the mountain, brought out with fierce and convulsive energy, full of expression, passion, and strength; the plains and the lower hills are the repose and the effortless motion of the frame, when its muscles lie dormant and concealed beneath the lines of its beauty, yet ruling those lines in their every undulation.

King also read about the Alps at about this time in a newish book by John Tyndall, a British physicist and lecturer. Tyndall had written a serious scientific treatise with Thomas Huxley called *On the Structure and Motion of Glaciers* in the 1850s and followed it in 1860, writing alone, with his more colorful *Glaciers of the Alps*. King wrote in his own Ruskinian work, *Mountaineering in the Sierra Nevada*, that "Ruskin helps us to know himself, not the Alps; his mountain chapters, although essentially four thousand years old, are, however, no more an anachronism than the dim primeval spark which smoulders in all of us; their brilliancy *is* that spark fanned into flame. To follow a chapter of Ruskin's by one of Tyndall's is to bridge forty centuries and realize the full contrast of archaic and modern thought."

By the end of January, King had moved to Manhattan to share an apartment with Jim Gardner, who was attending law school on Washington Square at what is now New York University. Jim was already feeling the strain of his legal studies but wrote his mother that Clare's upbeat nature was "as good as sunshine." They filled their rooms with books and pictures, and found themselves drawn to a group of what Jim called "practical Ruskinites of the city," who modeled themselves on the British Pre-Raphaelite Brotherhood and held similar views on nature and art. The American group, founded on February 18, 1863, by seven men including King but not Gardner, called themselves, with a solemnity that might have made King chuckle, "The Society for the Advancement of Truth in Art." The other members were an artist who had studied with Ruskin in England, a journalist who started a magazine devoted to Pre-Raphaelite ideas called *New Path,* an art student who would become a well-known professor of art, an architect, an architecture critic, and a future diplomat. Their credo was dogmatically Ruskinian. After much argument among the seven, the group's Articles of Organization held that, for visual art as well as for literary:

> We hold that the primary object of Art is to observe and record truth, whether of the visible universe or of emotion. . . . The greatest Art includes the widest range, recording, with equal fidelity, the aspirations of the human soul, and the humblest facts of physical Nature.
>
> That the imagination can do its work, and free invention is possible only when the knowledge of external Nature is extended and accurate. . . .
>
> That beauty . . . can only be appreciated and seized by those who are trained to observe and record all truths with equal exactness. . . .
>
> Therefore, that the right course for *young* Artists is the faithful and loving representations of Nature . . .

This Ruskinian concept of truth to nature was a reaction to the classical traditions of academic art, and in architecture as well the American Pre-Raphaelites echoed Ruskin's call for a return to the Gothic in reaction to the neoclassical standard of the time. ("In that hot-bed of the false and ridiculous in Art, Washington City, the ancient faith in the Greek colonnade still holds sway," an essay in *New Path* chided.) So carefully did *New Path* align itself with Ruskin's ideas that the great man himself soon wrote to the little magazine from England, offering "my thanks for the help you are giving me in carrying forward and illustrating the views which I have hitherto endeavoured to maintain almost singlehanded."

King turned twenty-one that January. How much different was his experience of New York now than it had been at eighteen, when he'd clerked for the flour merchant and ridden the ferry from Brooklyn. Now he was living near Washington Square, spending his evenings with artists and idealists, rooming not with his mother but his best friend. No word has come down the years of how King fared with the same sorts of young women who had inflamed his passions at eighteen. But his religious fervor had faded, he'd grown older and more self-assured, and judging by a photograph of him taken only a year or two later, he had become a dazzlingly handsome young man. King's mother had moved with her husband, George Howland, his surviving child from his first marriage, and their new daughter up the Hudson to Irvington, New York. Howland was almost certainly still paying Clarence's way. King would make the hour train ride to Irvington from time to time and go geologizing along the Hudson, but his days in Manhattan were free for reading and socializing. As a scientific who had lived off campus, King might well have missed out on the sort of late-night bull sessions in which college students begin to test their notions of philosophy and aesthetics. How much headier, then, must the meetings of the American Pre-Raphaelites have seemed, and how much more exotic their notions about painting and poetry and architecture. Still, King was not a one-dimensional science nerd. Thanks to his mother he was broadly educated, already a good talker and writer. And his family had an artistic tradition beyond his grandmother's anti-slavery novel. King's great-grandfather Samuel had been a painter and a successful teacher of painting in Newport. Among his students had been two miniaturists who were well known in their time, and Gilbert Stuart himself had taken art lessons from him. Stuart was now one of the bêtes noires of the American Pre-Raphaelites, part of the tradition they wanted to tear down.

For King, then, as he roamed the streets of lower Manhattan in the spring of 1863, truth to nature covered a lot of ground. Since boyhood he had been an enthusiastic natural historian. His scientific training had prepared him to observe, measure, and conduct experiments upon the earth and its mineral elements. Agassiz had reinforced the idea, going back to King's first schoolmaster, Rev. Park, that the natural world gave evidence of God's design. Ruskin and Tyndall had filled him with romantic notions about the power and beauty of mountains. And his fellow idealists in the Society for the Advancement of Truth in Art proposed that the artist and the scientist shared similar methods and similar goals in the objective observation of nature. It was at about this time that King wrote in a small notebook he carried, "You, Clarence King, never dare to look or speak of nature save with respect and all the admiration you are capable of."

The weather began to hint of spring, and it must have been clear to King that the canyons of Manhattan and even the cliffs of the Hudson were not going to hold him. As early as the end of January he had asked Professor Brush for a recommendation to work for the Whitney survey of California, "in any capacity from blow piper to mule driver." Already a skillful reader of men, King had promised, in return, to find specimens for the vast minerals collection that would be Brush's most passionate contribution to Yale. Not that Brush needed much prodding. In later years he would think of King as the Sheffield School's "greatest graduate."

Jim's struggles with his law studies, meanwhile, had pushed him to the point of nervous breakdown. As he tried to apply himself to the dry and for him unpalatable legal cases upon which he would be examined, he had undoubtedly listened to an unending stream of conversation from Clare about the wide-open continent he would like to cross and the breathtaking mountains on the other side. It would be like one of their youthful nature rambles, like their rowing trip to Canada, but it would never end. We know from Jim's decision to transfer to Yale that King could influence him to make even the biggest changes in his life. Besides, this time his emotional health was at risk. Could either of them have doubted for a moment that Jim would agree to go west with Clare? As it happened, a fellow they knew named William Hyde also wanted to go west, as far as the Nevada Territory, where his father owned a foundry in a mining boomtown near Virginia City and the Comstock Lode. Having a third companion must have made the prospect of the trip that much more palatable. But as it turned out, the presence of Bill Hyde would cost them all of their possessions and nearly cost them their lives as well.

## CHAPTER THREE

# Crossing the Continent

*Supply wagons and pack mules on the Great Plains.*

The Pony Express, with its teams of riders and mounts, covered the two thousand miles from St. Joseph, Missouri, to San Francisco in eight days. Clarence King would make his first transcontinental crossing by pony, too, leaving St. Joseph a year and a half after the first coast-to-coast telegraph connection, completed in the fall of 1861, made the Pony Express obsolete. His trip would take almost four months.

By May 1863, when Clarence, Jim Gardner, and William Hyde set off by wagon train from St. Joseph, crossing the continent in this way had a history of nearly forty years. The great migrations had begun twenty years earlier, in 1843, with large trains made up of many families heading to Oregon's Willamette Valley and elsewhere in the northwest by what became known as the Oregon Trail. The Donner Party left Springfield, Illinois, for California in 1846. Brigham Young established his desert kingdom in Utah in 1847, and thousands followed by wagon to people it. With the Gold Rush of 1849, tens of thousands more fortune seekers made the overland journey to the West. Yet even by 1863 the trip was far from routine. The passage west of so many settlers was highly unsettling, of course, for the many native tribes that lived along the emigrant trails. When King stopped off to see his mother in Irvington on his way to Niagara, where the three young friends would begin the railway portion of their adventure, Florence expressed her alarm that the Sioux had recently been in a state of agitation. Two years after King's wagon train went west, the Massachusetts newspaper editor Samuel Bowles took a stagecoach along much of the same route. In his account of his journey, *Across the Continent,* Bowles writes that as his party prepared for the first leg of its trip, from Atchison, Kansas, to Fort Kearney, Nebraska, a route by then well traveled by wagonloads of supplies and goods headed for the Far West, the incoming stage arrived

with the news that it had been attacked by Indians about one hundred and forty miles back . . . some of the Indians had broken through or run around the military lines. They commenced by ambushing a party of some twelve to twenty soldiers, mostly converted rebels, on their way up from Leavenworth to Fort Kearney, but without arms. Two of these were killed outright, and most of the rest they wounded so savagely that they will probably die. The next day they assaulted the incoming stage, which had some six or eight passengers, men, women and children, circling around and around the vehicle on well-mounted horses, and shooting their arrows fast and sharp . . . They numbered about twenty-five in all, and their appearance on what was supposed to be the safest part of the route, and the one least protected by soldiers, had made some excitement.

Two days later, when Bowles's stagecoach (traveling about half as fast as the Pony Express and many times faster than King's wagon train) arrived in Fort Kearney, Bowles wrote, "We came through the region of the Indian surprises and attacks of last week, but met no hostile red-skin. We found abundant evidences, however, of their last year's swoop through the line, in ruins of houses and barns which they burned, and stories of their terrible massacres."

Early in their trip, King's party would occasionally see Potawatomis in small bands, which would come closer at night when the train camped, but none seemed threatening. At least at first, the weather was so terrible that any attack would have had to take place in ludicrous slow motion, given the mud. The wagon train that King and his friends joined, formed by a horse and mule trader from St. Louis named Speers, left St. Joseph on May 1, late enough in the season for the plains grasses to sprout, providing feed for the stock they were driving to California to sell. Three covered wagons and a smaller conveyance for Mrs. Speers and her children accompanied the herd of mules and horses. They crossed the Missouri on a newly completed bridge—the Pony Express had had to take a ferry—and on their second day in Kansas the rains began, miring their wagons in the mud. Their route, an old military road that had become one of the principal paths from the Missouri to the Far West, took them across the northeast corner of Kansas into Nebraska, where they would follow the south bank of the Platte River west across the plains.

In Kansas, as King and his friends soon discovered, there was more to fear from the whites than from the natives. Ever since the Kansas-Nebraska Act had passed Congress in 1854, undermining the Missouri Compromise that had established a geographical dividing line between slave states and free states entering the Union, the territory had been wracked by guerrilla warfare between pro-slavery and anti-slavery groups, the latter led by John Brown himself. The territory would earn the name "Bloody Kansas" before entering the Union as a free state just before the Civil War began. But tensions did not end during the war years. In his January 14,

1863, inaugural message as governor of Kansas, Thomas Carney warned that

> Kansas has been disturbed by lawless bands, professing ability to executive law and to protect private property. Raids and robberies have followed. Our most populous cities have been controlled for hours, if not for days, by those who claimed, insolently, to be the defenders of right and justice. Demoralization of the worst kind has ensued. These bands and their agents, whatever their pretence or whoever they may be, must be put down and kept down, be the cost what it may.

The Speers wagon train had managed to cover only fifteen miles when King and his friends were grabbed by vigilantes and dragged before what Thurman Wilkins calls the "quagmire court" in Troy before Speers rescued them. If the rain and mud had not dampened the expectations of the three for the journey, surely this incident would have. Still, years later, what Jim remembered about the early parts of the trip was King's irrepressible interest in his fellow travelers. "In that journey," Jim wrote, "he showed his wonderful power of entering the lives and sympathies of every human being in the train, from the half-breed Indian hunter to the gaunt and bigoted Southwestern Missouri emigrant."

Samuel Bowles would make the trip from Atchison to Fort Kearney on May 22 and 23 of 1865, but he writes that the season was late that year, so the landscape he passed through must have looked very much like what the King party saw during the first two weeks of 1863. The newspaper editor wrote:

> The country up to fifty miles of [Fort Kearney], presents the characteristics of the finest prairie scenery of the West—illimitable stretches of exquisite green surface, rolling like long waves of the sea, and broken at distances of miles by an intervale with a small stream, along whose banks are scattered trees of elm and cottonwood. . . . Within the last fifty miles, the soil grows thinner, the

grass less rich, the sand hills of the Platte rise before the eye, and Plain, rather than Prairie, becomes the true descriptive name. The streams are few and scant, and the water muddy . . . It is too early yet for many of the prairie flowers; but the rich, fresh green of the grass satisfies the eye.

After King had his famous run-in with the buffalo, his guide took him to an army doctor at Fort Kearney, the oldest active military post in Nebraska, built on the Oregon Trail route on the south bank of the Platte. By 1863, it had a dozen buildings arranged in a square, some of sod or adobe, and comfortable officers quarters made of well-tended clapboard. The fort's chief feature, in the middle of the nearly treeless plains, was the tall, shady cottonwood trees that lined the parade ground surrounded by the buildings. In later years the trees, which had been planted as saplings in the late 1840s, would have trunks ten feet in diameter. As a place where two stagecoach routes met, Dobytown, outside the fort, was known for its good food and bad whiskey. It was both an oasis of civility in what was still known as the Great American Desert and a place to get your throat slit.

In other circumstances, at least later in life, King would have been drawn by both aspects of the little wayside's civilian nightlife. But the buffalo-hunting accident probably made fine dining as unlikely as tomcatting. King had managed not to break his leg when his hunting pony fell on him after the buffalo rammed it, but the weight of the animal had caused some damage that would take weeks to heal properly. The next day he would struggle onto the Overland Stage heading west until it caught up with the wagon train. Because of the accident, he had no fresh meat to share with the others, but he did have a good tale and a jaunty limp. That limp, along with his cowboy clothing and the muttonchop sideburns he was growing, added to the romance of his buffalo stampede story, one that he would tell for years to come. He'd already had two brushes with death, given the unpredictability of the kangaroo court in Kansas, and the myth of Clarence King had its first heroic chapter.

♦  ♦  ♦

The wagon train bounced west across Nebraska along the valley of the Platte the two hundred miles from Fort Kearney to Julesburg, just across the border in Colorado, where those who were not going to Denver along the south fork of the Platte forded the river and headed for one of the passes in the Rockies. Even during the war this was a heavily traveled road, filled with the Conestoga wagons of the emigrants (their white covers looking from a distance like sails on the oceanic plains, as the cliché went), convoys of military supplies, commercial freight wagons, and the regular coaches of the Overland Stage Line. Every dozen miles or so along the road was some sort of settlement, as small as a single cedar-logged cabin with a sod roof or as big as a handful of adobe buildings, which served the stagecoach, the post, and the telegraph. The river itself was wide, shallow and sandy, often lined with cottonwoods and spotted with islands where willows grew—at least until the passing hordes cut them all down for campfires. Travelers from the East like Clarence King remarked on the titanic thunderstorms and the large number of rattlesnakes along the way, and well out on the Plains on a bright day they would sometimes see their first glimmering mirages, which might look like an endless herd of buffalo or a twinkling inverted city, off in a middle distance that never grew nearer. In 1863, the Indians kept their distance along this stretch, although in the bloody summer of 1864 they would burn all but one of the stage stations, steal or drive away the stock, attack wagon trains, and murder ranch families, bringing the ever increasing traffic along the Overland route to a halt for several months.

The ford at Julesburg, first called the Upper California Crossing, had been used for years in spite of patches of quicksand that were a problem all along the Platte, but it would lose favor as a crossing only a few months after the Speers train went through. Julesburg had the largest buildings between Fort Kearney and Denver, but it was a rough town. Samuel Clemens had come west by stagecoach in 1861, traveling virtually the same route from St. Joe's to Carson City, which he describes under his pen name, Mark Twain, in his wonderfully high-spirited travel book, *Roughing It*. In the book, he calls Julesburg "the strangest, quaintest, funniest frontier town that our untraveled eyes had ever stared at and been astonished with," but he doesn't elaborate. In the winter of 1865, all of its buildings—the stage station, houses, barns, a warehouse, a telegraph office, a blacksmith shop, and sheds, mostly built of cedar logs that had been hauled a hundred miles from the mountains by mules—were burned by marauding Indians, and the town was abandoned until the Union Pacific Railroad went through the town in 1867 and built a station.

King's party passed all across Nebraska and into Wyoming Territory with no sign of hostile Indians, although King took his turn every third night standing watch as a precaution. An emigrant family traveling alone with two daughters, the older of whom especially interested Jim, would join their train near Fort Laramie because of rumors that the route had grown more dangerous. Once, beyond Fort Laramie in the Badlands, where the landscape turned dry and alkaline, King, whose leg had mended, rode with a companion miles off their route to find "cold pure water" in the mountains. As they rode back they came upon an Indian encampment and spent an anxious night hiding as best they could in the empty desert to avoid being discovered. They returned to the wagon train the next morning after the Indians moved on.

The Speers train would pass Fort Laramie in Wyoming Territory, and from there head west along the Main Emigrant Route following the North Fork of the Platte and then the Sweetwater River to South Pass in the Rockies. Once they crossed the Rockies at South Pass and turned south, still tracing the Overland stage route toward Fort Bridger and Utah, Indian parties lingered near their camps each evening. Shoshones were gathering in large numbers and would cut the road soon after the Speers party passed, but their wagon train reached Fort Bridger without incident.

By the end of June, almost exactly two months after they'd crossed the Missouri, they saw the Great Salt Lake and passed through its fertile valley into Salt Lake City itself. As they rested in the vast public square, watering their stock from a cold stream fed by melting mountain snows, they noticed all around them the bustling city's small buildings of brick or sod or wood, and nearby the great tabernacle under construction. In *Roughing It,* Twain notes Salt Lake's "broad, straight, level streets" and "a grand general air of neatness, repair, thrift and comfort, around and about and over the whole." While the Speers party was refreshing itself, a carriage pulled by two massive mules approached, bearing Brigham Young himself, who offered advice about the next leg of their journey, across the Great Basin to Carson City, Nevada. Hostile Utes were making raids along the route, but Young urged the travelers to offer "a biscuit instead of a bullet" if they encountered any Indians, with whom the Mormons were trying to keep the peace. The last leg of their journey took another month. Although they could see the signal fires of the natives winking all around them at night, their luck continued to hold. A member of an emigrant party that passed along the same route a few days later wrote, "For three hundred miles we rode expecting death in every canyon."

But King and Gardner were so exhilarated by their new experiences that they were able to put aside their fears. As Gardner wrote his mother a few weeks later, "Before we left the Plains we had become so fascinated with the life and so interested in the vast loneliness in these deserts . . . that I would gladly have turned around and traveled back over the same road." The variety and intrinsic interest of the lands they passed through, both men later said, would shape their scientific studies for years to come. Once the Plains give way to the Rockies, the landscape becomes more and more audaciously geological, offering dazzling evidence of the ways in which wind, water, and ice carve up the earth, leaving imposing buttes, strange rock formations, and narrow valleys defined by sheer red sandstone walls. As Samuel Bowles proved, you didn't have to be trained as a geologist to appreciate the wonders of what the elements have created in that area:

The effect of the high winds and blowing sands and sharp rains of this region upon the soft rock and clay of some of these hills, is certainly very curious. These agencies have proved wonderful miracle-workers. . . . the tall, isolated rocks, that surmount a hill, sometimes round, but always even and smooth as work of finest chisel; the immense columns and fantastic figures upon the walls of rock that line a valley for miles; the solitary mountains upon the plain, fashioned like fortresses, or rising like Gothic cathedrals, and called *buttes* (a French word signifying isolated hill or mountain), separated from their family in some great convulsion of nature; the long lines of rock embankment, one above another, formed sometimes in squares like a vast fort, and again running for miles, a hundred feet above the valley . . .

Many of the geological curiosities that King's party passed were already well known to the thousands of travelers who had trudged by for years. Near Fort Laramie, within view of the road, were Castle and Chimney rocks. As D. A. Shaw, a pioneer who saw them on his way to California in 1850 wrote, "One resembled an immense castle, with its walls and towering domes, and the other a column of an immense height, round and perfect as though built by human hands." Farther along the route, as they approached South Pass, King's party came near Independence Rock, where the Great Pathfinder John C. Frémont had carved his initials in 1842 and thousands of other travelers had followed suit.

Of the geological sights along the way, perhaps the least impressive was South Pass itself, where the momentous crest of the Continental Divide is difficult even to discern. As Frémont wrote in one of his exploration reports, "The ascent had been so gradual, that, with all the intimate knowledge possessed by [Kit] Carson, who had made this country his home for seventeen years, we were obliged to watch very closely to find the place at which we had reached the culminating point." To the north, though, the Wind River Mountains loomed, "gleaming like silver" and luring Frémont into them, where he would name one of the peaks for himself.

After crossing the Green River and arriving in Fort Bridger on June 24, the Speers train continued on to the southwest, passing through the Wasatch Range into Utah via Echo Canyon, where King and his companions undoubtedly gaped at the sheer red sandstone walls. Much of the territory through which they were now traveling, from as far back as Fort Laramie and ahead to Carson City, would be the subject of King's Fortieth Parallel Survey. His traversal of the Great Basin—the area between the Rockies and the Sierra Nevada (which, Frémont was the first to realize, acted like a basin out of which no rivers or streams drained)—clearly planted the seed for the mission King would lead only four years later. His first good look at the Sierra Nevada themselves probably came when the party reached the Carson River on August 6. Later, King would describe this view as being of a range "high against the west, its summits snow-capped, and its flanks shaded by a forest of dark green pines."

Their route from Salt Lake City to Carson City roughly followed today's US 50, weaving when possible through the many small mountain ranges of central Nevada. After Samuel Clemens had been in Carson City for several months, long enough to get the lay of the land, he wrote in a letter home to his mother that "the country is fabulously rich in gold, silver, copper, lead, coal, iron, quicksilver, marble, granite, chalk, plaster of Paris, (gypsum,) thieves, murderers, desperadoes, ladies, children, lawyers, Christians, Indians, Chinamen, Spaniards, gamblers, sharpers, coyotes (pronounced Ki-yo-ties,) poets, preachers, and jackass rabbits." This swirling mixture of the animal and the mineral, the sacred and the profane, surely continued to characterize the whole culture drawn to the Comstock Lode—that rich seam of silver and gold discovered in the mountains above Carson City in 1859—four years later when King arrived and Clemens had gone to work for the nearby Virginia City newspaper and taken the name Mark Twain.

At Carson City, King, Jim, and William Hyde left the Speers wagon train, which was pushing ahead across the Sierra Nevada into California on the Placerville Road. Clarence and Jim planned to accompany Bill Hyde home to Gold Hill, which required them to backtrack seven miles to Silver City and head north another seven miles, almost to Virginia City, above the Comstock Lode. Bill's father owned the Pioneer Foundry, built like everything in the town on the steeply pitched side of Mount Davidson, and business was booming. Presumably he had put so much effort into the business that the Hyde house was too modest to accommodate Bill's two guests, who slept in the wooden foundry building itself along with a dozen or so workers. On the very night they arrived the wind gusted so strongly that the building where they slept rattled and shook; it was a veritable Washoe Zephyr, the Nevada mountain wind about which Twain wrote in *Roughing It,* "It is by no means a trifling matter. It blows flimsy houses down, lifts shingle roofs occasionally, rolls up tin ones like sheet music, now and then blows a stage coach over and spills the passengers." At one in the morning Clarence and Jim awoke to the shouts of the foundrymen—the building was aflame and filled with smoke. Everyone managed to escape, but in the strong wind the foundry went fast, and Clarence and Jim lost all of their possessions except the clothes they were wearing and their ponies. Most troubling to them, probably, was watching their cash burn up, but from this distance it is easiest to regret the loss of notebooks each of them had been keeping about the geological features of the landscape they were passing through.

Bill's father estimated his own losses at a hundred thousand dollars, none of them insured, but such were the boom times that he immediately began to clear the site and rebuild. Clarence and Jim might well have pitched in to make enough cash to continue on their trip. One friend of King's in later life reports that the two went to work as day laborers in a nearby quartz mill. Whatever else they did for money, they also sold their ponies and toward the end of August set out on foot back to Carson City, around Lake Tahoe, and onto the Placerville Road to cross the Sierras into California. They had announced their intention to have a look at the Comstock Lode itself, but with the fire and the scramble for money that followed, they might not have seen it on that visit. But the Comstock Lode would be one of King's priorities for his survey of the Fortieth Parallel. He would return more than once, and the survey's photographer, Timothy O'Sullivan, would join him and leave some memorable images of the mining region, including Gold Hill, and of the mines beneath.

The Placerville Road was the primary wagon route into Northern California from the east, passing through the Sierra Nevada near Echo Lake and Echo Summit and eventually into the valley and on to Placerville itself. In the years after the Comstock strike, the roads through the passes had been filled with eastbound traffic, out of California and into Nevada. But by 1863, the traffic was again going mainly west, with supply wagons pulled by mules, emigrant trains like the Speers', and coaches filling the road.

Clarence and Jim found it easy to hitch a ride on a freight wagon, sitting alongside the teamster as the mules trudged up and over the mountains and eventually into the town of Placerville, named for the placers—the gravel or sand deposits in streams— where so much of the 1849 gold was found, and where so much more was sought. Placerville was far from tame even fifteen years after it was founded in 1848. The story goes that the teamster liked the two young men well enough to buy them dinner at a small hotel on the Saturday night of their arrival. In the bar of the hotel, a loudmouthed drunk began to talk secession, and his attention focused on King. Even wearing the dust and grime of the road, the youthful-looking and articulate King was obviously a college boy, always a good target for a bully in a bar. Perhaps King was uncharacteristically silent, perhaps not, but soon the secessionist's hand began to hover over the six-gun he was wearing. King's own Navy Colt had been lost in the fire, so he was very much unarmed. According to King's friend Edgar Bronson, in his book *Reminiscences of a Ranchman*, Colts were often sported by poseurs (like King himself, actually), whereas "one or more of the vest or trouser pockets of the really ready and artistic life-takers was sure to hold a short Derringer pistol, which was often, on due emergency, fired from within the pocket." Knowing this, King, who happened to have his hand in his right pocket at the time, supposedly "stuck forward his thumb until it looked like a muzzle of a pistol and then snapped a quill toothpick that fortunately happened to be in the same pocket." The sound was like that of a pistol being cocked, Bronson suggests, and upon hearing it the secessionist fled, Colt and all. At this, King turned to Jim and said, in a punch line surely honed by many tellings, "Gardner, in this country there are not many wolves in sheep's clothing, but there are a lot of sheep in wolves' clothing."

The next day the teamster drove on, heading south to Stockton, but Clare and Jim decided to honor the Sabbath, and because they didn't have clothes appropriate for church even in a town like Placerville, they climbed a nearby hillside and Jim read aloud from a Bible they had picked up somewhere, in that voice that had prevented him from becoming a preacher, the Sermon on the Mount. On Monday, August 30, they took a coach to the Central Pacific rail line and the train to Sacramento. By four that afternoon they had reached a dock on the muddy Sacramento River, where they set off on a paddlewheel steamboat filled with miners heading to San Francisco to spend their earnings. The miners, who wore flannel shirts and high muddy boots, and had revolvers stuffed under their belts, weren't wasting any time unburdening themselves of their troubles and their cash, drinking rowdily from a bar on the steamer's open deck. Jim noticed one man in a grubby gray shirt and a well-traveled hat, who stood out for not joining in the festivities, but sitting quietly smoking a pipe.

"Again and again I walked past him," Jim later wrote, "and at last, seating myself in a chair opposite and pretending to read a paper, I deliberately studied this fascinating individual." Jim then walked Clarence past the man several times to see if his friend was also struck by the look of him. The fascinator would give his own account some years later. "I noticed two young men conversing together in low tones, and curiously glancing from time to time at me, attracted, no doubt, by my costume and appearance, which indicated that I was engaged in rough mountain- or forest-work of some kind, yet not that of the hunter or the miner." Whether or not the two young men could yet read the subtleties of Western costuming, Jim and Clare both saw something in the man's calm expression that, despite his sunburned face and disreputable clothing, marked him as an educated person. After a while Clarence had an insight so remarkable that without the accounts of the other two people present we could doubt it as more mythologizing. King screwed up his courage and approached the bearded man.

"Is your name Brewer?" he asked.

"Yes," was the unlikely reply.

"Of the California Geological Survey?" King asked with growing relief.

"Yes."

"Well," King said, "I had a letter of introduction to you from Prof. Brush, but it burned up the other day!"

William H. Brewer had, of course, written that letter to Professor Brush about Mount Shasta, the one that had convinced King to go to California, so Brewer was the very man in California whom King most wanted to meet. As Jim reports, "Clare introduced himself as a student from Yale Scientific School and was warmly received. He then introduced me and we all spent the evening together." Brewer remembered that "I liked King from the first; he gave me much comparatively recent information concerning my old friends at Yale; I told him my plans; and we agreed to meet in San Francisco."

As the sky grew darker and the miners rowdier around them, Brewer told his two new acquaintances that he had

been making, that summer, a reconnaissance in the Sierra Nevada, beginning in the extreme southern part, at Tejon, and zigzagging six or eight times across the divide, my last crossing having been from the northern end of Lake Tahoe to Forest Hill. My party had been reduced by sickness and other causes until, during the last four crossings, I had with me my packer only. It was my desire to continue the reconnaissance northward as far as Lassen Peak; but another man, at least, was needed—especially as the Indians were reported to have broken out from Lassen Peak to the Shasta valley.

Imagine the excitement with which King must have heard these words. Not only had Brewer appeared as if by magic within a few days of their crossing into California, but now he was looking for an assistant to accompany him to within sight of mighty Shasta itself. If on his journey west King had been able to charm everyone from the Speers children in the bouncy railroad car to the teamster in his wagon crossing the mountains, how he must have turned it on in the presence of Brewer on the Sacramento River steamer. All of those qualities that had drawn people to King, the youthful energy and enthusiasm, the animal strength and grace, the intelligence and witty loquacity, and something like a strong dramatic presence, would have been fired up now for this solitary, contemplative man. Brewer must still have been wounded by the sudden loss of his young family back East several years before, but he was also consumed by the massive task of completing the puzzle of California's topography and geology.

By the time they had arrived in San Francisco, Brewer had urged King and Gardner to stay at his hotel. Brewer had hinted that he might need more than one man to join him as he went back in the field. The next day, after the two friends bought some presentable clothes, Gardner went with King to the California Geological Survey's offices, where the leader of the survey, Josiah Whitney, and other members of the group happened to be back from the field. Three rooms were filled with plant and mineral specimens they had gathered in their work. For whatever reason, Jim seems to have dropped out of the running for a job at this point, but Clarence made several more visits to the offices, "deepening on each occasion," Brewer remembered, "my affection and esteem for him." During this time Brewer had consulted with the Indian agent in San Francisco about the rumors that the natives were about to go to war north of Lassen Peak. The agent had told Brewer that it would be "madness" to try to go into the Shasta Valley, "but I decided to start anyhow, and go as far as I could." King had made it very clear that he wanted to go, too, even if he had to work as an unpaid volunteer. "The possible danger of the trip," Brewer wrote drily, "was an additional temptation to him." King undoubtedly turned his charm on Whitney, too, whose younger brother, William, King's German professor at Yale, he had charmed two years before. The two older men never had a chance in the face of this personality onslaught. Brewer reports that within a day or two "Whitney (who was likewise captivated by [King's] light and ardent nature) authorized me to engage him." King was just where he wanted to be.

## CHAPTER FOUR

# Into the Field

*Corps of the California Survey, Christmas 1863.*
*From left: Chester Averill, William M. Gabb, William*
*Ashburner, Josiah D. Whitney, Charles F. Hoffmann,*
*Clarence King, and William H. Brewer.*

Josiah Dwight Whitney was forty-three years old when Clarence King met him at the California Geological Survey offices in San Francisco in early September 1863. Whitney had been head of the survey since the California legislature established it in April 1860; the act's first provision had appointed him state geologist. Much of the rest of the act, spelling out the scope and goals of the survey, Whitney had very conveniently written himself. He had gotten the job in part through family connections with the most powerful politician in California at the time, Stephen J. Field, a legislator who was about to become chief justice of the California Supreme Court and would later be a U.S. Supreme Court justice. But Whitney's appointment was one of those rare cases of the fix being in for the man with the best possible qualifications (if not, as it would turn out, the best possible political skills) for the job.

The firstborn child of a Northampton, Massachusetts, banker descended from Puritans, Whitney attended Round Hill School, which had been established in Northampton by George Bancroft before Bancroft made his reputation as a historian and statesman. According to the *Dictionary of American Biography,* the school was "well known for its strict but kindly discipline, its thorough instruction on the plan of the German *gymnasium,* and the vigorous outdoor life and manly spirit it fostered." From there Whitney went to Yale, where he was elected to Phi Beta Kappa and graduated in 1839. The family expected him to go on to Harvard Law School, but Whitney, who wanted to be a chemist, instead went to work in a chemical laboratory in Philadelphia before becoming assistant geologist on the New Hampshire state survey. After two years in New Hampshire, he went to Europe to study chemistry under Justus Liebig in Germany and geology with Elie de Beaumont in France. He also went to lectures by the great naturalist Alexander von Humboldt, whose early conservationist approach to the natural world would shape a generation of California scientists, including Whitney, William Brewer, and King. When he returned from Europe, Whitney worked for several years on a survey of Lake Superior and then traveled the states east of the Mississippi to produce, in 1854, *The Metallic Wealth of the United States,* which became the standard work on the subject for the next twenty years. During the rest of the 1850s, he was the state geologist in Iowa, where he produced a survey with the paleontologist James Hall, and then helped conduct the surveys of Wisconsin and Illinois.

As early as the end of 1848, while Whitney was writing a report about the copper lands of Lake Superior, he responded to the first news of gold in California not by chucking everything and heading for the goldfields himself but by attempting to mine a different sort of geological wealth. In a letter to his brother, William, he playfully wrote that "California is all the rage now and poor Lake Superior has to be shoved into the background. We are planning to secure the geological survey of that interesting land, where the farmers can't plough their fields by reason of the huge lumps of gold in the soil." He didn't follow through, though, because he was soon appointed codirector of the Lake Superior survey. During the 1850s, others completed two perfunctory geological studies of California, and by 1859, Whitney was ready to propose a new and ambitious survey of the state. He got recommendations for the job from such scientific heavyweights as Agassiz, Dana, Brush, and Benjamin Silliman the elder and his son of the same name, who was now teaching at Yale. His own reputation, because of *Metallic Wealth*, was almost as substantial as theirs.

Less surprising than Whitney's landing the job were the terms of the survey. After the Gold Rush and then the recent 1859 Comstock Lode find, legislators in California, never apt to spend money on something as impractical as knowledge, were less interested than ever in pure science. They wanted to hire scientists who could tell them where the next big hit would be or who could find other ways to advance the commercial interests of the state. In the language that Whitney drafted for the legislature, though, there was no mention among the survey's goals of locating specific mineral deposits except as part of "a full and scientific description of [the state's] rocks, fossils, soils, and minerals, and of its botanical and zoological productions." Whitney would later tell legislators that "it was not the business of a geological surveying corps to act to any considerable extent as a prospecting party." But the defensiveness of that statement came after the relationship between the survey and the legislature had begun to sour. When Whitney arrived in San Francisco by ship on November 15, 1860, ready to begin his work, the newspapers took note and the governor himself hurried down to greet him. Whitney and Brewer, who had sailed with him from Boston, found the weather, both climatologically and politically, "perfectly heavenly."

♦  ♦  ♦

Before Whitney and his team could make a comprehensive study of the state's geology, charting the underground strata and establishing what minerals and fossils could be found in them, they needed a reliable map of the earth's surface, something that didn't exist yet for the state as a whole, although the coastline had been mapped and a boundary survey was under way. Whitney's plan was to divide the state into four bands running north to south: the coast, the western slope of the Sierras (where much of the richest gold mining had taken place), the summits of the High Sierras, and the eastern slope. His men would move up and down these bands fairly quickly, starting on the coast, to make an accurate topographical map of the state. In order to cover such a vast territory efficiently, Whitney decided to employ the relatively new surveying method of triangulation, using fixed spots to measure distances and then sketch in what was between them, building each new triangle from those that preceded it, and using barometers to measure heights, since a column of mercury would rise to a known level at a given distance above sea level. Slopes and other changes in terrain would be sketched in with hachuring or cross-hatching. When Charles F. Hoffmann, a brilliant young German topographer, joined the team the next summer, he refined these methods in ways that became the standard practice well into the twentieth century, used both by the great western surveys of the 1860s and '70s and by the U.S. Geological Survey, begun in 1879 with King as its first director.

Because the California survey was getting under way so late in the season of 1860, Whitney sent Brewer south to Los Angeles to start the work in that temperate climate. Brewer and three others boarded a steamer in San Francisco on November 24, stopping at San Luis Obispo and Santa Barbara before landing at San Pedro, the port for Los Angeles. Brewer notes in his wonderful journal of his years with the California survey, published in book form as *Up and Down California in 1860–1864*, that "The Boundary Commission, to run the line between California and countries east, were aboard, a hard set, who were making much noise and drinking much whiskey." The more abstemious Brewer party made its first camp on a plain twenty miles from the ocean and fifteen from the mountains at a spot overlooking the little city of Los Angeles, its population then less than four thousand souls. "The weather is soft and balmy," Brewer writes, "no winter, but a perpetual spring and summer." And then the rains started, and it rained for the next month, eliciting such journal entries as "rainy and cheerless enough in our tents" . . . "another rainy Sunday" . . . "it has now rained for seventy hours without cessation."

Despite the weather, the crew busied itself not only mapping the countryside ("This want of maps, as well as incorrect maps, is a very serious evil which we feel much," Brewer notes. "We have to make observations all the way"), but also making many side trips to climb mountains, visit ranches or vineyards, or inspect mines. In his journal Brewer seems to relish everything from camp life, even with its soggy deprivations, to the pleasures of taking readings with the survey's fine chronometers and brass-encased tube barometers to, on the occasional sunny day, the lovely mountaintop views of sunsets over the ocean or of distant ranges to the north and northeast. The only thing Brewer doesn't much like is being in charge. Until Whitney joined them on December 10, and later whenever the boss is called away, Brewer grumbles to his journal about the unwanted responsibility of leadership.

The members of the survey spent ten weeks doing their work in Southern California, climaxed by a climb Whitney and Brewer made up what is now called Santiago Peak, the tallest mountain in the Santa Ana Range. During the ascent, the rough chaparral literally tore the clothes from their bodies, leaving them with "parts out," as Brewer puts it. But the view from the 5,700-foot summit made them monarchs of all that they had surveyed so far, and more: 150 miles of coastline, the islands off the coast, the mountains to the north and northeast, and to the east and southeast, "dry almost desert . . . a country nature had not favored."

By the middle of February, they began to make their way north.

Soon after that, Brewer hiked off on his own one day, climbing to a ridge about two thousand feet above the camp. He found evidence there of vast geological changes over the millennia, "oyster shells by the cartload, clam shells, in fact many species," some of the shells so well preserved that he could still see the place on them where the muscle had been attached.

> I cannot describe my feelings as I stood on that ridge, that shore of an ancient ocean. How lonely and desolate! Who shall tell how many centuries, how many decades of centuries, have elapsed since these rocks resounded with the roar of breakers, and these animals sported in their foam? I picked up a bone, cemented in the rock with the shells. A feeling of awe came over me.

To read that passage is to know how fortunate King, the scientist with the soul of a romantic, would be in his choice of mentors.

As the survey team made its way up the coast that season, Brewer's journal shows how unreliable the state was in supporting them. Still, Brewer and his men accepted the consequences of too little money and kept working. By March 7, they had encamped at Santa Barbara to wait for more funds from Whitney, who had gone back to San Francisco. The official cash on hand had dwindled to $3.25; among the crew they could muster only an additional $3. "Five men in camp," Brewer wrote, "two weeks before another steamer, flour all gone, jerked beef ditto, onions ditto, potatoes ditto—long ago—have forgotten how some of them looked—bacon, small chunk, and even beans only a meager, lonely few left in the last corner of the sack." Still they made excursions out of camp every day, climbing the foothills and nearby peaks to take barometric readings, and visiting hot springs, the ruins of the old mission, a ranch, and the shore for fossil hunting. The steamer arrived on schedule, bearing Whitney and his purse, and he steamed back out a few days later, taking with him eleven boxes of fossils that the party had collected while waiting for a decent meal: "I think he was decidedly pleased with our work," Brewer wrote, "and concluded to leave the party in my command." Brewer was becoming more comfortable with the idea of being in charge.

The survey spent a month in Santa Barbara and then moved up the coast on a new wagon road and eventually reached San Luis Obispo, where they camped for two weeks while geologizing and taking measurements nearby. Two more weeks took them through the Salinas Valley to Monterey, where they stopped at a ranch on the present site of the Pebble Beach golf course and partook of such civilized pleasures as church and dinner at the nearby ranch of a judge with two attractive daughters, one of whom played the piano for them. Oddly enough, the whaling industry, which was growing in Monterey, created a nightly hazard for the geologists. Once the whales had been stripped of their blubber they were towed out to sea, where they would drift around the Monterey Peninsula and wash up on the shoreline of what is now Pebble Beach. Grizzly bears would emerge from the nearby hills at night to feed on the carcasses, and Brewer's camp was right on their path to the supper table.

In September the state of California ran out of money and, as state employees, Whitney, Brewer, and their men had to decide whether to quit or to work on without being paid. They chose the latter, and Whitney took out a loan of $2,500 for supplies, not the last time he would have to borrow to keep the survey afloat. The survey's goal for the year had been to work up the coast beyond the Napa Valley to Clear Lake, and a week short of a full year in the field they packed their wagons and headed for San Francisco, having met all their expectations. In that time, Brewer figured, he had traveled a total of 4,830 miles, more than a thousand of them on foot, and written a thousand pages of field notes and four hundred letters to Whitney reporting their progress, in addition to his journal notes and general correspondence. He remarks with modest understatement but clear satisfaction that "I have proved myself capable of successfully managing a party, carrying it through times of discomfort, and even hardship, accomplishing much labor, and doing it economically." He had barely settled into the survey offices at a building called Montgomery Block in San Francisco before he longed to return to the field. "To sit down in the office, write, compare maps, make calculations, and plot sections, is harder work than mountain climbing."

The next season, 1862, would feature one of the greatest adventures of the whole California Geological Survey, an ascent of Mount Shasta, although for much of the year the field to which Brewer longed to return was something much closer to an inland sea. During the winter, rain fell at a rate that had become at best alarming and in places astounding. In Sonoma County, seventy-two inches of rain was measured between November 11 and January 14. In San Francisco itself, the amount was less than half that, but still an astonishing amount of rain—nearly three feet—to fall in two months. As Brewer noted in his journal,

> The great central valley of the state is under water—the Sacramento and San Joaquin valleys—a region 250 to 300 miles long and an average of at least twenty miles wide . . . Although much of it is not cultivated, yet a part of it is the garden of the state. Thousands of farms are entirely under water—cattle starving and drowning.

The flooding, which utterly submerged Sacramento for weeks, prevented Brewer's team from returning to the field until late March, and then they stayed fairly close to San Francisco. Because of the high water, many state officials had moved temporarily to San Francisco, where Whitney continued to lobby them for money that had been appropriated to the survey months before. But the flooding also worsened California's shaky financial situation— farms and businesses that no longer existed would not be paying taxes; revenues were expected to dwindle by a third, the state treasurer told Brewer. Once the weather improved in May, Whitney began inviting legislators to visit their base camp near San Francisco at Mount Diablo where, like legislators in the field everywhere, they could be treated to a safe and not-too-strenuous adventure. Brewer would cook them dinner over a campfire, and after they ate he and the men would treat the visitors to "a jolly time." Grizzlies would be alluded to but discouraged from making an appearance.

Early in the summer, the party went down into the San Joaquin Valley with the idea of crossing the river at some point and meeting up with Whitney, who was working on the west slope of the Sierras. But even by the end of June, the whole length of the San Joaquin River was so swollen as to be impassable. Brewer and his men worked their way back up to San Francisco and by late August had set off from Sacramento for Mount Shasta. Throughout his months on the survey, Brewer had climbed every peak he could manage in the Coast Range. The highest peaks made great anchors and vantage points for the vast triangles he and his men were laying down to map the state, but it becomes clear as you read Brewer's journal that he could not have resisted a vista in any case. Still, the ascent of Shasta, which Frémont and others had guessed was 17,000 feet (giving it the reputation as the tallest mountain in the United States), was Brewer's first serious attempt at mountain climbing. Even at the 14,400 feet that Brewer reckoned and the final official height, established decades later, of 14,162 feet, Shasta was roughly twice as high as any mountain Brewer had climbed before it. And Whitney, who was far less field-hardened than Brewer and his crew, having spent his time mostly on administrative work, might have been expected to falter. They were not the first to climb Shasta, and many thousands of people have climbed it since. But they were the first to lug instruments to the top, and at a time when mountaineering clothing and equipment were still primitive. The camp from which they made the final ascent was located at about 7,400 feet. They left camp at 3:30 a.m. and by eight o'clock they had climbed to 13,000 feet, on a grade of about forty degrees, over twisted lava, loose ash, and snow. "The last thousand feet has been hard," Brewer notes, "the air is so light that one is very short winded, must stop often, and resting does not appear to restore the strength." Brewer and Whitney each had to lug a barometer the whole way, Whitney's fingers got frostbitten, and the final push to the summit took three and a half hard hours. Brewer notes that

. . . at about noon we reached the highest point. This is a mere
pinnacle of lava, shooting up into the air—difficult of access, and
only reached with some daring. One has but a small hold in
climbing on it; I would never trust myself to it on a windy day. It
is accessible only by a narrow ridge, while a fall from any one of
the other three sides would precipitate one many hundreds of feet
below on the rocks.

They lingered on the summit for an hour and a half, taking readings, although the thin air and exertion made all of them feel
drowsy, and "all complained of headaches, eyes were bloodshot
and red. My lips and fingernails were of a deep blue . . . But no one
bled at the nose, as is common." Still, once they ate their lunches,
several of the others became very nauseated and began to go back,
leaving Whitney and Brewer alone with their barometers. This was
when Brewer got his fine view of Lassen's Butte, the one he had
described in his letter to George Brush, the one that convinced
King to head to California.

If Clarence King was exhausted from his long trip across the continent, he didn't show it. By September 4, 1863, the Saturday after
he and Jim Gardner had met Brewer on the Sacramento river
steamboat, Brewer and King, now an assistant geologist with the
California survey, if an unpaid one, were back on the boat, steaming upriver to Sacramento. (Jim, who did not have a rich stepfather
and could not afford to work for nothing, stayed behind to help
build battlements for the U.S. Engineer Corps, a job Brewer helped
him snag.) On Sunday morning, Clarence happened to see Speers
riding on a Sacramento street and followed him to a large corral,
where he saw the wagons from his emigrant train lined up, and
under a shed were the "dear old mules I had watched so many
nights," as he wrote in a journal he began that very day. He was
warmly received by Speers, who told him that Dick Cotter, a wagon
driver whom King had befriended on the trip across the plains, was
now herding sheep in the countryside near Sacramento. King bor-

rowed a horse and rode out to find Cotter, and they chatted for an hour or so. Dick told him that he could get better-paying work but "in bad company," to which King responded drily in his journal, "he is evidently hard at work being good."

After the visit, King galloped the borrowed horse back to Sacramento and then himself worked at being good—he went to church for the first time since he had left the East, and enjoyed belting out the hymns again. The next day King went by train and stage to Grass Valley, in the Sierra foothills, where a horse was waiting for him, and he would wait for Brewer, who had gone elsewhere to get his own horse, some pack mules, and a packer. The mines around Grass Valley would produce more gold than any other place in California between the middle of the nineteenth century and the middle of the twentieth, and by the time King got there it had, like much of the rest of the state, made the transition from placer mining—loners washing gravel in streams—to industrial mining, which, in the 1860s, involved the use of hydraulic pumps to wash vast amounts of the hillsides down those streams, where the gold could be caught.

After Brewer and the packer, Jan Hoesch, arrived, King would renew one of his most enduring relationships in the West, involving him with any number of "that most grotesque and sober of beasts, the mule." In *Mountaineering in the Sierra Nevada*, King often lavishes his comic affection on the various mules he employs or encounters, and as he self-deprecatingly writes, "my regard for all mules rises wellnigh into the realm of sentiment." Because mules could go places and bear burdens that other animals could not, the mule packer was one of the most important members of any western traveling party. Not only could balancing the load increase the amount that each mule could carry, but proper packing and the ability to think like a mule could lighten the mood of the famously petulant four-wheel-drive vehicle of its day. King became Hoesch's enthusiastic apprentice in the mulish arts, learning techniques that would serve him well for decades of traveling over the roughest terrain of the West.

Brewer led them northeast directly into the Sierras along hot, dusty roads, King riding his new "fair gelding." From Nevada City ("a fine town in a rich mining area," Brewer writes) to Camptonville ("a miserable, dilapidated town, but very picturesquely located"), they then climbed more steeply uphill to Eureka, while passing through smaller burgs that had not been memorable even when placer mining had swelled their populations. Now that the gold panners had moved on, these makeshift towns were filled with empty shacks and squalid streets where Chinese mine workers lived. One of these places was Poker Flat, which King describes as "one of the most rudimentary of mining towns" and Brewer calls "a miserable hole" where "what we lacked in accommodations was made up for in [exorbitant] prices." Despite the squalor, there was still sufficient money around to support "houses of ill fame, hurdy gurdy and gambling houses of all kinds," King writes. Bret Harte would make the town's name famous in 1869 when he published his story "The Outcasts of Poker Flat."

They crossed two ranges of the Sierras, going east along the Middle Feather River and then northeast toward Honey Lake. Along the way, Brewer led them on a detour that would later help King make a significant discovery. Scientists were at the time looking for fossils of a known age in geological layers of the earth where gold had been determined to be. Such a discovery would tell when in geological time gold was formed, which would help miners know where to look for it. Brewer and King went into the Genesee Valley to an upland basin of land, where they looked for fossils "said to occur here in the auriferous slates"—meaning the gold-bearing strata. "We found them," Brewer says simply, "a most important matter geologically." Later in the year, King would build upon this discovery by finding fossils distributed widely enough in the layers of gold ore to be very much in the mining industry's debt.

The nights were growing colder, dipping into the twenties, and the terrain was sufficiently challenging to warrant their making camp early, leaving them long evenings by the fire to get acquainted, to reminisce about Yale, and for King to show off his education while sponging up what Brewer had to say. Brewer would later write to his friend Brush complimenting him on the general scientific knowledge of their young protégé, although, as Brewer would remember after King's death, "he was not so thoroughly informed or so deeply interested in geological problems as he afterwards became. In fact, he stood on the threshold of that fascinating study, saturated chiefly with Ruskin and Tyndall," and chattering constantly about glaciers in the Alps.

King undoubtedly also talked to Brewer about his recent journey west and about the geological wonders along their route. Brewer wrote later that in these first weeks together the two men discussed for the first time what Brewer called a "transcontinental section," a survey that would run west to east as King's Fortieth Parallel Survey would. Brewer remembered:

> This had been the dream of Whitney in 1862, when the construction of the Pacific railways was actively begun. He thought that . . . once a section across California had been completed the railroad companies might be inclined to pay for making one along their lines, across the interior basin and the Rocky Mountains, to the great plains.

On September 15, the day after Brewer's thirty-fifth birthday— "half my 'three-score years and ten' are past," Brewer noted somberly in the journal—King had cooking duties, another science he was only beginning to master. When he overcharred a steak for their breakfast, Brewer nonetheless tore into it hungrily, saying, "Thank God I'm omnivorous."

The three men spent time in the pleasant uplands to the west of Honey Lake and on September 21 veered back to the northwest, toward Lassen Peak in the southern Cascades, that "bare and desolate peak of snow and rocks," as Brewer describes it. At Willow Lake, "a pretty little sheet of water embosomed in the hills," Brewer caught his first trout. Lassen is a volcanic dome, formed by the slow buildup of lava from within, and although it had not erupted in a thousand years, there had been eruptions nearby only a few hundred years before, and Lassen would blow spectacularly in 1915. All around it were peaks and flows formed by volcanic activity, and bubbling, steaming hot springs. Brewer was interested in the story of this activity that the lava told. They camped beneath the mountain at a height of about eight thousand feet, which was as high as the grass grew to feed the animals, joined by three members of a hunting party from Sacramento, including a judge, whom they had befriended. On September 26, Brewer, King, and their companions made their first ascent of Lassen, bearing the pipe barometer with which they would test the mountain's height. When they reached the summit, "the wind howled and roared in fierce gusts," King wrote. "It was so strong that I was obliged to retreat" from a two-foot-wide ledge to which he had climbed. They were the first people known to have reached the 10,450-foot crest, but they would not be able to estimate the cone's height that day. As Brewer wrote, "The day was unpropitious for good barometric work . . . a storm was approaching, and the barometer was falling rapidly; and the whole Pitt river valley was filled with clouds, hiding everything below the altitude of 8000 or 9000 feet. But all was clear above, and Shasta, eighty miles away . . . rose from the white mountain of cloud, projected against an intensely blue sky." This was the mountain that Dana had seen decades before and that Brewer and Whitney had climbed the year before. King called Shasta "the magnet that drew him to the Pacific coast," and now as he struggled against the wind at the top of Lassen, he was dumbfounded by the view. Finally he shouted into the wind, "What would Ruskin have said, if he had seen *this*!"

King's exuberance did not end there. As Brewer relates, with something of the disapproval mixed with pride of a mother watching her brave but foolhardy child, "On the way back he wanted to try a *glissade* [a sort of skiing without skis] down one of the snow-slopes. I objected strongly, being uncertain whether it would be practicable for him to stop before reaching the rocks at the bottom. But he had read Tyndall; and what was a mountain climb without a *glis-*

*sade?* So he had his way, and came out of the adventure with only a few unimportant bruises." King had three days to recover at the camp they'd made at 8,000 feet, while the storm dumped rain, sleet, and snow on their campsite (his fingers got "numbish," King wrote, "and café glacé is not a very warming drink you know"). During a break in the weather their hunting friends departed. On the 29th, Brewer, King, and Hoesch made the climb again, taking advantage of a clear night when the moon was bright to rise in the eighteen-degree chill before two a.m. and climb through the crunchy snow, noticing that the sky grew blacker and the stars brighter as the air got thinner, and "the intense cold or something exhilarated me," wrote King. They reached the top of Lassen's cone before dawn and watched the sky grow pink in the east as the moon and Jupiter glistened above them, and then as the sun came up "it gild[ed] the peaks one after another" while, just below them, "an arctic sparrow sang out a sweet little melody to greet the day."

"The sky was cloudless," Brewer remembers, "and the atmosphere transparent in the highest degree." Brewer and King both believed that they could see Mount Hamilton, in what is now Santa Clara County, 240 miles to the south, "the longest distance, as far as I know," Brewer wrote, "I have ever seen a terrestrial object." Then Brewer and King beheld another amazing sight:

> Rising high above all is the conical shadow of the peak we are on, projected in the air, a distinct form of cobalt blue on a ground of lighter haze, its top as sharp and its outlines as well defined as are those of the peak itself—a gigantic spectral mountain, projected so high in the air that it seems far higher than the original mountain itself—but as the sun rises, the mountain sinks into the valley, and, like a ghost, fades away at the sight of the sun.

The cold was so pitiless that Hoesch returned to camp and King, who had no gloves, stuffed his hands into an extra pair of wool socks he had carried with him. One of King's ears went stiff "but thawed out later without much pain"—the word "much" added later to the entry. Brewer and King spent nearly ten hours on the summit of Lassen, and King filled his journal with page after page of Ruskinian descriptions of the views. All in all, Brewer writes, "that day stands out in my memory as one of the most impressive of my life."

If the day was impressive, the geological work was less so. King was still green as a geologist, and Brewer himself had been trained as an agricultural chemist, and would return to the Sheffield School the next year as a professor of agriculture. On the second ascent they got the height of Lassen approximately right, and were appropriately awed by lava flows and giant boulders, and noted the signs of glacial movement in the polished rocks and canyons the glaciers left behind. As volcanologists, though, they concluded wrongly that Lassen was extinct and accepted the general opinion that one of the nearby peaks to the north had been active only six years before, when it had been inactive for something like four hundred years.

In spite of the warnings about restiveness in the native tribes to the north, Brewer decided to strike off in that general direction. Armed with only two revolvers and a broken pistol rigged to look like it would work, they carried their notebooks in their pockets in case they had to abandon the rest of their kit quickly if attacked or chased. But the only Indians they came across were two solitary figures like characters in a Wordsworth poem gathering grasshoppers for their supper. King and Brewer made their way up Hat Creek to the confluence of the Pitt and Fall rivers, and eight miles up the Fall River (which John Muir describes in *Steep Trails* as "a very remarkable stream . . . springs beautifully shaded at one end of it, a showy fall 180 feet high at the other, and a rush of crystal rapids in between") to Fort Crook ("a dismal place"), where they camped while Brewer had his horse reshod. They traded with the local Indians, swapping worn blankets and clothes for salmon and trout and "a fine bow and a lot of arrows I shall take home," Brewer writes. King bought arrows and a bow, too.

After a few days they set off west and north toward Shasta, and then to Yreka and eventually across the top of California to Crescent City on the coast. They would spend a little more than a month getting from Lassen to Crescent City, and in all that time Mount Shasta, just over fourteen thousand feet, would dominate every place they visited. Brewer was drawn to describe it again and again in his journal, from various directions and distances, even apologizing for his obsession with it. The second most astonishing thing they saw in these weeks was Pluto's Cave, which had only recently been discovered north of Shasta. Beneath a lava slope was a room more than a mile long and as tall and wide as fifty feet in places, where cooling lava had apparently suddenly flowed out, leaving the large empty space with ceiling, floors, and sides of black lava, often in "fantastic shapes." They walked as far into the cave as they could and then blew out their lights to experience the "silent black darkness."

If the landscape often awed them, its inhabitants more often had the opposite effect. "What a strange country this is for loose solitary hermits," King notes in his journal. "It makes me sad to see men so sunken so devoid of noble ideas and high glimpses of something beyond the animal."

By October 20 the weather had grown cold enough to convince them to camp no more, and the next day Brewer sent Hoesch with two mules and a horse packed with specimens back to San Francisco, "a long and weary ride of 400 miles to make alone." Brewer and King followed the Klamath River through mining towns reminiscent of those at the beginning of their trip, also made desolate by the playing out of placer mines. "You have no idea," Brewer writes, "of the dilapidation of a mining town in its decline, before it is entirely dead." As they worked their way west they made a few jaunts up into Oregon, and once they got close to the Pacific Coast they came upon sites where copper had been found and some of the excitement of the gold times was in the air. But one senses in Brewer's journal that his energy is ebbing away (King's journal stops altogether on October 20)—the cold nights had made the arthritis from which he sometimes suffered flare up, and the landscape no longer inspired them. They sold their horses on November 1, and went on by foot. When King reached Crescent City he found letters calling him back to San Francisco, and he set off immediately, carrying their barometer and the beautiful Indian bows and arrows that they had traded for at Fort Crook. Two-thirds of the way home, in Marysville, the bows were stolen. That loss might have been the only regret King bore back to San Francisco from his first venture into the Sierra Nevada.

PART TWO

# The Highest Peaks

*Science I love, but geology is the only branch of science that could have held me to its active, persistent pursuit. For me the study or the laboratory would have been utterly impossible. The working geologist, on the contrary, dwells in close contact with Nature in her wildest and most savage moods. He seeks the solution of his problems where vast dynamic forces have in past ages crumpled the earth's crust and brought huge mountain ranges into being—ranges that expose its structure and tell much from which we may deduce how its structure was accomplished.*

*Our tasks take us out across the rolling yellow billows of the plains, through the profound silences of burning deserts, whose colors would fire the artist's brain to frenzy, up into the magnificent uplifts of the Sierras, with their singing brooks and roaring torrents, their majestic redwoods and fragrant pines, their smiling, flowery glades and sinister bald summits, their warm, sheltered nooks and grim, pitiless glaciers—out beyond civilization and settlements, where to sustain himself man must confront the raw forces of animate and inanimate nature, as did our forebears of the stone age, and conquer or succumb. It is a life that develops weird types. . . .*

—King quoted by Edgar Beecher Bronson
in *Reminiscences of a Ranchman*

## CHAPTER FIVE

# Man of Action

*The General Grant
Sequoia in Kings Canyon
National Park.*

At Christmastime in 1863, Clarence King posed for his first photograph as a member of the California Geological Survey, standing on the left of its director, Josiah Whitney, and between the seated figures of the cartographer Charles Hoffmann and the survey's field leader, William Brewer. Three other members of the survey, Chester Averill, William Gabb, and William Ashburner, are arrayed on Whitney's right. All seven of the men look stern and six of them are dressed in dark suits, their below-the-knee coats unbuttoned to show their vests. Only King, who had lost his clothes in the Nevada fire five months before and had spent most of his time since then as an unpaid volunteer in the field, couldn't muster a suit. He wears a dark lapel-less jacket cut short and buttoned at the top, perhaps to conceal a shabby vest, but open wide enough at the bottom to reveal trousers of a slightly lighter color. King was the newest member of the survey, but already the ruddiest, and in his makeshift outfit he was showing signs of leaving the serious East behind and embracing the rugged West. In the photograph, the four seated figures in front rest their polished shoes or boots on the Oriental carpet of the San Francisco photographic studio where they posed. Perhaps King was asked to stand so that his scuffed and muddy field boots wouldn't show.

Less than a year later, Brewer and King are back in the same studio, judging by the carpet, posed alongside two new members of the survey, King's childhood friend Jim Gardner and the new friend that King and Gardner had made on their cross-country trip, Dick Cotter. Once again King is standing and Brewer sitting, but everything else about the picture (the frontispiece of this book) is as different as it could be. King's boots do show now, and they're as scuffed and disreputable looking as you might expect—but so are Brewer's. The four are dressed as if they've just come back from their remarkable campaign in the field that year, a time when they climbed and named the highest peaks in the southern Sierra Nevada, showing incredible stamina and courage, all in the name of science. The photo indicates this because as they pose in their worn boots and wide belts, rough pants and shirts, they choose to display the instruments of their trade—a theodolite (a sextantlike instrument consisting of a small telescope that rotates to measure angles), two pipe barometers, a carbine and, in King's hand, a heavy-headed hammer. The poses they strike fall somewhere between the cocky and the comic. Cotter would say later that he had placed his left hand on Brewer's shoulder to emphasize his confidence in their leader, but Brewer's own pose, with his left hand grasping the shoulder strap for his barometer, suggests a man who is aping his own leadership role rather than portraying it; it's hard not to suspect that he and Cotter were goofing around when the shutter opened. King, with his right thumb hitched stagily in his belt, seems to be sharing in the fun. In their dress, the other three could almost be farmers or ranchers, but the jaunty King is unmistakably an adventurer. Only he has the truly theatrical touch of a light-colored scarf tied around his neck, cavalryman style. In less than a year he has transformed himself from a well-bred, Yale-educated eastern intellectual, whose unwillingness to fight in the Civil War ate away at his self esteem, to this rough and ready man of action, a man meant for the top of California, if not the world.

When King returned to San Francisco in November 1863, he learned that Whitney wanted to send him right back out into the field. Frederick Law Olmsted, who had in the late 1850s designed Manhattan's Central Park with Calvert Vaux, and who had until recently served for two stormy years as head of the U.S. Sanitary Commission—a precursor to the Red Cross authorized by Lincoln to oversee the health of federal troops during the Civil War—had now come west to manage the Mariposa Estate. This was a gold-mining operation on the western slope of the Sierras near the present city of Merced, on land that the legendary explorer of California and much of the rest of the West, John C. Frémont, had purchased by mistake in 1848, well before gold was discovered nearby. (He'd asked a friend to buy him a piece of land on the coast, but somehow the friend bought him this literal gold mine instead.) Las Mariposas, as it was called, made him a very rich man in the 1850s. But the Pathfinder was never much of a businessman (he would die broke) and, having run unsuccessfully for president in 1856 and got himself appointed by President Lincoln to what would be an unsuccessful Civil War generalcy, he had now managed to run the estate into the ground. Frémont sold it in 1863 to investors from the

East, who then offered Olmsted a handsome salary to manage it for them. Like the Pathfinder before him (and like Clarence King after him), Olmsted was tempted from a life of higher purpose by the possibility of growing rich from the glittering metals of the West. But two weeks after Olmsted got to the estate in the fall of 1863, he wrote home to his wife, Mary, that "Things are worse here than I dare say to anybody but you—and to you with a caution. There is not a mine on the Estate that is honestly paying expenses."

Olmsted quickly turned to William Ashburner, a mining expert who had been one of the original members of the California survey. A Harvard graduate who had studied in Paris at the Ecole des Mines, Ashburner had set off for Los Angeles with William Brewer in November 1860 on the survey's first expedition, but his health had been too frail to stand the rigors and deprivations of life in the field, so he worked out of the San Francisco office until he left the survey in 1862. He kept in close touch with his former colleagues, and perhaps went back to work with them from time to time, as evidenced by the Christmas 1863 photograph in which he was included. Olmsted hired him as a private consultant, and Whitney, seeing an opportunity to broaden the experience of his young assistant geologist, sent Clarence King along with Ashburner to conduct a general survey of the seventy-square-mile estate and poke around in the gold-bearing strata of its hills.

Ashburner and King set out on November 24 by stagecoach and arrived the next day. King was six weeks shy of his twenty-second birthday, healthy, and a good physical specimen. But he had now been on the road or in the field almost continuously since the previous April, and he might have been weary in body or soul. For whatever reason, King didn't distinguish himself with his hard work during the first month at Mariposa. One of King's favorite activities was to climb what Frémont had named Mount Bullion, a Sierra foothill that dominates Bear Valley, where Frémont's headquarters had been. The mountain's name is partly a reference, and perhaps a rueful one, to his father-in-law and patron, Thomas Hart Benton, the powerful U.S. senator known as Old Bullion because of his preference for gold over paper currency. From the top of Mount Bullion, where King would sit on a rock and lean against an oak tree, he had a sweeping view of the Sierra range, both north and south. To the west, King would write years later in *Mountaineering in the Sierra Nevada,*

> You overlook a wide panorama; oak and pine mottled foot-hills with rusty groundwork and cloudings of green wander down in rolling lines to the ripe plain; beyond are plains, then coast ranges, rising in peaks, or curved down in passes, through which gray banks of fog drift in and vanish before the hot air of the plains. East, the Sierra slope is rent and gashed in a wilderness of cañons, yawning deep and savage.

Upon returning to San Francisco at Christmas, King evidently tried out some of these Ruskinian ruminations on the blokes at Montgomery Block, the building where the survey was headquartered. One of them, William Gabb, a dour, self-satisfied but "decidedly smart" paleontologist, "said of me," King reports, "more in sorrow than in unkindness, yet with unwonted severity, 'I believe that fellow had rather sit on a peak all day, and stare at those snow-mountains, than find a fossil in the metamorphic Sierra.'" Unwonted as the criticism might have seemed to King himself, others on the survey, including Whitney and even Brewer, seemed to share Gabb's doubts about King's seriousness as a scientist. Ashburner would refer to King even a year later as "a confounded little 'blow-hard.'"

In a chapter of *Mountaineering* called "Merced Ramblings," King describes his stagecoach ride back to Mariposa after the Christmas holiday. He spends the first part of the trip drearily turning over in his mind the charges Gabb has made against him. "Can it be, I asked myself," King recalls; "has a student of geology so far forgotten his devotion to science? Am I really fallen to the level of a mere nature-lover?" Like any good Romantic, King finds a correlative for his mood in the world outside the stagecoach window. "The Sierras were quite cloud-hidden, and desolation such as drought has never before or since been able to make reigned in dreary monotony over all the plains from Stockton to Hornitas."

As the coach bounces up the approaches to the Sierras themselves, King writes, "I re-dedicated myself to geology, and was framing a resolution to delve for that greatly important but missing link of evidence, the fossil which should clear up an old, unsolved riddle of upheaval age . . ." Here the older King looks back from the distance of almost a decade at his still-callow self, and wittily undercuts this road-to-Damascus moment:

> . . . when over to eastward a fervid crimson light smote the vapor-bank and cleared a bright pathway through the peaks, and on to a pale sea-green sky. Through this gateway of rolling gold and red cloud the summits seemed infinitely high and far, their stone and snow hung in the sky with lucent delicacy of hue, brilliant as gems yet soft as air,—a mosaic of amethyst and opal transfigured with passionate light, as gloriously above words as beyond art. Obsolete shell-fishes in the metamorphic were promptly forgotten, and during those lingering moments, while peak after peak flushed and faded back into recesses of the heavens, I forgot what palaeontological unworthiness was loading me down, becoming finally quite jolly of heart.

We expect memoirists to fashion their histories for the greatest possible dramatic effect, and King was more prone to this than most. (His friend James D. Hague remembered after King's death that "in one instance, when I had intimated that his story of the slopes of Mount Tyndall might well seem pretty steep to an unimaginative reader, he offered to throw off five degrees for my flat acceptance.") Whether the sun broke through at this very moment or not, King makes a serious point here, even though he can't resist giving it a comic turn. To bring up Gabb's criticism so many years later shows how stung he was by it; of course he did not want to appear to be a lightweight to the other dedicated, hardworking members of the survey. But whether or not King realized it in the last days of

1863, as he approached Bear Valley, the older King recognized that the younger was not about to bury the poetic side of his nature beneath the scientific. King would become one of the ablest scientists of his generation, and he was about to prove himself to be one of the most tenacious members of the California survey, but he was not going to lose the enthusiasm for adventure and romance that sent him west in the first place. He would always be a gazer at mountaintops, and from them.

Still, when he returned to Mariposa, he got to work. Because Whitney's relationship with the California legislature had soured, and its four-year authorization of the survey was coming up for renewal, Whitney realized that he needed something dramatic to prove to the practical-minded legislators that the findings of his corps of scientists could be of value to the commercial interests of the state. But this realization did not mean he was simply going to sell out, to send his men off in search of gold, silver, copper, or even lead so that the mining interests that owned the legislature might be repaid for their patronage. Instead he sent his men after fossils. They would address the enduring question, both scientific and commercial, of where in the earth's strata gold was most likely to be found. Because paleontologists had a pretty good idea of when in the aeons of the past various fossils had lived, if they could find a fossil whose age was known in the so-called auriferous slates—that is, in the gold-bearing stratum—then they could date that stratum, too. Then miners wouldn't have to waste their time excavating layers of the earth where no gold could be.

This was one reason why Gabb, the paleontologist, was annoyed with King for not returning to San Francisco with boxes of fossils. And it's why Brewer, when he'd set off with King several months earlier to climb Mount Lassen, made a detour to the Genesee Valley to hunt for fossils. As Brewer noted in his journal for that trip, he and King had found fossils in the auriferous slates there, but because they had not found veins of gold adjacent to them Whitney had not considered the discovery conclusive. Now, with Gabb figuratively sitting on his shoulder, King found himself at Mariposa "leaving no stone unturned, and usually going so far as to break them open." He claims to have worn out two hammers in this way, and was at work with his third in a place called Hell's Hollow when "I noticed in the rock an object about the size and shape of a small cigar. It was the fossil, the object for which science had searched and yearned and despaired! . . . I knelt and observed the radiating structure as well as the characteristic central cavity, and assured myself it was beyond doubt . . . [a] plump, pampered" mollusk called a belemnite, which "the terrible ordeal of metamorphism had spared." For King it was a eureka moment—"The age of the gold-belt was discovered!" he wrote of the episode in *Mountaineering*—but it was not until he found other belemnites in the gold strata of the estate that Whitney gave him credit for the discovery.

Sometime after Christmas 1863 Whitney sent Charles Hoffmann, the topographer, down to Mariposa, perhaps to free King from his surveying duties so he could concentrate on the fossils. On Sundays in January, the two men would climb Mount Bullion, where the crisp winter weather offered a crystal-clear vista of the High Sierras. The two men were particularly struck by a view to the south of what King describes as "a vast pile of white peaks, which, from our estimate, should lie near the heads of the Kings and Kaweah rivers. Of their great height I was fully persuaded." It was to these peaks that Whitney would send a team including King five months later, and it was in these peaks that King would distinguish himself as a mountaineer.

Whitney had either become pleased with King, or continued to recognize his potential, or simply wanted to keep an eye on him, because twice in the spring of 1864 he asked his assistant geologist to leave Bear Valley to go along on trips he made. One, in March, was King's first chance to see Yosemite, an experience that was not likely to encourage him to suppress his Romantic enthusiasm for the glories of nature. The second, in April, was to the western part of Nevada, where Whitney wanted to study rock formations that were similar to some within the purview of the California survey. The stagecoach ride they took on the Placerville Road across the

Sierras was at first slowed by mud and then, near the crests, was stopped by snow, forcing them to go on by sleigh. Whitney left King on the south shore of Lake Tahoe to make barometric readings; when King caught up to his boss near the Comstock Lode he got an assignment to take a few soldiers for protection and cross the Carson Sink along the northern emigrant route to Salt Lake City (picking up the path of I-95 today) to the Humboldt Mountains, roughly a hundred miles to the northeast. King worked his way along the western slopes of the Humboldts, and climbed the tallest mountain in the range, the 9,800-foot Star Peak. To the west he could see Lassen's Butte, which he'd climbed with Brewer a little more than six months before. He pushed on to make a cursory inspection of the East Humboldt Range, and in spite of the hastiness of the whole journey Whitney later wrote that King had made "some important explorations" while they were in the territory.

When the two were together on these trips, King had undoubtedly bent Whitney's ear about the cluster of high peaks visible to the south from Mount Bullion. Whitney would write in his first report for the survey, *Geology* (1865), of King's "belief that here were the most elevated summits of the [Sierra Nevada] range," and because Whitney did not want to leave "a blank on the map of California," he finally agreed to let a small group go explore what King was calling "the new Alps."

Brewer, who King admits "was more sceptical than I as to the result," would lead the mission. Charles Hoffmann would be the next most senior member, King would be assistant geologist, and Jim Gardner, who had impressed Brewer from their first meeting, would join the survey with the title assistant surveyor. King and Gardner would be paid only for their travel expenses. For the fifth spot in the party, King convinced Brewer not to rehire as packer the Dane Jan Hoesch, whom King admits he detested "with great cordiality." But as Brewer notes, "To put a load of baggage on a mule and make it stay there, and at the same time not hurt the mule, is a great art." King wanted Brewer to hire as packer his friend Dick Cotter, the wagon driver from the emigrant train who had turned to sheepherding in California in order to avoid bad company. One drawback to this plan was that, as Brewer puts it, Cotter "most unfortunately knows nothing about packing." Brewer finally agreed to hire Cotter only if King would be responsible if things went wrong. "When the pack-saddles roll under the mules' bellies," Brewer warned, "I shall light my pipe and go botanizing."

These five gathered in San Francisco in late May and departed from Oakland, where their four horses and three mules—all of them "upon a footing of easy social equality with us," King writes—were stabled. They headed down the eastern side of the bay toward San Jose, and by the time they went through Pacheco Pass, King found himself wishing he hadn't lobbied so hard for Cotter, since the packs had come loose from the mules with "provoking frequency." To add to King's irritation, he had drawn a buckskin mount who was "incorrigibly bad":

> To begin with, his anatomy was desultory and incoherent, the maximum of physical effort bringing about a slow, shambling gait quite unendurable. He was further cursed with a brain wanting the elements of logic, as evinced by such *non sequiturs* as shying insanely at wisps of hay, and stampeding beyond control when I tried to tie him to a load of grain. My sole amusement with Buckskin grew out of a psychological peculiarity of his, namely the unusual slowness with which waves of sensation were propelled inward toward the brain from remote parts of his periphery. A dig of the spurs administered in the flank passed unnoticed for a period of time varying from twelve to thirteen seconds, till the protoplasm of the brain received the percussive wave, then, with a suddenness which I never wholly got over, he would dash into a trot, nearly tripping himself up with his own astonishment.

As the party struck out to the southeast across the San Joaquin Valley they saw the effects of a devastating drought that had followed hard upon the devastating floods of the year before. At one ranch where they stopped, "Where there were green pastures when we camped here two years ago," Brewer writes, "now all is dry, dusty, bare ground. Three hundred cattle have died by the miserable water hole back of the house, where we get water to drink, and their stench pollutes the air." A hot wind blew dust that covered everything and sometimes reduced visibility to fifty yards. Past Fresno they saw towering whirlwinds of dust, as many as twenty-seven at a time, Brewer reports. Then when they camped at Elkhorn Station, one of their pack mules, Jim, became sick and was "in a terrible agony." They stayed up with him through the night, nursing him as best they could, but he died in the morning. Brewer offers a heartfelt tribute. "He had been a faithful beast, was very sagacious and true. . . . I did not think that I could feel so sad over the death of any animal as I did over that faithful old mule."

When they reached Visalia it was so hot that the soldiers at a post there begged Brewer to requisition them for protection as he headed into the cool mountains, but Brewer declined for the time being. King became the beneficiary of Jim the mule's death when Brewer decided to buy another horse as a replacement and somehow King ended up with him. "We named him Kaweah," King writes, "after the river and its Indian tribe. He was young, strong, fleet, elegant, a pattern of fine modeling in every part of his bay body and fine black legs; every way good, only fearfully wild, with a blaze of quick electric light in his dark eye."

On June 8, they left Visalia and headed east toward the Sierras. The temperature soon climbed to a sickening one hundred degrees, but their path took them steadily uphill and by the middle of the second day they had reached an area between the Kings and Kaweah rivers where the pines began to grow, offering cool shade. They came upon a mountain-fed stream of cold, delicious water— "our first real good water in many a long day!" Brewer writes. By the next day, they had reached an elevation of about five thousand feet and the forest had grown dense and dark. Soon they came to a beautiful meadow of about two hundred acres watered by a clear brook, and pitched camp. They shared the meadow with a lumber operation called Thomas's Sawmill. Here, "far above the heat and dust of the plain," they would stay for the next week, "during which we were to explore and study all about the neighborhood."

They were camped in what is now known as the Grant Grove Area of Sequoia and Kings Canyon National Parks, several miles south of what is perhaps the most famous living tree in the world, the General Grant Sequoia. Also known as the Nation's Christmas Tree, it is the only living U.S. national shrine, dedicated by President Eisenhower to commemorate Americans who have died at war. Like the tourists they partly were, the five men spent part of the week at this camp among the gigantic trees, gawking at their height and beauty, measuring their girth and in the case of the General Grant, then known as the "King of the Mountains" (although it turns out to be the third largest tree in the mountains or anywhere else), using triangulation to estimate its height. They figured it was 276 feet; today, it measures 268. Like a few tourists who preceded them and millions who followed, they were especially drawn to the fallen sequoias. One in particular, "burned out so that it is hollow," Brewer writes, tempted them to stunts that were not exactly scientific. "We *rode* into it seventy-six feet and turned around easily. For forty feet *three* horsemen could ride in abreast, but we had but one horse along, which we took up on purpose to take this wonderful ride." At the fallen tree's greatest width and height, Brewer writes, "I *stood* erect in the saddle and could just fairly reach the top!"

While Brewer was filling his journal with italics and exclamation points, King and Cotter rode off to the east and north, perhaps as far as Lookout Peak, from which they had an excellent view of Kings Canyon, just to the north, and the snow-covered crests of the Sierra's highest peaks, twenty miles to the east. In places Kings Canyon dropped off thousands of feet to the river below. Noting that the granite "ridges upon one side are reproduced on the other," King pondered the question of how this remarkable geological structure could have been made. Still influenced by the catastrophic theories of Agassiz at Harvard, and of Whitney himself, King decided that "actual rending asunder of the mountain mass determined the main outlines. Upon no other theory can we account for those blank walls." In other words, the sheer cliffs were not formed over aeons but in one great cataclysmic crack, when the earth broke in two. Plausible, this theory, but wrong. The canyons and other dramatic geological features of the region—waterfalls, upland valleys, and lakes, and the jutting peaks of the mountains themselves—were caused by the movement and melting of glaciers that appeared at least four times over a period of ten million years, a few of which still exist in the neighborhood today.

He and Cotter spent several hours on the "isolated crag," sketching, looking to the east where their party would be heading and, as King writes, "getting acquainted with the long chain of peaks, that I might afterward know them from other points of view." They stayed on the mountaintop until the shadows darkened in Kings Canyon and the forest below them turned purple, and then galloped their horses downhill through the trees until the "shadow deepened into an impressive gloom" and they slowed their mounts, relying in the darkness and then in the surreal moonlight on Kaweah's homing instinct to retrace their path. "At last, descending a hill, there shone before us a red light; the horses plunged forward at a gallop, and in a moment we were in camp."

Brewer's party lingered in the beautiful high-country environs of Thomas's Mill until a lumber wagon brought the rest of their supplies up from Visalia. Then they pushed off toward the east over terrain at first so "terrible" with pathless forests and rocky slopes that they led their animals rather than rode them, passing through groves of the Big Trees until at last they found a path cleared by cattlemen who had driven their herds up from the drought-weary valley for grass and water in the mountains. They camped for another week in the vicinity of Big Meadows in what is now Sequoia National Forest. Although it was late June, because they had reached an elevation of nearly eight thousand feet the temperature at night fell into the teens. On the summer solstice there was a violent snowstorm. "Wind howled fiercely through the trees," King remembers in *Mountaineering*, "coming down from the mountains in terribly powerful gusts. The green flower-covered meadow was soon buried under snow; and we explorers, who had no tent, hid ourselves under piles of brush, and on the lee side of hospitable stones. Our scant supply of blankets was a poor defence against such inclemency; so we crawled out and made a huge camp-fire, around which we sat for the rest of the day." Brewer, on the other hand, records that King and Cotter were off trying without luck to shoot a bear when the storm struck, and that he himself saved the day by greeting the two on their return, "wet and numb with cold," with a big kettle of soup.

So desperate was the heat back in Visalia that two cavalrymen from the company stationed there were dispatched to find Brewer and beg him again to request an escort; then at least some of the soldiers might escape the heat in the cool mountains. The two caught up with the survey party at Big Meadows, and reminded Brewer of rumors that hostile Indians had been forced into the region north of them, where the explorers were eventually headed. Brewer took pity and thought he might make use of them even leaving aside the possibility of Indians, so he agreed to the escort.

After stocking up on venison and bear meat from two hunters they befriended, the party pushed off on June 24. Brewer suggests that they knew just where they were going, but King writes that "after several days of marching and countermarching, we gave up the attempt to push farther in a southeast direction, and turned north, toward the great cañon of the Kings River, which we hoped might lead us up to the Snow Group." One of their marches or countermarches did take them south to the crest of the Kings-Kaweah divide, where on June 28 they named an eleven-thousand-foot peak Mount Silliman, in honor of the younger Benjamin Silliman, a Yale geology professor who taught at the Scientific School when Brewer, King, and Gardner had been students, and who would soon be Brewer's colleague there. The name holds to this day, and also graces a nearby creek, a pass, and the crest of the divide running to the northwest of Mount Silliman itself.

After working their way northeast along Sugarloaf Creek and reaching the Roaring River, they could plainly see to the southeast "the lateral moraines of a vast extinct glacier," the valley of which would lead them by way of what is now called Brewer Creek up "a comfortable grade" to what is now called Big Brewer Lake, on the western slope of the Great Western Divide. There they camped, in full sight of the awesome peaks around them:

> A thousand upspringing spires and pinnacles pierce the sky in every direction, the cliffs and mountain-ridges are everywhere ornamented with countless needle-like turrets. Crowning the wall to the south of our camp were series of these jagged forms standing out against the sky like a procession of colossal statues. Whichever way we turned, we were met by some extraordinary fullness of detail. Every mass seemed to have the highest possible ornamental finish.

An awesome sight but also a daunting one, to these young men with their thin blankets and ranchers' boots and clothing, with nothing in the way of mountaineering equipment but wool socks and a coil of rope. But King had learned something a few days earlier, back at Big Meadows, that filled him with fire. Two hunters they had met there, who were shooting deer for their skins, had claimed that "they themselves had penetrated farther than any others" into the High Sierras, "and had only given up the exploration after wandering fruitlessly among the cañons for a month." Then came words that would fill King with ambition and an almost reckless energy: "They told us that not even Indians had crossed the Sierras to the east, and that if we did succeed in reaching this summit we would certainly be the first." Never mind that these hunters—one a half-blooded Cherokee in buckskin breeches and "a sort of Trovatore hat," and the other dressed in butternut jeans and "a greasy flannel shirt . . . pinned together with thorns in lieu of buttons"—really had no way of knowing where Indians had or had not been. King was twenty-two, his head was still filled with John Tyndall's tales of Alpine mountaineering, and he had much to prove to his colleagues and to himself. Here was his big chance.

## CHAPTER SIX

# The Top of California

*King the mountaineer.*

Wiliam Brewer and his field party retraced the path of an ancient glacier from the canyon of the Roaring River up into what looked like a vast amphitheater of rising ground surrounded by crests and ridges. They crossed a moraine and followed a narrower gorge at the head of which was a pyramid-shaped mountain. At sunset on July 1, 1864, the five men camped at a height of 9,750 feet by a bold stream near a beautiful lake. Grass to feed their mules and horses was thin at this elevation, but winter avalanches had conveniently felled some of the scattering of pine trees, so there was a good supply of dry firewood.

Before dawn the next morning Brewer and Hoffmann ate breakfast, slung their instruments over their shoulders, and set out on foot toward the mountain that, from their camp, dominated the view to the east. At first the three men who remained in camp, James Gardner, Richard Cotter, and Clarence King, could follow the progress of their friends with field glasses, "their minute black forms moving slowly on among piles of giant débris; now and then lost, again coming into view, and at last disappearing altogether." Brewer reports that in their ascent of what they believed to be the highest peak in that part of the Sierra Nevada, he and Hoffmann "had a rough time, made two unsuccessful attempts to reach the summit, climbing up terribly steep rocks and at last, after eight hours of very hard climbing, reached the top." They were the first men known to have stood on the crest of what Brewer's men would insist should be called Mount Brewer. Apparently they approached the summit directly from the west, although their route would have been easier from either the south or the north. But the path they took created a moment at the top that went beyond exultation to utter disbelief. Not only were they not on the highest peak in the vicinity, but arrayed before them about five miles farther east were a dozen other mountains as tall as the one they had crested or taller. And the barometer suggested that they were, at something above 13,600 feet, a thousand feet higher than they had expected the summit to be. (Mount Brewer, as it is still called today, measures 13,570 feet.) Once they got over their shock, Brewer was able to describe the view:

> Such a landscape! A hundred peaks in sight over thirteen thousand feet—many very sharp—deep canyons, cliffs in every direction almost rivaling Yosemite, sharp ridges almost inaccessible to man, on which human foot has never trod—all combined to produce a view the sublimity of which is rarely equaled, one which few are privileged to behold.

They had reached the summit at about two p.m. and lingered there while taking readings and while Hoffmann sketched the views. Although they were able to begin their descent by sliding down a snowbank from the top of the mountain, traveling in minutes an eight-hundred-foot stretch that had taken them several hours to climb, they did not get back to camp until dusk, about eight o'clock. King remembers their return, how "as they sat down by our fire without uttering a word, we read upon their faces their terrible fatigue." Soon they were revived with hot tea and coffee, venison soup and bread, and they began to tell the story of their day. In addition to the line of mountains of which Mount Brewer is a part, in what we now call the Great Western Divide, and the range of even taller peaks farther east, Brewer described "a tremendous cañon which lay like a trough between the two parallel ranks of peaks." Hoffmann pulled out his sketches of the eastern range, and King immediately saw that these were the same peaks he had viewed from Mount Bullion on the Mariposa Estate, "whose great white pile had led me to believe them the highest points in California." The others had begun to rib King about what he thought he had seen from Mount Bullion, and now he had been proven right. But Brewer and Hoffmann were also saying that they did not think it was possible to cross the gorge between the two ranges and climb the peaks of the eastern range.

King lay awake that night. He was exhilarated by what Brewer and Hoffmann had seen, but "Their verdict of impossible oppressed me." Although King was young and bold and ambitious, he was no fool. He knew that to try what Brewer thought could not be done involved real danger. But the next morning, while the exhausted Brewer and Hoffmann slept in, King led Cotter away from the campfire and "I asked him in an easy manner whether he would like to penetrate the Terra Incognita with me at the risk of our necks, provided Brewer should consent." Probably there was never any question of asking his longtime friend Jim to join him on this adventure, given Jim's relatively frail health. Yet in King's description of Cotter there is a bit of the ardor for the new friend at the expense of the old:

Stout of limb, stronger yet in heart, of iron endurance and a quiet, unexcited temperament, and, better yet, deeply devoted to me, I felt that Cotter was the one comrade I would choose to face death with, for I believed there was in his manhood no room for fear or shirk.

"Why not?" Cotter responded with understated bravado, and then the only barrier was Brewer. Their leader was also excited about the prospect of "a campaign for the top of California." Brewer felt that King had the enthusiasm and endurance to succeed if anyone could, but he also felt a paternal reluctance to let these two young men go off on such a dangerous quest. In the end Brewer agreed to let them try, and King and Cotter spent the rest of the day, July 3, getting things ready for their attempt.

Our walking-shoes were in excellent condition, the hobnails firm and new. We laid out a barometer, a compass, a pocket-level, a set of wet and dry thermometers, note-books, with bread, cooked beans, and venison enough to last a week, rolled them all in blankets, making two knapsack-shaped packs strapped firmly together with loops for the arms, which, by Brewer's estimate, weighed forty pounds apiece.

After King spent another restless night and Cotter, as he later confessed, did not sleep at all, the whole party rose before dawn on July Fourth and had breakfast. Brewer and Gardner had decided to accompany King and Cotter for about five miles, to a height of thirteen thousand feet, and then climb to the summit of what they were now calling Mount Brewer in order to retrieve some instruments that Brewer and Hoffmann had left behind. And Jim was anxious to see the view of the eastern range that Brewer had described. When they set off in the darkness, Brewer carried Cotter's pack so that Dick could save his strength. After about five hours of crossing snowfields, climbing huge boulders, and skirting sky-blue lakes, they reached a saddle pass at the southern foot of Mount Brewer, from which they could see the eastern range of the Sierras. They laid down the packs and sat together in silence, contemplating what stood before them: "the most gigantic mountain-wall in America, culminating in a noble pile of Gothic-finished granite and enamel-like snow."

"I looked at it as one contemplating the purpose of his life," King writes in *Mountaineering*, "and for just one moment I would have rather liked to dodge that purpose, or to have waited, or have found some excellent reason why I might not go." But the blood rose in him and when he glanced at Cotter "there was such complete bravery in his eye that I asked him if he was ready to start." As the men said good-bye there were tears in every eye. King writes that when Brewer asked him what his plan was, "I had to own that I had but one, which was to reach the highest peak in the range." King and Cotter took up their packs and started to the south, planning to walk along the western range until they found a likely spot to descend into the abyss that they would have to cross to get to the eastern range. The other two headed north up the slope of Mount Brewer, where they would plant an American flag in honor of Independence Day, and King remembers that every time he and Cotter stopped to rest they could see their companions, growing smaller and smaller until they appeared at the summit as "microscopic forms."

King and Cotter climbed a peak south of the pass, but when they peered down its eastern face they saw a sheer drop. Farther along they found a snowy slope that they considered sliding down, but when they tossed a stone along their intended path the way was so steep that the stone took bounces of hundreds of feet. So they set off instead for a ridge several miles to the south that ran perpendicular to the two ranges, bridging them. To reach the ridge they managed to descend partway down the eastern slope of the Great Western Divide, a dangerous maneuver because their packs made them top-heavy and threatened to tip them head over heels to their deaths. Because of this and because their shoulders were already bruised by the pack straps, they took the packs off and lowered them with a rope, with one man climbing slowly down to a resting place to receive them and then the other following and then forging on down to the next spot. "In this manner," King writes, "we consumed more than half the afternoon in descending a thousand feet of broken, precipitous slope." They had reached one amphitheater, but the walls surrounding it were too steep to climb. They were able to get out of the canyon by following a creek bed, "and then up again over a long, difficult debris-slope and across several fields of snow, into another amphitheater." The sky darkened then, and they hid under the overhang of some rocks as a massive hailstorm passed by. At sunset they reached the cross ridge between the two ranges. They found a flat place under an overhang in which to camp, having thought to fill their canteen from a stream before darkness turned everything around them to ice. They ate cold venison and bread and, because there was no firewood at that height, cut small strips of wood from the barometer case to make a tiny fire with which to warm a cup of "miserably tepid tea." After supper there was nothing to do but roll up in their blankets and contemplate the view, watching as the shadows from the western range grew darker and the light on the eastern range went from yellows to oranges to violets to pinks to grays.

When the sunlight disappeared entirely, "A sudden chill overcame us. Stars in a moment crowded through the dark heaven, flashing with a frosty splendor. The snow congealed, the brooks ceased to flow, and, under the sudden leverage of frost, immense blocks were dislodged all along the mountain summits and came thundering down the slopes." They had been lucky in their choice of camping place, because the ledge of stone above them gave protection from "these missiles, weighing often many tons." By nine o'clock the temperature was twenty degrees Fahrenheit, and by morning it would be two degrees. With only blankets protecting them from the cold granite beneath and the colder surrounding air, "How I loved Cotter!" King writes, "how I hugged him and got warm, while our backs gradually petrified, till we whirled over and thawed them out together!" King does not generally show Brewer's fondness for exclamation points; his use of them here suggests his awareness that the image of two robust young men spooning on a ledge far out in the wild could have its homoerotic overtones. Still, given their level of exhaustion, the nature of their bed (which, besides being hard and far from smooth, sloped downward so that they had to chock themselves with small rocks to keep from sliding away), and the unimaginable cold, eroticism of any sort would seem to be so incredible as to make the exclamation points unnecessary. And they slept with a version of Tristan's sword separating them—the canteen, which their body heat kept from freezing. In spite of all this discomfort, King eventually sank into "an industrious slumber which lasted with great soundness until four," when they arose, ate some frozen venison, took a swig from the canteen, and were off.

In his *History of the Sierra Nevada*, Francis P. Farquhar refers to King and Cotter's crossing from the western range of the Sierras to the eastern range as "a new era in American mountaineering. Never before had anyone attempted to traverse such a complex maze of ridges and canyons as those that confronted them. To venture into such unknown country, scantily equipped and without experience on steep snow and precipitous rock, required more than ordinary courage." What King and Cotter would do before they slept again would be the centerpiece of this accomplishment, and King's account in *Mountaineering* of the feats of July 5 makes blood-pounding reading. King gave a soberer and yet still exciting account of their trip to their boss Josiah Whitney for his first book about the California Geological Survey, *Geology*. The tale in *Mountaineering* was written more than six years after the fact, based on notebooks and his report to Whitney. The dramatic effects that King achieves in this later telling have led Farquhar and others to take a slightly condescending tone toward the *Mountaineering* account, but there is no diminishing the difficulty of what they achieved in the face of real danger. To have done it at all is amazing; to have been able to fashion it later into a powerful literary work would seem reason enough to praise rather than to patronize.

As King and Cotter set off in the dark of the morning of July 5, the temperature was still just above zero. By moonlight reflected off the peaks to the east, they worked their way along the ridge connecting the two ranges, looking for a likely place to ascend. They walked up a frozen snowfield until it became so steep and slippery that they were forced to cut steps in it using Cotter's bowie knife. After about an hour the light of day began to penetrate the shadows cast by the eastern range. "To look back when we stopped to rest was to realize our danger,—that smooth swift slope of ice carrying the eye down a thousand feet to the margin of a frozen mirror of ice; ribs and needles of rock piercing up through the snow, so closely grouped that, had we fallen, a miracle only might save us from being dashed." King writes drily that "this led to rather deeper steps."

After two more hours of climbing in this way, they reached a rock field and crawled laboriously up it for two more hours until they came to a ravine that they couldn't climb with their packs on. They again used the rope, with Cotter climbing up its length and then hauling the packs and instruments up, and King following. "Constantly closing up in hopeless difficulty before us," King writes in *Mountaineering*, "the way opened again and again to our gymnastics, till we stood together on a mere shelf, not two feet wide, which led diagonally up the smooth cliff." With their backs against the mountain, they shuffled along this ledge until they reached a flat spot where they could rest and contemplate their next step. The way up offered no likely foothold and the way down now seemed impossible, too. They sat for an hour. King recalls that they felt disheartened, but paralyzed by fear might be a more likely description of their state of mind. Thirty feet above them was another ledge that had several granite spikes along its edge. They had no way of knowing whether the spikes were attached to the rock or simply loose boulders, but what alternative did they have? After fashioning the rope into a lasso they began to toss it at the spikes while trying to keep their balance on the narrow ledge. Both men tried flinging the rope until at last King looped one of their targets and pulled the lasso tight. He slowly put his 150 pounds of weight on the rope and the spike held, so Cotter added his weight as well. Something

moved above—either the spike tilted or the rope itself stretched—
but either way they had to try.

> I began to climb slowly. The smooth precipice-face against which
> my body swung offered no foothold, and the whole climb had
> therefore to be done by the arms, an effort requiring all one's
> determination. When about half-way up I was obliged to rest,
> and, curling my feet in the rope, managed to relieve my arms for
> a moment. In this position I could not resist the fascinating temp-
> tation of a survey downward.
>
> Straight down, nearly a thousand feet below, at the foot of the
> rocks, began the snow, whose steep, roof-like slope, exaggerated
> into an almost vertical angle, curved down in a long white field,
> broken far away by rocks and polished, round lakes of ice.
>
> Cotter looked up cheerfully and asked how I was making it; to
> which I answered I had plenty of wind left. At that moment,
> when hanging between heaven and earth, it was a deep satisfac-
> tion to look down at the wild gulf of desolation beneath, and up to
> unknown dangers ahead, and feel my nerves cool and unshaken.

King climbed the rest of the way up, slung himself onto the shelf,
and called for Cotter to send the barometer and then the packs up.
Dick, who was evidently even stronger than King, then "came up
the rope in his very muscular way without once stopping to rest."
The shelf on which they now stood led to the summit of the perpendicular ridge that connected the western and eastern ranges of
the Sierras. When they reached the summit and looked over the
south side they saw a sheer thousand-foot drop—an "almost
Yosemite cliff." And when they looked to the east, along the summit itself, they saw that it was impassable in that direction, broken
by notches going down hundreds of feet and topped with rocks that
looked unstable. So much for using it as a bridge.

Because it was now midday, they put down their packs and ate
lunch. Ever since King's first sight of these mountains from the top
of Mount Bullion, he had suspected that both the Kings and Kern

rivers had their headwaters here, and one of the survey's goals for the Brewer party's summer campaign was to find just where these two rivers began. Now King and Cotter could see that the crest on which they sat was the divide between the two rivers, that everything to the north of them flowed into creeks that fed the Kings, and everything to the south fed the Kern. "Thousands of rills poured from the melting snow," King remembers, "filling the air with a musical tinkle as of many accordant bells." They could see the path of glaciers down the Kern Valley and to the west they could see some of the peaks of the Coast Range. "The view was so grand, the mountain colors so brilliant, immense snow-fields and blue alpine lakes so charming, that we almost forgot we were ever to move, and it was only after a swift hour of this delight that we began to consider our future course."

They knew they could not go east along the top of the divide as they had hoped. Even if they could get back down the north slope of the divide, which they had just climbed, it would not help, because the Kings Cañon, as they called it, "seemed untraversable." That left only the Yosemite-like wall to the south, which, should they actually make it to the bottom, offered a fairly uncomplicated path to what looked like the highest peak in the eastern range, a mountain several miles to the south of them. King went west a little way on the divide and Cotter went east to see if either of them could find a likely place to begin their descent, but when they met back where they'd eaten their lunch they concluded that it was as good a place as any: "Down it we must," King writes. They lay on their stomachs looking over the precipice for some minutes until King suggested that he might tie the rope around his chest and after attaching it to a sturdy rock, lower himself until he found a place from which they could stage the next part of the descent. Over he went, and about forty feet down he came to a notch just big enough to hold him and Cotter, but not the packs. He asked Cotter to lower the packs, and then tied them together with his silk handkerchiefs and looped them on a little jutting point of rock. Once Cotter came down the rope they "whipped the noose off its resting-place above, and cut off our connections with the upper world."

As the rope sailed down on them, Cotter said with his usual understatement, "We're in for it now, King." They were standing on a two-foot-wide shelf, and there was no likely place to tie the rope as an anchor for the next stage, "so I determined to try the climb with only as little aid as possible. Tying [the rope] round my breast again, I gave the other end into Cotter's hands, and he, bracing his back against the cliff, found for himself as firm a foothold as he could, and promised to give me all the help in his power." King was able to find enough rough places in the smooth granite face to crawl down about ten feet without having to test Cotter's balance and strength, but then he reach an utterly smooth patch about eight feet above a three-foot shelf. He had gone down with his stomach against the cliff but now managed to turn so that his back was to the granite, hands clinging to two protuberances but feet dangling below him because the rock his back was hugging overhung the shelf below.

> I thought, possibly, I might, by a quick slide, reach [the shelf] in safety without endangering Cotter. I shouted to him to be very careful and to let go in case I fell, loosened my hold upon the rope, and slid quickly down. My shoulder struck against the rock and threw me out of balance; for an instant I reeled over upon the verge, in danger of falling, but, in the excitement, I thrust out my hand and seized a small alpine gooseberry bush, the first piece of vegetation we had seen. Its roots were so firmly fixed in the crevice that it held my weight and saved me.

Whether the little gooseberry bush was placed in just that spot by nature, by God, or by King's imagination, we can never really know. Nor can we know whether Cotter might have been able to hold him if the bush had not, because surely Cotter would not have heeded King's advice to let him go. Leaving loyalty aside, if King had plunged to his death Cotter would have had no way down from his own ledge unless a passing condor had thought to give him a lift. Cotter came down by the same dangerous maneuver, after lowering the packs, but this time King held one end of the rope and braced himself in case Cotter should slip. "As he came slowly down from crack to crack, I heard his hobnailed shoes grating on the granite; presently they appeared dangling from the eaves above my head. I had gathered in the rope until it was taut, and then hurriedly told him to drop. He hesitated a moment, and let go. Before he struck the rock I had him by the shoulder, and whirled him down upon his side, thus preventing his rolling overboard, which friendly action he took quite coolly."

The next stages down were not difficult by comparison, but when they had gone about 250 feet, "the rocks were so glacially polished and water-worn that it seemed impossible to get any farther." Then King noticed a crack in the rock about a foot deep and several inches wide at the surface, the only possible way down. "As the chances seemed rather desperate, we concluded to tie ourselves together, in order to share a common fate." They left about thirty feet of rope between them, maneuvering slowly down the ladder, as King called the crack, faces to the cliff and packs on their backs. They descended another eighty feet in this way and then reached "a rude granite stairway that led to the snow." They were down.

But not entirely safe. They quickly hopped down the stairway, leaping from rock to rock across what was a strip of glacial debris, until they reached the snowfield, which swept down about 750 feet at a steep angle onto an iced-over lake.

Without untying the lasso which bound us together, we sprang upon the snow with a shout, and glissaded down splendidly, turning now and then a somersault, and shooting out like cannon-balls almost to the middle of the frozen lake; I upon my back, and Cotter feet first, in a swimming position. The ice cracked in all directions. It was only a thin, transparent film, through which we could see deep into the lake. Untying ourselves, we hurried ashore in different directions, lest our combined weight should be too great a strain upon any point.

The cliff they had spent the last three hours descending had been in shadows. Now, standing in warming sunshine, their spirits continued to rise. A look back at the sheer cliff told them that they were very lucky to have gotten down it alive, and after the strain of climbing, "walking was a delicious rest" as they headed around the lake and toward the mountain they intended to climb. At its base they could see "a little grove of pines, an ideal bivouac," and they made that their destination. Soon the snow and glacial leavings turned to occasional small fields with thin grass and wildflowers, and little basins of clear water. After their hours of seeing only rocks, snow, ice, and that one lucky gooseberry bush, "it was a relief to find ourselves again in the region of life," King writes. "I never felt for trees and flowers such a sense of intimate relationship and sympathy." The grove of pines was farther than it appeared, and they didn't reach it until dark. They made a camp within a mile of the base of the mountain they would climb the next day, lighting a fallen log so full of pine resin that it flamed brightly. In the fire they could boil water from a nearby stream for a steaming cup of tea, char venison on a stick until it sizzled, and heat their beans until they became "seductively crisp upon our tin plates." The meal seemed to them "the quintessence of gastronomy," and after a little conversation they made beds of pine needles near the fire's warmth and slept deeply until three-thirty, when they arose to the still-blazing pitch and made breakfast.

They set off by moonlight, leaving their packs and carrying only their instruments, lunch, and the canteen, laboring over rocks and frozen streams till they got to the base of the mountain. Although they were in the mountain's shadow as the sun began to rise, they could soon see that the ascent was impossible from the west, where the granite cliffs were vertical or worse. But to the north, the mountain rose gradually enough to be worth a try, so they spent an hour circling around to the foot of that face. The boulders at first were large and apt to move when they leapt over them, but soon they reached a field of smaller rocks. As they began to climb the sun rose higher and started to melt the ice holding bigger boulders above them, sending them down the mountainside, where they created avalanches of smaller rocks. King and Cotter climbed side by side, about a hundred feet apart, because climbing in file as they usually did created the additional danger that the higher climber would unloose a rock that would hit the lower one. Farther up they reached places where they had to negotiate granite faces by clinging to cracks and protuberances, and other places where they had to cut steps in the frozen snow.

At one spot the only way up was to walk between the sheer granite face of the mountain and a thick wall of ice that had melted where it touched the warmed granite, creating a space. "We entered this crevice and climbed along its bottom," King writes, "with a wall of rock rising a hundred feet above us on one side, and a thirty-foot face of ice on the other, through which light of an intense cobalt-blue penetrated." Near the top of this formation they again had to cut steps in the ice to proceed. "We were now in a dangerous position: to fall into the crevice on one side was to be wedged to death between rock and ice; to make a slip was to be shot down five hundred feet, and then hurled over the precipice." The view opened to the east, and almost straight below them they could see the blue waters of Owens Lake; today, the runoff feeding the lake is diverted to Los Angeles, and the lake bed is dry.

The final crest of the mountain was surrounded by smooth blank walls, as "if Nature had intended to secure the summit from all assailants," but in one spot there was a strip of frozen snow leading directly to the top—"a great icicle-column frozen in a niche of the bluff." The two men began to cut stairs in it, and as they rose they were constantly afraid that it would break off from the cliff. Near the top it was too thin to cut anything deeper than tiny toe-holds, but the ice column had grown so narrow that they could wrap their arms around it and shimmy up like they were climbing a tree. When they got to the top, they managed to flop across the space between the ice and the rock, onto a flat granite shelf from which a gentle slope of ice and rocks led to the summit. They reached the crest at exactly noon. "I rang my hammer upon the topmost rock,"

King writes; "we grasped hands and I reverently named the grand peak MOUNT TYNDALL."

Like Brewer and Hoffmann several days before them, King and Cotter felt a sense of triumph only for the few seconds it took them to look into the distance and realize that they had not climbed the highest peak in the state, or even in the neighborhood. The dominant peak was about six miles to the south along the eastern range of the Sierras on which they stood. Mount Whitney, as they would name it, was some five hundred feet taller than Mount Tyndall's fourteen thousand feet. From the perspective of Mount Tyndall it looked like "a cleanly cut helmet of granite . . . fronting the desert with a bold square bluff which rises to the crest of the peak, where a white fold of snow trims it gracefully." King concluded that "its summit looked glorious, but inaccessible." The other peak that was clearly taller than Mount Tyndall was about a mile and a half due east. This they would name Mount Williamson in honor of Robert S. Williamson, an army officer and topographical engineer who had probed the whole length of the Sierras in the 1850s for likely railroad passes and who would before long be a crucial ally in King's quest to launch the Fortieth Parallel Survey. King and Cotter saw at least two other peaks that seemed as tall as theirs.

The view from the top of Mount Tyndall deeply impressed the two primary aspects of Clarence King's nature. For King the scientist, the topography of the whole region that they were exploring was laid out in very plain detail. He saw the parallel ranges of the Sierras, the perpendicular divide between them that separated the headwaters of the Kings and Kern rivers, the hard left turn around the base of Mount Brewer that the Kings watershed takes, flowing west in a canyon of its creation through the western ridge of the Sierras and down to the long, broad valley of California. South of the divide was the Kern River Canyon, "once the rocky bed of a grand old glacier," as King reports to Whitney. To the north and south, the range on which they stood dropped off steeply to the desert, "a vast expanse of arid plain intersected by low parallel ranges, traced from north to south." Beyond these low ranges were endless plains stretching to the horizon. Not only could you get the whole immense landscape in one slow pirouette, but you could see deep into the oceanic history of that landscape. "Traced in ancient beach-lines, here and there upon hill and plain, relics of ancient lake-shore outline the memory of a cooler past,—a period of life and verdure when the stony chains were green islands among basins of wide, watery expanse."

But Mount Tyndall's summit also affected the Romantic side of King's personality, in an almost overwhelming way. King's article "The Descent of Mount Tyndall," which includes his observations and musings from the summit, followed by a month his account of the ascent in the *Atlantic Monthly* in the summer of 1871. Although both accounts were written years later, King's ability to recall so many details, and especially pictorial details (remember Jim Gardner's assertion when they were young explorers of the Hartford suburbs that King had a photographic memory of all they saw on their outings), it seems safe to assume that King remembered his emotional responses to what he saw with great clarity, too. When King and Cotter reached the top of Mount Tyndall, they were dog tired, both from the efforts of that long morning and from several days of hard climbing, from the ebb and flow of adrenaline in countless dangerous situations, and from too little warmth, too little rest, and too little nourishment. The emotional rush of reaching the summit had been followed by the disappointment that they had not gained the "top of California." After King took his readings and made his scientific observations, he saw the landscape through weary eyes, and the images fell upon a soul prepared by his readings of Ruskin. In his 1987 book, *Pacific Visions: California Scientists and the Environment, 1850–1915,* the historian Michael L. Smith observes that King used the language of John Tyndall's writings about mountaineering in the Alps while fighting his way up a mountain or glissading down it, but "At the summit, King's narrative shifted from Tyndall's mountaineering language to that of Ruskin's sublime."

For Ruskin, in *Modern Painting,* landscape became more beautiful as it became more mountainous: "Paradise is in the slope of the meadows, orchards, and corn-fields on the sides of a great Alp," he wrote. The prospect of a mountain is beautiful chiefly because of the variety and subtlety of colors it displays, especially as the light changes throughout the day. But these observations are *of* mountains, not *from* them. When King stood at fourteen thousand feet atop Mount Tyndall and looked back at the western ridge, he praised its "wonderful profile." But when he looked east the view was down, far down, on almost everything he could see. From this godlike perspective he could perceive Ruskin's definition of mountains as the bones of the earth, skeletons that had to shake off the rocks and soil and sand that covered them in order to be exposed. As if images of premature burial were not enough, the whole scene was bleached of the warm colors of Ruskin's Alpine meadows, orchards and cornfields; instead "lay plains clouded with the ashen hues of death; stark, wind-swept floors of white . . . No greenness soothes, no shadow cools the glare." On the polished granite mountain walls "has been written the epitaph of glaciers now melted and vanished into air." Even the sky at this height was too blue: "You look up into an infinite vault, unveiled by clouds, empty and dark." He goes on in this vein for several pages of *Mountaineering,* at one point saying, "I have never seen Nature when she seemed so little 'Mother Nature' as in this place of rocks and snow, echoes and emptiness." Just in case we don't get it yet, he adds, "looking from this summit with all desire to see everything, the one overmastering feeling is desolation, desolation!"

Then the dark cloud passes over his Romantic's soul and he is himself again, enjoying the silence, making a Ruskinian observation about how Gothic architecture must have been inspired by mountains, bustling again with his readings, taking pride that he and Cotter feel no altitude sickness, making a witty observation about the rich European tourists who will eventually follow them: "They are already shooting our buffaloes; it cannot be long before they will cause themselves to be honorably dragged up and down our Sierras, with perennial yellow gaiter, and ostentation of bath-tub."

After a little while they gathered their instruments and started back; given their exhaustion and dwindling supplies, there was no thought of trying for the higher peaks. But the descent of Mount Tyndall and the return to their friends on the other side of Mount Brewer would be as dangerous as anything they had gone through so far. When they walked down the slight incline from the summit and looked over at the ice ladder, they saw that with the rising temperatures the top half had now indeed broken off, its white pieces smashed on the rocks far below them. "I saw," King writes, "that nothing but the sudden gift of wings could possibly take us down to the snow-ridge." But they worked their way round the top of the mountain clockwise, overhanging the steep cliffs to the east, and when they reached the southwest corner they found a face that was not smooth polished granite but "rough-hewn walls of rock and snow." They were able to descend it without using the rope, at the relatively quick rate of two thousand feet in two hours, reaching a snowfield and the topmost of a series of glacial lakes. On its south side the mountain formed the opening of a horseshoe, and when they made their way down and around the westernmost spur of the shoe they were below the snow line. They walked three miles north through groves of pines on flat granite floors, reaching their camp an hour before sunset, and found their pitch log still burning. The feeling of satisfaction they shared was mitigated by the bad shape of Cotter's shoes, "which were rapidly going to pieces." They thought about how they would make him a pair of moccasins out of one of their provision bags and a part of the blanket, then talked about what they'd done and seen that day and fell asleep, not waking until well after dawn.

Following a breakfast of venison, bread, and weak tea, they took up their packs "upon toughened shoulders" and set off. They could not go back the way they'd come, because the southern face of the perpendicular Kings-Kern divide was not climbable. Instead they decided to go north, crossing the divide where it met the eastern ridge of the Sierras, and take their chances going due west across Kings Canyon to the base of Mount Brewer, a route that had seemed impassable from the other direction just two days earlier. But since then "we had gained such confidence in our climbing powers, from constant victory," that they decided to give it a go. Besides, they didn't have another plan. Crossing the Kern River and approaching the western range from the east did not seem promising. In King's report to Whitney, published in *Geology*, King writes that "all this range, from Kings River gateway to Kaweah Peak, presents a series of blank, almost perpendicular precipices, broken every mile or so by a bold granite buttress." The plateau at the north end of Kern Canyon led gradually up the divide to the north, and by noon "we came suddenly upon the brink of a precipice which sunk sharply from our feet into the gulf of Kings Cañon." Due west of them now was Mount Brewer, and "straight across from our point of view was the chamber of rock and ice where we had camped the first night."

As uninviting as they found the "sharp and rugged" thousand feet of wall below them, they were more concerned about the two thousand feet below that, which they couldn't see. King rolled a boulder down the slope and after it traveled the first thousand feet it completely disappeared, suggesting a straight drop. Still, they could see the pass south of Mount Brewer where they had last been with their friends, and its sight encouraged them to descend. They went slowly down about eight hundred feet, the face becoming smoother and more slippery the closer they got to the brink. From there they sent more rocks tumbling below them, and "only heard the sound of their stroke after many seconds, which convinced us that directly below lay a great precipice."

Just at this time Cotter's shoes fell apart, so they stopped to make the moccasins as they had planned, tying them on with strips of buckskin. The next 150 feet down to the edge was so steep that they worked their way slowly on their backsides, digging in with the heels of their feet and hands. Although no gooseberry bushes presented themselves, there were stunted pines growing in the crevices of the granite face, and they edged downward from one to the other as they approached the precipice, King moving ahead of Cotter since he had the better footwear. Cotter was having trouble getting traction with his makeshift moccasins, and had just announced that he would try to go barefooted when King heard "a startled cry, and I looked around to see him slide quickly toward me, struggling and clutching at the smooth granite. As he slid by I made a grab for him with my right hand, catching him by the shirt, and, throwing myself as far in the other direction as I could, seized with my left hand a little pine tuft, which held us." They were only twenty feet from the precipice, and when King tied the rope to the pine tree and lowered himself down its edge he saw a drop of several hundred feet. But he also saw that to their south a pile of debris rose up to the very edge of the precipice. They scuttled slowly sideways about a hundred feet to a point above the spot, and King lowered Cotter down to it with the rope and then himself slid down.

Once they descended the debris slope and the rocky field below it they came to a meadow and their last test before they got back to camp—how to cross the gorge of what they called Kings River but was probably Vidette Creek, which leads to the Kings. Their choices were to get wet in the very brisk air or to go around the stream and a lake that fed it by climbing partway back up the divide. They chose the latter course, which involved chipping steps into another ice column and then climbing a difficult forty-foot face. At first King could not make it up the face, so Cotter went ahead, lowering the rope and assuring King that he had him if he fell. King tied the rope around his chest but decided to go up if he could without Cotter's help. He climbed carefully to the ledge, reproducing Cotter's climb, which King called "the most splendid piece of slow gymnastics I ever witnessed." King rested a moment and looked up at Cotter, who

was sitting upon a smooth roof-like slope, where the least pull would have dragged him over the brink. He had no brace for his feet, nor hold for his hands, but had seated himself calmly, with the rope tied around his breast, knowing that my only safety lie in being able to make the climb entirely unaided; certain that the least waver in his tone would have disheartened me, and perhaps made it impossible.

King generously writes about his friend that "it is one thing, in a moment of excitement, to make a gallant leap, or hold one's nerves in the iron grasp of will, but to coolly seat one's self in the door of death, and silently listen for the fatal summons . . ." We can never know whether this really happened as King says it did, and it's hard not to wonder why Cotter didn't simply tell King it was too risky and suggest that they find a safer solution. But acts of courage tend to be irrational, and King's sense that they often grow out of the moment smacks of truth. Even Cotter's decision to sit coolly listening for the fatal summons was an act of the moment. One feels the justice of King's assertion that "in all my experience of mountaineering I have never known an act of such real, profound courage as this of Cotter's." And whether the passage is fact or fiction, reading it makes one understand the nature of courage a little better.

A little higher up they found a grove of pine trees and a small stream, and camped there for the night on a bed of pine twigs, sleeping until the sun had risen high enough above the eastern ridge to fill the canyon with light. They made the hard climb to the pass south of Mount Brewer, which they reached at two o'clock. The day was uneventful except for the lack of proper footwear for Cotter; he now wrapped his feet in pieces of an old flour sack, which did not protect them from the sharp rocks, so that he left a bloody path in the snow where he walked. When they tramped down from the pass to their former camp they found a note saying that their companions had moved five miles lower, where there was better feed for the animals. The two men hurried on, and King claims that once they saw the smoke from the campfire even Cotter ran on his bloodied feet. "Our shouts were instantly answered by the three voices of our friends, who welcomed us to their camp-fire with tremendous hugs."

King and Cotter stretched out by the fire's warmth and told their friends of their adventures. Eventually their leader, William Brewer, admitted to King that "you have relieved me of a dreadful task. For the last three days I have been composing a letter to your family, but somehow I did not get beyond 'It becomes my painful duty to inform you.'" They had been gone five days in all, and though they had not reached the top of California, Brewer would note simply in his journal that "It was by far the greatest feat of strength and endurance that has yet been performed on the Survey."

## CHAPTER SEVEN

# Tall Tales

*Mariposa Trail, entrance to Yosemite Valley.*
*Photograph by Carleton E. Watkins, circa 1865.*

larence King had not abandoned but only postponed the idea
of climbing Mount Whitney, which he now believed to be the
highest peak in California. On July 10, 1864, the day after King and
his bloody-footed companion, Dick Cotter, rejoined the other
three members of William Brewer's field party, the five men
returned to the camp at Big Meadows, where some supplies had
been stored. Brewer writes in his journal that, as they had waited for
King and Cotter they had run "out of flour, salt, bacon, and sugar—

in fact we had nothing but venison and beans to eat." In his report, *Geology*, the director of the California Geological Survey, Josiah Whitney, writes that Brewer, Charles Hoffmann, and Jim Gardner "had been out of provisions for several days, with the exception of a few strips of jerked bear meat." Whatever the true state of their supplies, upon returning to Big Meadows, King writes, they were treated to "such bounties as the potato, and once a salad, in which some middle-aged lettuce became the vehicle for a hollow mockery of dressing."

The food and rest soon put the men "in excellent trim for further campaigning." The exception was Brewer himself, who had developed a toothache while waiting for King and Cotter to return. The tooth had now become agonizingly infected, and King tried three times to extract it using his bullet mold. That having failed, Brewer decided on July 12 to travel the seventy miles to Visalia and a dentist, and King accompanied him. As Brewer and King rode out of the mountains through the beautiful stands of sequoias and down into the Sierra foothills, the brutal heat of that California summer reached up to them. By afternoon it was too hot to travel farther, so they rested at a small ranch until, spurred on by the pain in his jaw, Brewer decided that they should push ahead at sunset and ride all night. The moon set after midnight and they got lost in the dark, wandering a couple of hours out of their way, but they reached Visalia at sunrise "in a state of reeling sleepiness quite indescribably funny," at least to King. As it happened, the ulceration in Brewer's mouth had burst just before dawn, ending two days of "terrible" pain that had left his face temporarily misshapen. They ate breakfast, slept till noon, and then Brewer had the tooth pulled.

At some point King hatched a plan to make an attempt at Mount Whitney by a more southerly route, following the Kaweah River east and thus avoiding the western range of the Sierras, now known as the Great Western Divide. Brewer engaged two of the Visalia cavalrymen so anxious to escape the heat, and they accompanied King, packing a week's worth of provisions. They would follow a trail recently blazed by a cattleman named Hockett, across the

Sierras to Owens Lake. Before King and his men got very far back into the mountains, the Kaweah River divided, and they followed the Hockett trail along the south fork, making their first camp forty miles from where the foothills had begun. From there they continued east across a high plateau, eventually passing below the western range of the Sierras and crossing the south fork of the Kern. King noted that between the south and main forks of the Kern the granite, which almost everywhere in the region was shaded tones of gray from light to dark, was here tinted varieties of red by iron oxide in the rock. Whitney's account of this trip in *Geology*, based on King's field reports, says that "Where the trail crosses the main Kern, the river is twenty-five or thirty yards wide; the water is clear and cold, and abundantly supplied with trout." On the far bank of the Kern the cattle trail turned sharply to the southeast so that it could cross into Owens Valley by a pass that would be easiest on the cattle. King left the cattle route once he crossed the Kern, and headed north "without any other guides than the eye and the compass," as Whitney reports in *Geology*.

Nobody knows just where King went from this point. He apparently reached a creek several miles to the north and then followed it east to a pass in the eastern range of the Sierras, about eight miles south of Mount Whitney. From wherever this left him, he spent three days "in the midst of every difficulty" getting those eight miles to the base of the mountain. At some point during this time he left the soldiers and horses behind, and was on his own. King told Whitney that he got to within 400 feet of the summit, and that barometric readings at the spot suggested he was at 14,740 feet. Since we now know that Mount Whitney is 14,500 feet, King's measurements were off by a considerable amount. This could be explained by the cold, windy, and snowy weather conditions, which would affect the readings, making the charts that translate barometric pressure to height useless. Why King stopped where he did might be explained by the weather and might be explained by his climbing alone. Although he had been an only child, he had rarely been on his own in his life. First his mother had been his constant companion, and then Jim Gardner, William Brewer, and, most recently, Dick Cotter. The one previous time that he had been sent out by himself was when he went to Mariposa—when he drew the ire of others on the survey for getting too little accomplished. King's natural theatricality by definition required an audience. When there wasn't one, King did not tend to distinguish himself. All we can know now for certain is that, whatever happened once he crossed the Kern and left his men, he did not want to write about it.

*Mountaineering in the Sierra Nevada,* King's 1872 book, devotes half of its fourteen chapters to the summer and fall of 1864. Two chapters dramatize the five-day Mount Tyndall trip and two describe events in October and November at and around Yosemite. But the Mount Whitney excursion gets only two clauses: "After trying hard to climb Mount Whitney without success, and having returned to the plains . . ." Not only does King avoid focusing on his failure, but he actively distracts the reader by insulating this brief admission with two tall tales, one that supposedly happened soon after he left Brewer and Visalia with his army escort, and one set in time after he returned to Visalia from Mount Whitney and headed north to rejoin Brewer.

The first of these two tales is called "The Newtys of Pike," which like the Mount Tyndall chapters first appeared in the *Atlantic Monthly* in 1871, as part of an article called "Wayside Pikes." "Pike" refers to Pike County, Missouri, and its environs, whose westward-traveling natives became a comic literary type— poor backwards wanderers, always looking for a better life in the next place on the frontier, but too broke and too slow-witted to ever take advantage of any opportunity. While traveling with Brewer in Northern California the year before, King had written in his notebook about "loose solitary hermits . . . so sunken so devoid of noble ideas and high glimpses of something beyond the animal." Another writer who focused on the literary type described them as "the Anglo-Saxon relapsed into semi-barbarism." Bret Harte also helped turn the Pikes, with their hill country drawl, into a subgenre of the Western humor school, and King had befriended Harte by the time he wrote his own sketch. John Hay, who would become King's bosom friend several years later, was writing wildly popular poems in dialect, which he collected as *Pike County Ballads*. One critic described the whole Western humor genre of the time as "a muddy tide of slang, vulgarity . . . impertinence and buffoonery that is not wit," and it must be said that even Mark Twain in this mode can sometimes be a little wearying. King's sketch of the Newtys, as he called a family of pig farmers he says he happened upon as he entered the mountains from Visalia, is fairly brief and verbally exuberant. Although it has a thick overlay of social superiority, he keeps the dialect under control, especially the highly irritating practice of cacography, or deliberate misspellings, that typified the genre.

Like any good tale, this one begins with the implicit assertion that it is true, picking up from the narrative of his summer with the Brewer party. But as soon as he leaves Visalia with the cavalry escort he begins to blur reality, suggesting that he cannot tell the reader just which road he was on because if he identifies the people he meets on the road too closely it would endanger him if he went that way again. The absurdity of this statement, given that he is writing about peripatetic people some years later, signals that King has wandered off the factual path. He comes to an open meadow beside a large stream and makes camp with the soldiers. On his side of the stream is a group of hunters, who share their whiskey jug with him, but whose "old eternal way of making bear-stories out of whole cloth" drives him away, he says, a nice touch given that he has just launched a sort of bear story of his own. On the other side of the stream he finds the Newtys, a family stretched out by a campfire in a "thick strata of what is known to irony as comforters," with "their feet to the fire, looking as if they had been blown over in one direction, or knocked down by a single bombshell."

Five Newtys emerge from the jumble of bedclothes, the parents at either end and between them two young children and a "huge girl . . . her mind absorbed in the simple amusement of waving one foot (a cowhide eleven) slowly across the fire, squinting, with half-shut eye, first at the vast shoe and thence at the fire." The fictional King speaks first, saying, "You seem to have a pleasant camp-spot here," to which the bony, sharp-faced mother replies, "They's wus, and then again they's better." The father points out that it's a good spot for feed for the three thousand hogs they are tending. Later, when King returns to the Newtys' fire after supper, he gets down in the dirt beside the family of pig herders, his feet to the fire, and tries to ingratiate himself to them with "such sentiments as 'A little piece of bacon well broiled for breakfast is very good,'" and "Nothing better than cold ham for lunch."

This is not only funny for the reader, but it puts King in good stead with Susan, the big girl, even though her mother dislikes him because he admits that he has never shot a coon. Mr. Newty tries to defend King with "Maybe . . . that they don't have coon round the city of York." Soon Mr. Newty and Susan get it into their minds that King would be a good match for her. Later in the evening, after the younger children are asleep, Mr. Newty asks Susan to check on the hogs, and when she rises from the fire and shows off her "amusing proportions," King nonetheless describes her in terms that are distinctly sensual. He notes that she is as supple as she is large and "as her yawn deepened, she waved nearly down to the ground, and then, rising upon tiptoe, stretched up her clinched fists to heaven with a groan of pleasure." She asks King to go off with her in the night to see the pigs and her father urges him, too, bragging that his is the "pootiest band of hogs in Tulare County!" Susan and King walk through the woods together and climb a hill above where the beasts are bedded down for the night. They lean against a tree and look down over the family's "two acres of tranquil pork," slumbering in the moonlight.

Susan and King then stroll back to camp, and King crosses the stream to his own bedroll, but lies awake half-dreaming about Susan and her family. Next morning the two meet at either side of the stream, where each is performing morning ablutions, and the narrator once again mocks Susan's size but admits to an attraction:

". . . as she sprang back across the brook [after borrowing King's comb] and approached her mother's camp-fire, I could not fail to admire the magnificent turn of her shoulders and the powerful, queenly poise of her head." After breakfast Susan bounds off again to let the hogs out to feed in the woods, and King listens to Mr. Newty while he tells the sad story of his family's wanderings since they had left Pike County in 1850. Newty's conclusion is that "These yer hogs is awkward about moving, and I've pretty much made up my mind to put 'em all into bacon this fall and sell out and start for Montana." Later, King sends his escort ahead as Susan and her father ride with him for a way along the Hockett trail. When the father is ready to turn back, he calls King aside and says, "Thet— thet—thet man what gits Susan *has half the hogs!*"

This moment is the story's comic, if condescending, denouement. Susan rides on with King for another half mile, and when they shake hands to part she says, sweetly, "Say, you'll take good care of yourself, won't you, say?" King does not hurry to catch up with the soldiers and, "as I rode along for hour after hour the picture of this family stood before me in all its deformity of outline, all its poverty of detail, all its darkness of future, and I believe I thought of it too gravely to enjoy as I might the subtle light of comedy which plays about these hard, repulsive figures." There is as much social superiority in his gravity as in his comedy, but the most interesting thing about the story, perhaps, is what it tells us about King's taste in women. The very qualities that might have made Susan a repulsive figure for his audience—her unkemptness, her Amazonian size and athletic strength, her lack of sophistication—were qualities that were alluring to King, and would appeal to him more and more as he got older.

The other tale, "Kaweah's Run," also begins with factual autobiographical detail. King returns to Visalia, where he rests for two days, thawing himself out after the Mount Whitney attempt, sitting the "whole day on the quiet hotel veranda accustoming myself again to such articles as chairs and newspapers, and watching with unexpected pleasure the few village girls who flitted about during the day." In the evening he chats with strangers under the oak trees of the side streets and buys figs across the garden gate of a "rustic sister." Then he introduces two Mexican mountaineers who may or may not have been fictional, whom he sees while standing in line at the Wells Fargo office, where he has gone to withdraw some gold for his trip north to meet Brewer and the others at Wawona, near Yosemite. Even granting Jim Gardner's belief that King had a photographic memory, King describes these two Mexicans in more detail than he would probably have been able to muster had he not invented them. His conclusion, though, might well be something he could have taken in at a glance: "I thought them a hard couple, and summed up their traits as stolidity and utter cruelty."

As the stableman helps him saddle Kaweah for the 120-mile leg of his journey to Millerton, King claims to have heard the two "greasers," his unfortunate but common-in-his day Anglo slur for Mexicans, ask both the stableman and the hotel keeper where he is heading. It seems doubtful that they would ask this question within King's hearing—why wouldn't they simply wait until he had left town to do their reconnaissance? But this is a detail King thinks he needs for the tale that follows. King trots Kaweah out of Visalia under shady oaks and past lush farms irrigated by mountain streams until they get onto the hot dry plain, where the summer's heat and drought have killed all the foliage. Man and horse pass uneventfully through this "lonely sort of landscape" for the rest of the day, arriving at dusk at a ferry for the Kings River. Here, after being served an inedible dinner, King goes out to the corral to check on Kaweah and notices two men on horseback fording the river in the dark a quarter mile below the ferry. "So dangerous and unusual a proceeding could not have been to save the half-dollar ferriage," King writes ominously. The next morning at dawn the ferryman takes him across the river, and King and Kaweah follow the road along the far bank, past cottonwoods and willows that welcome the eye after his day on the hot plain, to which he is about to return.

Soon Kaweah's head bucks up and King sees the two Mexicans 150 yards ahead of him, camped by a place where the road takes a

sharp turn away from the river. The two are hurriedly trying to saddle their horses, and King spurs Kaweah off the road and cuts a
hypotenuse across the open range where he can pick up the road
again after it turns the corner. As one of the robbers cinches the
horses the other picks up a shotgun and runs at King, shouting
"Hold on, you—!" King gets back onto the road as the men mount
their mustangs, and the chase is on, much like the chases in a
hundred cowboy movies of the century between King's and our own.
Kaweah easily outdistances the bandits, but then King slows
Kaweah down to save his strength, and as in any good chase scene,
the Mexicans get the chance to catch up so that the drama may be
prolonged. Kaweah plunges ahead again, "Foam tinged with blood
fell from his mouth, and sweat rolled in streams from his whole
body, and now and then he drew a deep-heaving breath." The
bandits get so close that King (ever the man of science) claims to be
able to count the breaths of the two mustangs and compare them to
Kaweah's relatively lower count, proving to himself that his mount
has the greater endurance. He urges his horse on and "the thing of
nervous life under me bounded on wilder and faster, till I could feel
his spine thrill as with shocks from a battery." Soon King looks back
and sees that the two men have stopped and one of the mustangs is
down. A little farther up the road is a way station, where the propri-
etor sits by the barn holding a rifle, having watched the chase and
seen the horse fall. The two Mexicans had tried to steal horses from
the station man in the night, he tells King, which is why he is still
guarding his stock now. He and King cover Kaweah and walk him
until he cools, watching all the while for the bandits.

King sees them make a wide circle around the way station,
heading for the Millerton Road to the north, having gotten the
fallen mustang back on its feet. King waits till the last light of sunset fades in the west and, with directions from the station man, sets
out across the plain, avoiding the road. Soon a partial moon rises,
helping to light his and Kaweah's way. They come eventually to the
San Joaquin River, upstream from Millerton, and King stops to let
Kaweah drink and graze, and then heads down a path along the

river toward the village. Soon he hears a spur tinkle, and hides himself and Kaweah as the two Mexicans pass by on their mustangs, heading upstream. At this point King cannot resist a pure touch of romance: one of the bandits bursts into song, the "delicious melody" accompanied by the deliberate jingling of his spurs. King takes this operatic moment to observe that "these Californian scoundrels are invariably light-hearted; crime cannot overshadow the exhilaration of outdoor life; remorse and gloom are banished like clouds before this perennially sunny climate. They make amusement out of killing you, and regard a successful plundering time as a sort of pleasantry."

Still, at this moment the bandits will have to content themselves with the climate and the song, or find someone else to murder. After they pass, King and Kaweah head into Millerton, arriving at "about the time the drunk were conveying one another home." King gets a good meal and rest at a hotel, and well before dawn the next morning he and Kaweah cross the river and head into the Sierra foothills toward Mariposa. Once he realizes that Kaweah's tracks are the only fresh ones on the road, he relaxes and luxuriates in the balmy late July foothills weather—although he apparently doesn't give voice to an aria from *Traviata,* or even whistle one, as he has reported doing earlier on the trip. He does comment on the joy of allowing his naturalist side to simply appreciate the world around him:

> No tongue can tell the relief to simply withdraw scientific observation, and let Nature impress you in the dear old way with all her mystery and glory, with those vague indescribable emotions which tremble between wonder and sympathy.

Like his more truthful tales of mountain climbing, "Kaweah's Run" creates real dramatic tension, offering just the right sorts of details—the bloody foam from Kaweah's mouth, the jangling spurs—to make it real, and the descriptions of the landscape were undoubtedly drawn from the ride he actually made at that time from

Visalia to Clark's Ranch, at Wawona, going by way of Millerton and Mariposa. "Many readers were to take this tale for sober truth," King's biographer Thurman Wilkins writes, "even in California." But King would refer to it as "an adventure with Mexican bandits" and in a report to Whitney would write of the actual ride that "I have nothing of interest." When he got to Clark's on August 1, he learned that Frederick Law Olmsted and his family were camped there, as was William Ashburner, an early member of the survey, and his wife. Brewer's party would arrive at Clark's Ranch more than three weeks late, so King had plenty of time to relax with these friends in the cool weather of the Sierras.

William Brewer returned to Big Meadows from Visalia and on July 17 he, Hoffmann, Gardner, and Cotter, along with an escort of seven soldiers and sixteen mules and horses, set off to the northeast with the expectation of crossing the south fork of the Kings River and then finding a route across the Sierras to the north to the peak they would name Mount Goddard, some twenty-five miles away. In the general region of Mount Goddard they hoped to study the headwaters of the San Joaquin River. With difficulty, including the occasional hillside tumble of a packed mule, they made their way into the steep canyon of the south fork and followed the river east, eating well after hooking dozens of trout from the cold water. Like many others since, they found the sheer-walled beauty around them to be the rival of Yosemite. When they reached the head of the canyon, they camped in a grassy meadow where the rattlesnakes were too abundant for comfort, and fanned out to look for routes to the north that could accommodate their animals. A soldier found what is today called Copper Creek and the party headed up it, but the way soon became too rough to proceed except on foot. On July 22, they climbed a ridge, as Brewer writes, "over eleven thousand feet that commands a stupendous view. The deep canyons on all sides, the barren granite slopes, clear little lakes that occupy the beds of ancient glaciers, the sharp ridges, the high peaks, some of them rising to above fourteen thousand feet, like huge granite spires—all lay around, forming a scene of indescribable sublimity." The peaks in their vicinity were a little shorter than they guessed, 12,000 to 13,000 feet. A few miles to the east were a pair of mountains that would turn out to be 12,905 feet and 12,907 feet, respectively. The northernmost of the two, which looked to be the tallest but wasn't, they named Mount King. (After a peak near Yosemite was named for the San Francisco preacher Thomas Starr King, it was known as Mount Starr King and this one was known as Mount Clarence King.) The other one became Mount Gardner, for Jim (now Mount Gardiner, because Jim would add the "i" to his name later in life). A third mountain a little farther away became Mount Cotter, for Dick. It would turn out to be 12,725 feet tall. Mount Brewer was about five miles to the south. Charles Hoffmann, the fifth member of the Brewer party, had already had a peak north of the Yosemite Valley named for him the previous summer. All five peaks still go by the names of these Sierra explorers.

Brewer and his party soon gave up the idea of approaching Mount Goddard from the south, so they went east up what is now Bubbs Creek and then Charlotte Creek, taking Kearsarge Pass through the eastern range of the Sierras, and then down into Owens Valley by Independence Creek. The valley where it is not watered by Sierra streams is desert, and Brewer's party suffered from the over one-hundred-degree heat and alkali dust as they made their way north along the Owens River. Indians watched them the whole way, signaling from the hills with brief intense fires when the party stopped or started, but thanks to the military escort, never attacked or even approached them. Brewer's party went almost as far north as Yosemite and then went into the mountains by Mono Pass and cut southwest by Mono Creek into what is now called the Vermilion Valley. As their supplies dwindled, they attempted to get to Mount Goddard, farther southwest, suffering deprivations and taking risks that King might well have turned into another rousing adventure story had he not been cooling his heels at Wawona. Dick Cotter was once again the star, making a final assault of the mountain with one of the soldiers, named Spratt, after Brewer and Hoffmann could not go on and headed back to camp. Brewer writes that

> Dick and [Spratt] did not reach the top, but got within three hundred feet of it. They traveled all night and had no food—they had eaten their lunch all up at once. Dick is *very* tough. He had walked thirty-two hours and had been twenty-six entirely without food; yet, on the return, he had walked in four hours what had taken Hoffmann and me eight to do.

On August 15, after a couple of days of recovery, the whole party started north, weary and footsore and beginning to run out of provisions, over very hard terrain. Hoffmann began to complain of a pain in his leg, and soon he couldn't walk and could barely ride a horse. They had several days of rain, which made all of them miserable, and Hoffmann grew alarmingly worse. Finally, on August 23, they made it to Clark's Ranch at Wawona and met up with King and the Olmsteds and Ashburners, who were still there. "We were a hard-looking set—" Brewer writes, "ragged, clothes patched with old flour bags, poor—I had lost over thirty pounds—horses poor." They camped there for three weeks, enjoying the company and waiting for Hoffmann to get better, but in fact he grew worse and asked to be seen by a doctor. On September 10, his four companions carried him by litter over a six-thousand-foot hill to Mariposa, the path so narrow that only two could carry at a time. From there King and Cotter rode with him by coach to Stockton, a hundred miles away, and then by steamer to San Francisco. Whitney reports in *Geology* that it would take Hoffmann several months to recover from what was apparently an infection.

Brewer would make a trip to Yosemite with Olmsted and do a day trip or two, but in effect the California Geological Survey's work for the season was done. They had made the first serious exploration of the High Sierras, adding to the map of California a region that was, in the words of Whitney's biographer Edwin T. Brewster, "as big as Massachusetts and as high as Switzerland." As William H. Goetzmann writes in *Exploration and Empire*:

> Thus concluded perhaps the most spectacular exploration ever made in the High Sierras. In the course of their adventures, the Brewer and King parties had not only managed to scale the heights. They had measured them, charted their position, sketched in the topography, and in so doing had changed the entire map of the West in a significant way.

By the middle of October, Brewer had gotten word of his appointment to a professorship at the Sheffield School at Yale. He left California by steamer on November 14, headed for New Haven four years to the day after his arrival in San Francisco. His work with the California Geological Survey was at an end. According to his calculations he had traveled more than fifteen thousand miles in the state doing survey work, half of that on horseback and about three thousand miles of it on foot. He does not say how many of those walking miles he spent going straight up the side of a mountain, or straight down, and he does not say how many of those miles he traveled with frosty toes and too little in his stomach. But despite the hardships, he must have been in person the unfailingly genial companion he is in *Up and Down California*, and King must have been very sorry to see him go.

But by the middle of November, King had already almost completed another great adventure of his own. On June 30, 1864, as Brewer's party was heading east toward the camp from which they would climb Mount Brewer and Mount Tyndall, President Lincoln signed into law a bill promoted by Frederick Law Olmsted and others to grant Yosemite Valley and the Mariposa Grove of Big Trees to the state of California. The bill placed two conditions on the grant: "The premises shall be held for public use, resort, and recreation" and the two spots "shall be inalienable for all time." Private ownership within the boundaries of Yosemite and the Mariposa Grove would end, and the concept behind the great system of national parks in the United States was born. California governor Frederick F. Low set up an eight-man commission to study the grant and make a proposal to the state legislature, which had to vote on whether to accept it. The commissioners included Olmsted, Whitney, Ashburner, and Galen Clark, who had first seen Yosemite in 1855 and whose ranch at Wawona near the Mariposa Grove had been the meeting place for King and the rest of the Brewer survey party. A fifth commissioner was Israel W. Raymond, a San Francisco businessman involved with the steamship lines; he had been crucial in translating some of Olmsted's ideas about the preservation of Yosemite and the Big Trees into law, and had devised the phrase "for public use, resort, and recreation" that ended up in the bill.

One of the first things the commission did when it was formed in September was to hire King and Jim Gardner to make a boundary survey around the rim of the Yosemite Valley. The commission wanted the survey completed before the legislature met in December and in any case, according to King in *Mountaineering,* "we undertook the work, knowing very well we must use the utmost haste in order to escape a three months' imprisonment,—for in early winter the immense Sierra snow-falls would close the doors of mountain trails." This was foreshadowing of the most direct kind, because King and his men would come very close to losing their lives when an astonishing snowfall closed those doors in a dramatic and dangerous way.

A week after reaching San Francisco with the ailing Charles Hoffmann, King and Dick Cotter, who had since been joined by Jim Gardner, left for Yosemite and reached it by October 5. King had seen Yosemite once before, on a trip with Whitney the previous spring, and the valley was already a famous tourist destination that more than a thousand non-Indian people had visited. The first white man to see Yosemite was probably the trapper and explorer Joseph Walker, in 1833. Others might have wandered into the valley after him, but the first party of whites to explore it and report its glories to the public consisted of about fifty members of the Mariposa Battalion, which had been formed to subdue the Indians in the years after gold was discovered at John C. Frémont's Mariposa Estate in 1849. In March 1851, these men were led into the valley by a member of a tribe whose name the whites heard as Yosemity, with the goal of herding up his fellow tribesmen and their families and persuading them to live on a reservation. One member of the Mariposa Battalion party, Lafayette Bunnell, would later write that with his first glimpse of the valley "a peculiar exalted sensation seemed to fill my whole being, and I found my eyes in tears with emotion." The Mariposa Battalion men camped in the valley on March 27, and Bunnell proposed that they name the place for the tribe, which had abandoned its huts there just before the whites arrived. The group that included Bunnell returned to Yosemite Valley a few weeks later and explored it more extensively, attaching names still in use today to some of its natural wonders, such as El Capitan, Three Brothers, Yosemite Falls, and Mirror Lake. It would take another year of treaties signed and broken and of violence on both sides before what became known as the Mariposa Indian War ended and tranquillity returned to the valley.

Real tourism did not begin at Yosemite until 1855, when an Englishman named James Hutchings took a small party there in June and, based on his account, three other parties followed, one of which included Galen Clark, who would settle nearby and live there on his ranch until 1910, when he died at ninety-six. By 1857, a primitive hotel had been established in the valley for visitors, which were increasing in number in part because of a monthly that Hutchings began publishing in 1856, *Hutchings' Illustrated California Magazine,* which ran illustrations and eventually photographs of Yosemite's wonders. The other major influence upon the growth of Yosemite's fame was a series of letters written in 1860 and 1861 for the *Boston Transcript* by the Reverend Thomas Starr King (no relation to Clarence), of the First Unitarian Church of San Francisco. His letters about visits to Yosemite Valley ratcheted up the excitement of readers in the East.

King's boundary survey party included three men besides himself, Gardner, and Cotter. One was a general assistant. One would help Cotter with the surveying chains. The third, named Longhurst, lived in the valley and did the cooking. King makes a halfhearted effort to turn Longhurst into a western character in "Around Yosemite Walls," a chapter of *Mountaineering* that describes the first half of the Yosemite expedition. But King is soon so absorbed by the sights and the geology of the valley that he drops Longhurst and rarely mentions the other members of the party at all. The survey began at the western end of the valley, starting north of El Capitan; they ran the boundary line to the northeast and east, at a distance of about a mile from the edge of the valley itself, as Congress had mandated. King tends to mix descriptions of the scenery with sober scientific observation, not wishing to fall too far into the abyss of Yosemite cliché already well established. Later, when they began to survey the southern border of the park they again started at the far western edge, near Inspiration Point.

I always go swiftly past this famous point of view now, feeling somehow that I don't belong to that army of literary travellers who have here planted themselves and burst into rhetoric. Here all who make California books, down to the last and most sentimental specimen who so much as meditates a letter to his or her local newspaper, dismount and inflate.

As they moved the chains across the northern border of what would become the new park, resorting to triangulation in spots where the chains could not easily go, King only occasionally slipped away to peer over the precipices—Three Brothers, Yosemite Falls, and Yosemite Point, North Dome and the Royal Arches. He traced Yosemite Creek, mostly dry in this dry season, the twelve miles up to Mount Hoffmann, which King climbed. Wherever he looked King found evidence of glacial activity, which we now know is what created Yosemite Valley in its present form. King's boss, Josiah Whitney, accepted the partial role of glaciers, as evidenced by the lesser valleys they plowed into the main valley, the markings they left on the granite, and several moraines that King identified. But Whitney, who was a doctrinaire catastrophist, believed that the Yosemite Valley itself was caused by a series of faster, more dramatic events, in which the floor of the valley actually dropped out, creating the sheer cliffs everywhere in evidence. The reasons for his theory were not only the height and verticality of the walls but the relative absence of glacial debris along the valley floor. Whitney did report in *Geology* King's belief that glaciers converged in the valley into one glacier a thousand feet thick. But since many of the vertical walls are as high as three thousand feet, this tended to reinforce Whitney's theory in his own mind. Whitney believed that the glaciers came on after the dropping out of the valley bottom, which would have happened as the mountains themselves were being thrust up. But he rightly concluded in *Geology* that "the time which has elapsed since the Yosemite was inhabited by a glacier cannot have been very long." John Muir would discover an active glacier there in 1871.

By the time the boundary party moved to the south side of the valley, King had grown bored with the work's daily routine, which he left in Gardner's charge while he went exploring. As the surveyors drew their chains east along a line a mile from the valley's edge, King moved east, too, exploring the features that bordered the valley on the south, starting with Bridalveil Falls and Cathedral Rocks. "From our camp," King writes, "I explored every ravine and climbed each eminence, reaching at last, one fine afternoon, the top of that singular hemispherical mass, Sentinel Dome." The view from that point, more than 8,100 feet high, opened up in every direction, but King was especially interested in Half Dome, three miles to the northeast and, some eight miles away to the east, an 11,500-foot peak named the Obelisk by an earlier Whitney party but now coming to be known as Mount Clark, for Galen Clark. "This peak," King writes, "from its peculiar position and thin tower-like form, offers one of the most tempting summits in the region. . . . I had longed for it through the last month's campaign, and now made up my mind, with this inspiring view, to attempt it at all hazards."

On November 10, King and Cotter set off on two mules for Mount Clark with a blanket apiece and supplies to last a week. They left the western end of Yosemite Valley and turned east, passing to the south of Yosemite's southern rim, crossing frozen meadows until they reached "the most eastern affluents of Bridalveil creek," where they camped for the night. In King's telling, a lost mountaineer, nearly frozen on his frozen mustang, approaches their roaring campfire, too cold to speak, and stands by it thawing himself, "turning round and round until I could have thought him done to a turn." The man finally warms enough to be able to say, "I was pretty near gone in, stranger!" King and Cotter fill him with "about two quarts" of warm tea, feed him a slice of fire-broiled beef, give his hungry horse a "tolerable supper" of grain. Then all of them bed down near enough to the fire to feel its warmth but far enough not to be struck by its "rain of sparks." Next morning the mountaineer, who had been without food for three days, regained his wits, recognized his surroundings, and headed west for the Mariposa Trail. The encounter is probably too insignificant to have been made up, but it does serve as more foreshadowing of the dangers that lay ahead.

King and Cotter headed east on their mules, crossing Illilouette Creek and following the "long parabolic curve" of a moraine that connected the creek basin with a point just south of Mount Clark. They reached the head of the moraine in the late afternoon and camped in a little meadow fed by a brook and surrounded by pine trees. Things were almost too good to be true. "One of the great charms of high mountain camps is their very domestic nature. Your animals are picketed close by the kitchen, your beds are between the two, and the water and the wood are always in most comfortable apposition." But his peace of mind did not last long. Before they went to sleep King noticed a moist wind from the south. The next morning the weather was ominous, the sky having turned a leaden gray, the clouds low enough to block out the Obelisk down almost to its base. Not only that, but "a strange moan filled the

air. The winds howled pitilessly over the rocks, and swept in deaf-
ening blasts through the pines." King realized at that moment
that he ought to turn back and get out of Yosemite, but instead they
waited in the camp, geologizing among the boulders that surrounded them, hoping the storm would clear up. King shrugs off
their bad judgment, explaining only that "I am naturally an optimist,
a sort of geological Micawber." By nine o'clock that night, November 12, the wind died down and the snow began to fall.

> Once or twice in the night I woke with a slight sense of suffoca-
> tion, and cautiously lifted the blanket over my head, but each time
> found it growing heavier and heavier with a freight of snow. In the
> morning we awoke quite early, and, pushing back the blanket,
> found that we had been covered by about a foot and a half of
> snow. The poor mules had approached us to the limit of their
> rope, and stood within a few feet of our beds, anxiously waiting
> our first signs of life.

After a quick breakfast, they wrapped themselves in their blankets and headed back, following the gradual curve of the moraine to
the bottom of Illilouette Creek. "Snow blew in every direction,"
King writes, "filling our eyes and blinding the poor mules, who often
turned quickly from some sudden gust, and refused to go on."
Who could blame the beasts, especially since balls of ice formed on
their hooves, causing them to slip around when they were spurred
forward. When they tried to ascend the hill on the other side of the
creek, the men had to dismount and lead the mules, taking turns
flopping into the snowdrift to clear a path. When they got to the
plateaus and meadows south of the Yosemite, they were able to
make steady progress, relying on a map with compass readings that
King had wisely sketched on the way to Mount Clark. After eight
hours they reached the Mariposa Trail, which excited the mules into
a trot in the direction of Inspiration Point. But the weather turned
fierce again, a high wind blowing ice and sleet horizontally into the
eyes and faces of man and mule alike. "The brutes refused to carry

us farther," King writes. "We were obliged to dismount and drive them before us, beating them constantly with clubs." When they got to Inspiration Point the storm was still so bad that they couldn't go on. King and Cotter left the mules in a grove of trees and took shelter in a nook in the cliff face above the valley. When King checked on the animals a short time later the snow was up to their bellies, they were covered in a "thick coating" of frost, and they looked at him with imploring eyes. All he could do was pat their noses and return to the cliff.

Then the weather broke above them and the sky showed a warm blue, although the Yosemite Valley below was still shrouded in clouds and mist. But as they watched, the clouds rolled off the Sierras to the east, glimmering with fresh new snow, and then the mist blew out of the valley and the air became still except for the late-afternoon light shimmering through it. Suddenly a sound like thunder broke the silence, an avalanche falling from El Capitan and disappearing into mist on the valley floor, followed by booms up and down the valley as other peaks and ridges "shot off their loads." King and Cotter drove the mules hurriedly down the zigzag path to the valley floor, where they were able to remount and ride to the east to cabins in front of the Sentinel Gorge. There the rest of the party was anxiously waiting for them, and soon the men and mules had both been fed. After dinner they sat outside with their friends and watched the stars until another monster storm blew up, bringing wind, rain, sleet, snow, lightning, thunder, the sounds of falling trees, and even an avalanche of rocks down the Sentinel Gorge behind them, "crashing through the trees by our camp."

In the moment of lightning I saw that the Yosemite Fall, which had been dry for a month, had suddenly sprung into life again. Vast volumes of ice and water were pouring over and beating like sea-waves upon the granite below. Our mules came up to the cabin, and stood on its lee side trembling, and uttering suppressed moans. After hours the fitfulness of the tempest passed away, leaving a grand monotonous roar.

The next morning, after one other apocalyptic thunderstorm had passed through the valley, Cotter and two of the assistants set off for Clark's Ranch with instruments and equipment tied to the pack mules, but King, Gardner, and another assistant named Frederick Clark dallied for one more day, watching as the Merced River overflowed its banks and threatened to fill the valley. They also watched the torrent flowing over Yosemite Falls across from them, fascinated by the way gusts of wind could stop the flow, or cause it to flare out in great loops to one side or another, or even send the water back up in the direction from which it had come.

They still had a few barometric readings to make along the Mariposa Trail, and when King set out the next morning to take the readings and break a path for Gardner and Clark, more than half a foot of new snow was on the ground. The snow fell steadily now with no sign of stopping. This was clearly the storm they had feared. It would seal off Yosemite from the outside world until spring. King labored for nine hours to reach a cabin halfway to Clark's, having stopped twice to take his readings. He got a fire going and was soon joined by the other two men, both of them frozen and weary, but he was afraid for all of them to stay there without anyone at Clark's knowing they were there, in case the continuing storm should trap them with no supplies. "Accordingly," King writes, "I volunteered to go on myself, Clark and Gardner expressing their determination to stay where they were at all costs."

Just then Cotter reached the cabin, having climbed the whole day through the storm from Clark's. He also thought that someone should let the others know where they were, and offered to accompany King back where he had come. After eating a meal by the fire, they set off into the dangerously snowy night, following Cotter's tracks for the first mile or so. But then the ever falling snow obliterated all sign of Cotter's trail, even as it began to obliterate almost all the features of the landscape. The trail marks that had been blazed on trees were now below the level of the snow, so that King and Cotter had to feel down below the snow line to find the blazes, often growing hopeless until they found the right tree. At midnight they came to a steep ravine that had to be the canyon of the south fork of the Merced River, which would lead them to the ranch. But Cotter was too cold and sleepy to go on. If they stopped they would undoubtedly freeze to death. King unwrapped a long scarf from around Cotter's neck, ran it under his arms, and then wrapped it around his own chest, so that he could drag Cotter far enough to "exasperate him to rise and labor on." King began to pull his friend and "In a few minutes it had its effect, and he sprang to his feet and fell upon me in a burst of indignation." Soon Cotter became himself again. They stumbled down the ridge and followed the river to their destination, arriving safely at two a.m. The next morning the weather was clear, and Gardner and Clark showed up at about noon.

By the following morning, more than two feet of new snow had fallen. They left their heaviest equipment at Clark's Ranch until spring, and men and mules headed out, the old one-eyed mule, Napoleon, steadfastly breaking the trail for them. Eventually they made their way down out of the mountains to an elevation where the snow turned to rain. But then the challenge was swollen streams of runoff, muddy banks that gave way, mules needing rescue from the current of fast creeks, men and beasts fording impossibly swollen rivers with the help of ropes. Finally they reached a ranch at which they found "two bachelors, typical California partners," who would not offer much hospitality to King's bedraggled crew. King demanded food and lodging for his men, and they were obliged, but the next morning the two ranchers charged them "first-class hotel prices." That day the survey party made it to Mariposa at last, very glad to be alive. Two days later, after struggling through a now muddy San Joaquin Valley, they reached San Francisco in time to catch a steamer on the first leg of their journey back to New York.

First they gave Olmsted the notes and sketches from their survey. Although King and Gardner met the Yosemite Commission's deadline, the commission would turn out to be in no hurry to complete its work for the state legislature. Still, as King and Gardner boarded the SS *Moses Tayler* in the middle of December, headed for Nicaragua, the physical exhaustion they felt must have been accompanied by a deep satisfaction of the soul. Twenty-one months after leaving home as boys barely out of college, they were returning to the East as experienced scientists and mountaineers, whose apprenticeship had quickly transformed them into notable figures in their field. Gardner, who had gone west with King to heal emotional and physical frailties, had borne up under some of the most extreme challenges that the continent could throw at him. King, who had gone west with his wrestler's strength and rower's endurance, along with the supreme self-confidence of a beloved only child, had been places and done things in the Sierra Nevada that were unprecedented. When they reached the "slumberous haze" of tropical Nicaragua just before Christmas, they went by carriage across the country to Lake Nicaragua to wait for the boat to New York. But they were in no hurry to push on to the winter weather at home. They lolled beside the lake, where King was quick to notice "a bewitching black-and-tan sister strumming her guitar while the chocolate for our breakfast boiled." Home would come soon enough; for now, though, "Warmth, repose, the verdure of eternal spring, the poetical whisper of palms, the heavy odor of the tropical blooms, banished the grand cold fury of the Sierra, which had left a permanent chill in our bones."

PART THREE

# GEOLOGIST IN CHARGE

*In the winter of '66, Professor Whitney sent Jim and me out to meet General McDowell in Prescott, so we might make a study of the deserts of California and Arizona. We shipped down to San Pedro from San Francisco in December, and there assembled the instruments and provisions we would need, as well as a troop of soldiers for protection. When we met the members of our escort, who had apparently "volunteered" for the army as an alternative to a noose or a long acquaintanceship with a jail cell, Jim and I wondered if we wouldn't be safer taking our chances with the Indians along our route. We set out after Christmas, managing to pass through the Sierra Madre and into the Mojave Desert without being murdered in our sleep by our guards, and we crossed due east through the desert with all haste, stopping over only when we reached Fort Mojave on the Colorado. The Mojave natives were living peacefully in reservation on the California side of the river, but we were warned of what we already knew about the tribes on the Arizona Territory side, that they were itching for a fight. Still we forded the river and went along the Prescott Road with no trouble, Jim and I wandering off to geologize and study the flora and fauna.*

*One day, January 24th as I recall for reasons that are about to be made plain, Jim and I left camp early and were riding well ahead of the cavalry troop. We had grown distracted by our work and careless of any dangers that might surround us, when two Apaches sprang from behind a clump of junipers and positioned themselves right under the noses of our horses, their bowstrings fully drawn and their arrows trained on our hearts. Jim went for his Colt, but I urged him not to draw it, sensing that these two would never be so bold if they were acting alone. Just as I feared, fifty of their brethren proved to be hidden almost in plain view, and instantly had us surrounded. As we had no Apache and they had no English, what happened next proceeded by way of pantomime. They showed us their determination that we should dismount and disrobe, and we knew then what we feared, that they meant to torture and then murder us. A well-known ritual of the Apaches is to strip their enemies, stake them to the earth, and place burning fires on their chests. The brilliance of this method is not only the slowness with which their victims die, but it requires less wood-gathering than, say, tossing their victims on a bonfire or burning them at the stake.*

*Our only chance for survival was to delay them long enough for the cavalry to show up. To that end, I pulled the tube barometer off my back, slipped it out of its case, and held it out for them to see. Then I made as if I were sighting through one end of it, and pantomimed a missile flying out of the other end, as though it were a deadly new weapon. I nattered on a bit in broken Spanish, which they might not have understood even had they spoken that language, but the sound of my voice seemed to promise more possibilities for the barometer-cannon. After perhaps a quarter of an hour they were growing bored with my little show, and all the while some of their fellows had been cutting thongs with which to bind us, gathering cedar branches, and igniting a small fire. Jim tried to prolong the hour of our fate further by unpocketing his compass. That was an instrument with which the savages were apparently all too familiar, for they angrily waved him off and signaled again that we should disrobe. As we fumbled with our buttons and out of our shirts, the cavalry managed to catch up. Seeing the fire and our state of undress, they knew instantly the trouble we were in, and came at a charge. Although our lads were outnumbered, the Apaches scattered. Perhaps the savages found the faces of our soldiers to be as brutally frightening as we ourselves did. In any case, the troops managed to apprehend only two Indians, whom they later gave over to a neutral chief, rather than subject them to the fate they would have dealt to us. We still had miles of the region to pass through, and it would do no good to further enrage their fellow tribesmen, who were already, according to the chief, mad for war.*

## CHAPTER EIGHT

# Making the Leap

*Clarence King in 1869*
*after three seasons of the Fortieth*
*Parallel Survey.*

A fter Clarence King's exertions in the California mountains in
1863 and 1864, the year 1865 would turn out to be one of
mental and physical recuperation. His weariness paralleled that of
the nation itself, as the Civil War wound down to the surrender at
Appomattox Court House on April 9, Palm Sunday, followed five
days later, Good Friday, by the shots in the presidential box at Ford's
Theatre and Lincoln's death the next morning. Half the country was

beginning to grasp the meaning of its defeat, the other half of its despair. King himself would write of the time that "The nation and its people went out as from some black tragedy into the sunlight of every day, and resumed a suspended life."

When the ship from Nicaragua reached New York, King went to Boston to see his boss, Josiah Whitney, and then traveled to his mother's house in Irvington, New York. There he fell ill with malaria that he presumed he had caught while passing through the swamps of Nicaragua, and he was sick with it for weeks, with recurrences continuing on for months. King worked when he could on his field notes from Yosemite, and when he felt well enough he would pop over to New Haven and sit in on Professor Chester Lyman's course on astronomy. At the Sheffield Scientific School at Yale he also visited with Professors Brush, Dana, Whitney (Josiah's brother, William), and of course the new professor of agriculture, King's friend and mentor, William Brewer. During this time William Whitney wrote his brother of King, "We enjoy having him here . . . and my real respect for his ability, as well as my liking for his disposition and engagedness in his work, grows every time that I see him." Clarence stayed in touch with his bosom friend Jim Gardner, too, who was working on a map of Yosemite for Whitney's second survey volume, *The Yosemite Book*. Together King and Gardner decided to return to California and the survey if Whitney could solve the ongoing problem of funding from the California legislature. The weeks and months of 1865 passed in this way, the intermittent malarial fevers lessening their grip on King even as the country began to look ahead after the devastations and deprivations of the war years.

By fall King and Gardner joined Josiah Whitney and his wife on the new three-thousand-ton Pacific Mail side-wheeler the *Henry Chauncey*, headed from New York to Aspinwall (now Colón, Panama), the Atlantic terminus for the Panama Railroad. When they crossed the isthmus and shipped on to San Francisco, they found that the legislature had still not come through with funds to continue the survey. Later in the year Whitney would be able to reappoint King to his job as assistant geologist for the California survey, and also to rehire Gardner, but in the meantime he needed to find something for the two men to do. What he found would not only lead to the sort of adventure and hardship that was beginning to define King's experience in the West, but it would introduce the two of them to scientific exploration in a radically different landscape, one in which King and Gardner would spend much of the rest of the 1860s. Whitney conceived the idea of convincing the U.S. Army, in the person of General Irvin McDowell, headquartered as commander of the Department of the Pacific at the Presidio in San Francisco, to employ King and Gardner in survey work. One aspect of the California survey that had not been addressed was the Mojave Desert region in the southeastern part of the state, including the Colorado Desert, along the border with Arizona Territory. The regular U.S. Army had begun to establish itself in Arizona after the Civil War ended, and had declared war in particular on the Apache, deeming all Apache males hostile, and determining to kill or imprison them and destroy or confiscate their belongings. Companies of volunteer troops from California and Arizona had been battling the Indians for several years, and the regular army would continue these struggles until the 1880s, ending with the extermination, deportation, or settlement of the many native tribes. General McDowell, the goat of the battles of both First and Second Manassas, who had been sent out west in 1864 into a sort of internal exile, eventually saw the need for survey work in "the unknown parts of Arizona" that could lead to recommendations about where new military roads should be laid. King and Gardner could do the California desert studies on the way to Prescott, the capital of Arizona Territory, and nearby Camp Whipple, from which their Arizona work would be staged. McDowell agreed to the plan in December and King and Gardner were soon on their way. Whitney wrote that "I quite envy them the privilege of a winter in Arizona, and only hope they will be prudent and not let the Apaches get their scalps." It was not an idle comment, because many of the native tribes were now on the warpath in response to the army's hostile actions.

King and Gardner did not lose their scalps, and they did manage to pass the winter months in Arizona, but the campaign could not be called a success. One mishap led to another, and although they were able to make notes about the Mojave Desert that were of use to the Whitney Survey and their Arizona studies would be published elsewhere, they produced little of value to the army before McDowell lost interest in the project. The two most memorable things about the trip happened en route, one on the way to Prescott and the other on the way home two months later. King made an oft-told tale of his and Jim's capture by Indians whom King would call Apaches but who were in reality Hualapais. Gardner wrote his own account of the road-to-Prescott incident, when they were accosted by two young males, then surrounded by as many as fifty members of the tribe, all intent on stripping the two white men and placing burning coals on their chests.

For a man of his time, King had an unusual sympathy for the Indians of the West. With friendly tribes he took an anthropological interest in their ways, and the more time he spent in the remote desert and mountain regions where they lived the more he respected their strategies for survival. Perhaps it is the pacifist influences of his Moravian grandmother at work again when, at one point in *Mountaineering* he writes that "any policy toward the Indians based on their being brutes or devils was nothing short of a blot on this Christian century." But as an explorer and surveyor of the West, King was the servant of the military and economic interests that would push the Indians off their lands and lead to their widespread slaughter. Nothing suggests that King felt personally implicated in the treatment that the native peoples received, and perhaps it is unreasonable to think that he might, even remembering his grandmother. In one other passage it is clear that he at least understood the guilt the society as a whole deserved, writing with heavy irony that "the Quakers will have to work a great reformation in the Indian before he is really fit to be exterminated." Yet King does not say this naïvely. However much justice rests with the other side, abstractions don't mean much when your scalp is at immediate risk. Not only were he and Jim very nearly killed themselves on the Prescott Road, but once they arrived in Prescott they learned that white people in the area were regularly being waylaid and murdered by local tribes. Because any serious work they might do there required a substantial guard, and the protection they got was intermittent at best, they gave up and returned to California at the end of March 1866.

The two men headed back to Los Angeles by a more southerly route than the one they had taken, roughly following the path of Interstate 10 from the Colorado River across the Colorado Desert to the San Gorgonio Pass near the present city of Palm Springs. King makes an amusing anecdote of this parched journey, adding especially to his ongoing investigations into the psychology of his favorite beast of burden. "My mount was a tough, magnanimous sort of mule," King writes in the first chapter of *Mountaineering*. But Jim's mule was "altogether wanting in moral attributes."

> He developed a singular antipathy for my mule, and utterly refused to march within a quarter of a mile of me; so that over a wearying route of three hundred miles we were obliged to travel just beyond the reach of a shout. Hour after hour, plodding along at a dog-trot, we pursued our solitary way without the spice of companionship, and altogether deprived of the melodramatic satisfaction of loneliness.

The two men and their mules moved westward in this way until on the third day they came out of a rocky mountainous patch where they could look down upon a "great basin . . . a level floor, as white as marble," plainly the bed of some aeons-old sea, even surrounded by a shoreline—"a white stain defining its former margin as clearly as if the water had but just receded." King would sometimes say that geology required the imagination of a novelist, and this is just one example of King's ability to look at a vast landscape and see how it had once been. But not only was the seawater long gone; "springs which looked cool and seductive on our maps prov[ed] to be dried up and obsolete upon the ground." They were thirsty and down to one canteen of water filled "with liberal traces of Colorado mud, representing a very disgusting taste, and very great range of geological formations."

As they looked out at the desert in front of them, mirages tricked their minds with images of rippling blue lakes, "spire-crowned villages, and cool stretches of green grove." The only things they could see in the distance that didn't shimmer and disappear were "two great mountain piles lifted above the general wall of the Sierra," peaks they knew to be San Bernardino and San Jacinto, which framed the San Gorgonio Pass toward which they were headed. Off they went in that direction, their mules carrying them for hours 150 miles across the desert until a particularly stubborn mirage resolved itself into an actual oasis. They hurried forward to revive themselves in the "blood-warm" water, while the mules feasted on rich grass.

Once they reached the pass many hours later King looked down toward the desert they had crossed and saw it in the same Ruskinian terms of death he had used on the top of Mount Tyndall.

> Spread out below us lay the desert, stark and glaring, its rigid hill-chains lying in disordered groupings, in attitudes of the dead. The bare hills are cut out with sharp gorges, and over their stone skeletons scanty earth clings in folds, like shrunken flesh; they are emaciated corpses of once noble ranges now lifeless, outstretched as in a long sleep.

But the landscape ahead of them could not be more different than the one they had passed through, offering up "tranquillity, abundance, the slow, beautiful unfolding of plant life," as well as shady oaks, gurgling streams, birdsong and "the soft distant lowing of cattle." They passed through this Eden and reached Los Angeles, where they boarded a steamer that took them to San Francisco. General McDowell at the Presidio was no longer interested in the Arizona project. Whitney called him "the greatest ass ever to wear epaulets," and gave King back his former job with the California survey.

After a few weeks of writing up the Arizona notes and preparing for another field expedition, King left San Francisco in early June with a botanist and a cook and went to Bear Valley, near Mariposa. Frederick Law Olmsted and his family had gone back east the year before so that he could work on Prospect Park in Brooklyn, but King made a sentimental Sunday morning ascent of Mount Bullion, noting a bench where Mrs. Olmsted had liked to sit. Gardner and Whitney soon arrived in Bear Valley, and the party went on to Galen Clark's ranch. "Another day's end," King writes in *Mountaineering*, "found us within the Yosemite, and there for a week we walked and rode, studied and looked, revisiting all our old points, lingering hours here and half-days there, to complete within our minds the conception of the place." King makes it all sound carefree, but below the surface the tension coiled. Whitney was trying to pull together his thoughts as well as his source material for *The Yosemite Book*, which would finally be published in 1868. He had already expressed his exasperation at King's notes from the earlier Yosemite work as well as at King's contribution to the map that Gardner was still laboring over, and he would later find King's notes from this trip inadequate as well. Much of the problem stemmed from the two men's differing opinions of the role of glaciers in the formation of Yosemite, a difference that would trouble their relationship for years to come.

But the notes that King was taking on this 1866 Yosemite trip would be the basis for his last great tale of Sierra mountaineering with the Whitney Survey, the ascent of Mount Clark, aka the Obelisk, which King and Cotter had been ready to attempt in 1864 before being driven back from the base by a huge snowstorm. King and Gardner rode from Yosemite to the 1864 campsite. The late-afternoon sunlight exhilarated them, and as they looked up at the Obelisk's "sharp summit" they found it "alluring as we had ever thought it." King tries to assure the reader, but not very convincingly, that the allure was not the "mere desire to master a difficult peak." Rather, we are to know, Mount Clark was "a station of great topographical value, the apex of many triangles, and, more than all, would command a greater view of the Merced region than any other summit."

They began their climb at five p.m. on July 11, Gardner carrying a "Temple [a Boston instrument maker] transit, his blanket, and a great tin cup," while King packed a "field-glass, compass, level, blanket, and provisions for both, besides the barometer which, as usual, I slung over one shoulder." Why they started so late in the day King doesn't say. Heat could have been a factor, but a better guess might be that King and Gardner wanted to see a sunset from the spectacular vantage of the Obelisk's slopes. They zigzagged up through the tree line and into "open granite country," and then followed a ridge that curved from the south slope of the mountain upward and around to the east. The sun began to race down the western sky as they hurried up through bands of rocks and snow to the crest of the ridge. To the east, "over the great gulf, rose terraces and ridges of sculptured stone, dressed with snow-field, one above another, up to the eastern rank of peaks whose sharp solid forms were still in full light." An amphitheater formed by the ridge they'd curved along opened out to the west, collecting the "pure red light" of the setting sun. "Snow-fields warmed to deepest rose, gnarled stems of dead pines were dark vermilion, the rocks yellow, and the vast body of the Obelisk at our left one spire of gold piercing the sapphire zenith." They settled under an overhanging rock with a view directly to the west, and lay on their blankets looking as the sun set suddenly below the Coast Range; then for another hour they watched the changing light. "Over two hundred miles of horizon a low stratum of pure orange covered the sky for seven or eight degrees; above that another narrow band of beryl-green, and then the cool dark evening blue." The colors lasted in the sky past eleven p.m., and when King took a reading at midnight there was still to the west "a low faint zone of light."

The next morning at dawn they started out, having quickly eaten some sliced bacon, and headed for the south face of the Obelisk, judging the east and west sides to be "utterly inaccessible." They climbed straight up piles of large rocks stacked upon each other, sometimes having to double back when the stacks did not lead anywhere. The two old friends reached a point where only the eastern summit, which had cracks along its face, offered a precarious ascent route; for an hour they climbed slowly from one crack to another, carefully passing the equipment between them as one climbed ahead without it and the other followed after the transfer had been made. When they reached what they believed to be the top, they found themselves "only on a minor turret, the great needle still a hundred feet above." Gardner picks up the tale in his own account. "We moved along a little shelf about three inches wide till we got to the edge." From there they could see a flat wall of granite in which there was a crack jammed with loose stones. It was the only way up. If the stones held in the crack they could have a foothold, but to get to them they had to leap across a precipice that King says was seven feet wide. If the rocks did not hold, the crack opened up beneath them and they would fall 1,500 feet straight down.

"Summoning nerve," King writes, "I knew I could make the leap, but the life and death question was whether the débris would give way under my weight, leaving me struggling in the smooth recess, sure to fall and be dashed to atoms." Gardner writes, "It was, I think, duty's call that nerved us. . . . Another winter's frost may break those stones caught in the crack and then Mount Clark is inaccessible." First King leapt, and in his telling the loose rocks shifted and then held. The instruments were passed across and then Gardner himself leapt. King writes, "I shall never forget the look in his eye as he caught a glimpse of the abyss in his leap. It gave me such a chill as no amount of danger nor even death coming to myself could ever give." The stones shifted for Gardner, too, King reports, and once again held. In the adrenaline rush of their relief, "We sprang up on the rocks like chamois, and stood on the top shouting for joy."

The summit was not big enough for Gardner, King, and the bulky transit, so King moved to a spot just below the top to take notes. Although he had been on higher peaks than the 11,600-foot Mount Clark, here, at the top of a narrow spire, "The sense of aerial isolation was thrilling. . . . At all sides I could look right down at the narrow pedestal" on which the spire rested. To the east the tributaries of the Merced lay below them like a map. To the west he could see "the white line of Yosemite Fall" and beyond that, "half submerged in warm haze, my Sunday mountain"—Mount Bullion. Gardner writes that "our view of the southern Sierra was very fine. In the extreme distance, yet clear and prominent, was the double-peaked summit of Kaweah Mountain, always most easily distinguished in the southern group." To the southeast was a cluster of peaks, then called Mammoth Mountain but now known as the Ritter Group. Gardner writes that from their vantage it was "one of the most striking peaks in the Sierra, from its great size and from the needle-like pinnacles that rise from a mountain at its southern end. King names them the Minarets." As King's biographer Thurman Wilkins puts it, it was "a name that would be preserved for its aptness."

They spent four hours on the summit, during which, as King writes, "the thought that we must make that leap again gradually intruded itself, and whether writing or studying the country I could not altogether free myself from its pressure." Now they would have to jump from the shifting stones jammed into the crevice onto the small platform from which they'd leaped on their way up. But they "sprang strongly, struck firmly, and were safe," and they made their way carefully down the piled rocks of the pinnacle and then more hurriedly as they got to lower ground, "well pleased that the Obelisk had not vanquished us." Once again, King's talent as a mountain climber is only exceeded by his talent for building narrative suspense. To read the tale in *Mountaineering* is to get a little moist in the palms as you hold the book. But today Mount Clark is not considered a particularly difficult peak. As Thurman Wilkins drily puts it, "subsequent climbers could [not] duplicate his perils."

King and Gardner would make several more uneventful ascents or attempts of mountains in the vicinity, including a first ascent of a 12,500-foot peak they would name Mount Conness, after John Conness, the powerful U.S. senator from California who had pushed the Yosemite bill through Congress. In August they would make a partial ascent of Mount Ritter, and although they would identify in a shady wrinkle on its slopes an ice field half a mile long that had moved fifty feet during the warm season, they did not recognize it as a small glacier, as John Muir would a decade later. Nothing they did during the rest of the summer of 1866 could compare with the climbing of Mount Clark; it would be the last good story produced by their years with the California survey.

As early as 1863, when Clarence and Jim crossed the continent with the Speers wagon train, they had been deeply impressed by the showy geological landscape on the western side of the Rocky Mountains. Despite the danger they faced from Indians as they crossed the Great Basin—the name that Frémont had given the territory between the Rockies and the Sierra Nevada in 1844— Gardner had written to his mother that he would gladly retrace his steps, agreeing with the Pathfinder's assessment that the deserts of Utah and Nevada amounted to "a rare and singular feature" of the continent. Among the possessions Jim and Clarence lost in the fire at the Virginia City foundry were notebooks each had kept of the geological curiosities they had seen on this leg of their journey. Most travelers whose ultimate destination was California found the Great Basin a trial to be endured, and moved through it quickly and without much curiosity. But for King and Gardner, as for Frémont before them, this land of desert and mountain from which no water could escape was a place that would repay further study. King had spoken of his interest in the region to William Brewer in the fall of 1863 as the two men wandered through the northern Sierras in sight of Nevada, even suggesting the possibility that a survey of it might be undertaken. Then in the spring of 1864 his boss, Josiah Whitney, had taken King on the Placerville Road over the

Sierras to the foot of Lake Tahoe and then sent him on to do some preliminary inspecting of Nevada's West Humboldt Range. Whitney had thought a survey of the Great Basin might follow his long California project, but this 1864 probe into Nevada was only for comparative purposes for the California work. Whitney may well have been the first person to link the possibility of a Great Basin survey to the route of the transcontinental railroad, which would soon snake its way across that territory. Once the route was completed, the knowledge that a survey could produce would be valuable for both military and economic reasons. Knowing the landscape itself would be necessary to protect the trainloads of passengers and freight passing through; understanding the potential mineral wealth and availability of water would dictate how the inevitable settlement of the land near the railroad could develop.

From Mount Conness and some of the other peaks they climbed late in the summer of 1866 King and Gardner could see across Mono Lake into the Great Basin. As Gardner would remember decades later, after King's death, "Sitting on the high peaks of the Sierra, overlooking the deserts and ranges of Nevada to the eastward, we worked out the general outlines of the 40th-parallel survey-work. It was the natural outgrowth of our journey across the plains, our experience on the California survey, and our exploration of Arizona, coupled with King's great aggressive energy and consciousness of power to persuade men to do the things that he thought ought to be done."

Given the ambition of the plan, there was one pretty daunting hitch. Both King and Gardner were only twenty-four years old. Yes, they had worked for one of the most respected survey geologists in the country at the time, and yes they had tested themselves physically and intellectually. Gardner had absorbed the lessons of their gifted colleague, the German topographer Charles Hoffmann, and in the mountains in the summer of 1866 he and King talked about how to improve upon Hoffmann, using larger triangles from higher peaks, and checking their work with the astronomical calculations that King had been learning at the Sheffield School the year before. They convinced themselves that their improved methods would allow them to cover larger amounts of territory more quickly and thoroughly. By following the path of the railroad from the Great Plains to the Sierras and adding their findings to what they had learned on the California survey, they would in effect be making a cross section of the whole western half of the continent. Much of what they found would have practical implications for mining companies, for the military, and for potential settlers— although large stretches of the area they would survey is unsettled to this day, given its bleak, hostile landscape and weather. But the greater promise was scientific, a kind of information that could not be converted into gold but only into knowledge. They would complete the story of how the continent was formed.

King and Gardner weren't just content to set their own ambitious course; it was important for them to find a project that was not only bigger than Whitney's but more important. Who can guess what sort of Oedipal role the paternalistic Whitney might have been playing for the fatherless Clarence King? At the very least, Whitney, whose problems with the California legislature would never reach a satisfactory conclusion, had always been grumpy about King's brashness. Rightly or wrongly he felt that King's bravery and ambition, which had driven him to accomplish things for the California survey that others had not, were sometimes offset by an indifference to detail and, early on at least, a susceptibility to sloth. King, who inspired the admiration of so many of his peers, would almost certainly have suffered from Whitney's occasional blunt disapproval. Even the year before, as he was staying in Irvington at his mother's house while his malarial fevers raged, King had doodled in his notebook words that showed his need to outshine Whitney: "THE U.S. INTERIOR SURVEY, C. R. KING, SUPT."

Now as King and Gardner drifted through their last days in the Sierras for the Whitney Survey a telegram came from Irvington. King's stepfather, George Howland, who had put him through Yale and almost certainly underwritten his adventures in the West, had died of a brain fever, possibly encephalitis or meningitis. King would tell Henry Adams in a letter many years later, "I found myself at 24 years of age with eleven people dependent on me alone." Florence had two children by George Howland and the responsibility for his son by his first marriage, and King still had an aunt living in Newport; perhaps the other six people were members of his mother's household. King and Gardner responded to the telegram by quitting the Whitney Survey and hurrying back to the East by ship. To his other reasons for leaving Whitney, King added the need for a more reliable source of income than the California legislature was likely to provide. What was his alternative? He and Jim would sell their idea for a Great Basin survey to the U.S. Congress. Only someone naïve to the ways of the world would consider that a better way to secure the financial future of his family and himself. But without that breathtaking naïveté, the great thing itself could never have been accomplished.

## CHAPTER NINE

# Strong Men

*Clarence King on the shore of Lake Uinta in 1869. Photograph by Timothy O'Sullivan.*

Whatever it was that made Clarence King decide to go out west for the first time in 1863—the need, for example, to prove to himself that his reluctance to fight in the Civil War was not the result of cowardice—it still took a big dose of brashness for him to talk Jim Gardner into it and actually set out. Four and a half years later, King returned to the East with his brashness intact. He was only twenty-four years old, and for all his newfound knowledge of his chosen field and his mastery of the complicated fieldwork required to pursue it, his understanding of the ways of the world, and more specifically the ways of the East and more specifically still the ways of Washington politics, would not have been greatly enlarged by his years in California. Being so inexperienced, he had no reason to think he might fail by walking into the Capitol and asking Congress to fund a major scientific undertaking. R. S. Williamson, for whom King had named a peak in the southern Sierra, and now a colonel in the U.S. Army Corps of Engineers, wrote in a letter at about this time that "King has an idea that it would be easy to make a successful application to Congress for a small appropriation. Of this I know very little but should think it no easy thing to get."

But even King's robust self-confidence allowed the capacity for doubt. Thurman Wilkins reports that when King did get home to Irvington and found the family's finances in bad shape, he briefly considered returning to Colorado to work in mining, a likelier source of steady income than selling Congress on his Big Idea. But a visit to his old friend and mentor William Brewer in New Haven steadied his nerves. Brewer thought the Great Basin survey was not only an exciting proposal but a necessary one, that the transcontinental railroad should not be expected to pass through lands that were essentially unknown. He wrote as much to Secretary of War Edwin Stanton, as did King's two most influential professor friends—Louis Agassiz of Harvard and James Dwight Dana of Yale. Before King had set off for home from the West he had asked for a recommendation from his boss on the California survey, Josiah Dwight Whitney. At first Whitney declined. He had tried to convince King to stay on by offering to put him in charge of economic geology for the survey, and perhaps he was annoyed by King's decision to leave in spite of this offer. Or perhaps he was unhappy about King's appropriation of the Great Basin idea itself, which, according to Brewer, had first been Whitney's. But soon the voluble Whitney relented and wrote a letter to John Conness, the California senator after whom, like Williamson and indeed like Whitney himself, King had named a Sierra peak. Whitney wrote that King was "well qualified to make geological and geographical explorations" and that "the cause of science will be subserved and the material interests of the country advanced by such exploration" as King proposed, "and I therefore have not hesitated to ask you to favor his plan, if you find it in your power to do so." Whitney had hesitated, but never mind.

When King set off for Washington in late fall of 1866, he had lined up not only these endorsements of his abilities as a scientist and of the project itself, but in a postwar capital where scientists were rapidly becoming more influential, his backers were able to help him make the right political and social connections as well. Whatever his experience in matters of politics, King had an instinctive understanding that his physical magnetism and the force of his personality were his greatest assets. From an early age he had been able to inspire Jim Gardner and others to do what he wanted them to do. Now he understood that "my credentials make me a good fellow" and that, as Jim would write years later, "I can see that this gift of friendship made possible the carrying out of our plans that could never have been accomplished on their mere merits" and "brought to him at Washington the support of the strong men who aided him to create the Fortieth Parallel Survey."

The first of these strong men was Stanton himself, who had served as war secretary to Lincoln and now to President Johnson—with whom he would soon quarrel. Stanton was a formidable man, a lawyer who had also served briefly as attorney general under President Buchanan and who had longed to be chief justice. Lincoln would not oblige him in this wish when an opening occurred, deciding that he could not spare Stanton in his cabinet. Meeting Stanton in the brick War Department building on the corner of 17th Street and Pennsylvania Avenue, the building to which Lincoln had trudged many nights during the war to read the latest cables from the battlefront, King must have been more than a little awed. But Stanton, who had lived in California himself before moving to Washington, was immediately won over by King's plan, especially given the War Department's backing of the transcontinental railway because of its value for moving troops around quickly. Stanton turned King's idea over to the army's chief engineer, Brigadier General A. A. Humphreys, himself a former western explorer, who did some research and then also supported King's proposal, based in part on what he believed to be the likelihood that King would discover coal deposits in the eastern portion of the Great Basin. In his report back to Stanton, Humphreys mentioned the lack of timber along the railroad's proposed route between the Rockies and the Sierra; the coal deposits would be valuable as fuel for the locomotives. In fact, an article in *The New York Times* about the impending expedition would say that the discovery of coal "may be of more value to the railroad than a gold mine." If the coal deposits were significant they would also bolster King's assertion that the territory could be rich in commercial possibilities.

With these two men from the executive branch on his side, King turned to Congress itself. James D. Hague, in his memoir of King, writes that

> Senators, representatives and government officials of every grade became at once his admiring friends. Fessenden, of Maine, after an evening's companionship with King at Sam Hooper's genial dinner-table, was himself almost persuaded to be a scientist, and professed his conversion in saying, "If I were not United States Senator I would be United States Geologist."

King soon realized how significant an ally Senator Conness could be. The Californian attached a provision for the survey to an appropriations bill already moving through the Senate and persuaded his colleagues to support it. The bill passed both houses at the beginning of March 1867. In *The Education of Henry Adams*, Adams would write that King "had managed to induce Congress to adopt almost its first modern act of legislation," calling it that because its support for scientific inquiry was not directly tied to military necessity. Adams emphasized that the King survey arose out of "a civil—not military—measure."

Still, the resulting federal statute did direct itself to the War Department, authorizing "a geological and topographical exploration of the territory between the Rocky Mountains and the Sierra Nevada mountains, including the route or routes of the Pacific railroad." No specific appropriation was made for the new survey at first, but Congress directed that the funds come from an existing pot of money they had authorized for the survey of a wagon road through the territory. What made King's exploration different, and in Adams's estimation, modern, was that it would be run by a civilian—Stanton quickly appointed King geologist in charge—and that King would have full control over staffing. He picked no military men, only civilian scientists.

King was required by Stanton to report directly to General Humphreys, the chief of army engineers, a line of authority that both King and Humphreys would take seriously throughout the years the survey lasted. By March 21 the general had produced a letter, based on a plan King had devised, giving King specific marching orders:

> The object of the exploration is to examine and describe the geological structure, geographical conditions and natural resources of a belt of country extending from the 120th meridian eastward to the 105th meridian, along the 40th parallel of latitude, with sufficient expansion north and south to include the line of the "Central" and "Union Pacific" railroads, and as much more as may be consistent with accuracy and a proper progress, which would not be less than five degrees of longitude yearly. . . . It should examine all rock formations, mountain ranges, detrital plains, coal deposits, soils, minerals, ores, saline and alkaline deposits . . . collect material for a topographical map of the regions traversed . . . conduct barometric and thermometric observations [and] make collec-

tions in botany and zoology with the view to a memoir on these subjects, illustrating the occurrence and distribution of plants and animals.

"As I sketched them myself," King wrote lightheartedly to Smithsonian assistant secretary Spencer Baird a week after receiving the orders, they "naturally satisfy me."

According to Hague's memoir, when Stanton gave King his appointment as geologist in charge he also gave him a piece of advice. "Now, Mr. King, the sooner you get out of Washington the better—you are too young a man to be seen about town with this appointment in your pocket—there are four major-generals who want your place." King, who had turned twenty-five in January, now had what he'd come to Washington to get, and he was wise enough to do exactly what Stanton advised. He got out of town.

King went first back to the old family home on Church Street in Newport, where he recovered from his Washington campaign. He apparently did not waste much time wondering whether he was up to the very big task he had wished for; if he was going to get into the field that year, he had to work quickly. His first move was to recruit Jim Gardner, the friend of nearly half his young life, and the person with whom the dream of a Great Basin survey had taken shape as the two sat on Sierra peaks looking eastward into the distances the survey would cover. Nobody would have blamed King had he chosen a friend like Gardner merely out of a sense of loyalty, or out of a need for the loyalty that Gardner had for King. Clarence was not only still a young man, but he looked even younger than he was, and would now be in charge of several dozen people, many of them older than he, in territory as vast and lonely as the sea the Great Basin had once been. But Gardner had not just proven his allegiance and his friendship; he had also proven that he had the physical and mental stamina for prolonged fieldwork, and thanks to his apprenticeship with Charles Hoffmann, that he had the mapping skills the undertaking would require. King probably never considered the possibility that Gardner might refuse the position of first topographic assistant and second in command, but Jim did have to weigh the offer. Josiah Whitney had moved to Harvard's Lawrence Scientific School and offered Gardner the chair of geodesy there. Jim would later want to be out of Clare's shadow, but he now passed up this excellent chance to be his own man. He and King met in New York, where they worked in an office provided by the Olyphants, who had been partners in the King family's China trade business. Together King and Gardner began to assemble a team of scientists and the instruments they would need to do their work.

After consulting with Jim, King wrote letters to three other topographers, who accepted positions: Henry Custer, who was Swiss, and recommended by General G. K. Warren, a famous Western topographer and Civil War officer; F. A. Clark, who had worked with King and Gardner on the Yosemite boundary survey; and A. D. Wilson, who would be chief topographer for the Hayden Survey a decade later and would have a peak in Colorado named for him.

The group of geologists working directly with King were the brothers James and Arnold Hague and the younger Hague's friend Samuel Franklin Emmons. All three men were from Boston. James was six years older than King, a graduate of Harvard. He had worked on a South Seas exploration and had served in the navy during the Civil War. He had studied at a string of important European universities and mining schools, as his brother and Emmons would after him. Arnold Hague was a year older than King but had been a year behind him at the Sheffield School at Yale. Arnold had met Emmons, like James a Harvard graduate, at the Royal School of Mines at Freiberg, Germany, where they had become close friends. William Whitney Bailey, a Brown graduate who was now at MIT, took the position as botanist despite "a lively imagination" that produced a mental picture "in which naked and savage Indians danced about my tortured body." His health did not permit him to stay with the survey for long, but his lively diaries draw a good portrait of King and of the early days of the survey.

King's most idiosyncratic recruit was a largely self-taught teenaged ornithologist from Illinois named Robert Ridgway. Like King and Gardner themselves, Ridgway had taken up the amateur study of natural history as a result of spending his youth in the woods. From the time he had been old enough to pick up a pencil, if not yet a gun, Robert would make drawings of the birds he observed while out hunting with his father, a pharmacist in Mount Carmel, in the southern part of the state. Soon Robert was painting and cataloguing these birds. When at age fourteen he spotted his first purple finch and couldn't identify it, he wrote for information to the federal government in Washington and his letter ended up in the hands of the Smithsonian's Spencer Baird. Baird kindly wrote back, identifying the bird, and thus began a correspondence between the boy and the scientist that, two years later, resulted in Baird's recommending Ridgway to King as the expedition's zoologist. In late February of 1867, Baird wrote Ridgway asking, "How would you like to go to the Rocky Mts. and California for a year or two as collector of specimens. There would probably be a salary of about $50.00 per month and all expenses necessary." He added a line at the bottom of the letter asking, "Are you strong and is your health good?" When Ridgway agreed he rode the train to Washington, where Baird himself trained his sixteen-year-old friend in preserving and classifying specimens, and by May Ridgway was a member of the first party of King's scientists to ship out to California. Ridgway would work for King for more than two years, collecting hundreds of samples of birds, reptiles, fish, and other fauna. Later, he would have a long and distinguished career as the chief ornithologist for the Smithsonian.

The most famous person to join King's party was not a scientist at all, and at the time King hired him he was not as well known as the work he had already done would one day make him. This was the Civil War photographer Timothy H. O'Sullivan. Born in Ireland in about 1840, O'Sullivan had moved with his family to the United States in 1842 during the potato famine, eventually settling on Staten Island in the same neighborhood where the fashionable New

York photographer Mathew Brady had moved. Brady, who was about seventeen years older than O'Sullivan, had learned to make daguerreotypes from Samuel F. B. Morse within a few years of the invention of the photographic process in France. Morse had learned it in Paris from Daguerre himself. Brady opened his first portrait gallery on Fulton Street and Broadway in Manhattan in 1844, and before long he was approaching the important people of the day to pose for him. Among them was Dolley Madison, who sat for his camera in Washington in 1848. Soon afterward he would photograph John Quincy Adams, Henry Clay, John C. Calhoun, and Daniel Webster. As Brady's business grew and he opened more galleries, his eyesight began to fail, and much of the actual photography was done by talented assistants, although, as was common at the time, every image was credited to Brady himself. Brady moved to Staten Island in 1853, the same year O'Sullivan's parents bought a house there.

Not much is known about O'Sullivan's early life, but Brady himself said he had known the younger man since Tim was a boy. Tim began to work in Brady's Fulton Street studio in his early teens, where he learned the new wet-plate photographic process and other innovations as they came along. Eventually O'Sullivan moved to Washington, where Brady had an impressive studio on Pennsylvania Avenue run by a Scot named Alexander Gardner, who would himself become one of the most important figures in American photography. Business was very, very good. Photography had moved swiftly, as so many technological innovations would after it, from magic act to necessity, with Americans by the hundreds of thousands clamoring to have their portraits made, whether as daguerreotypes in the forties, or in the fifties as *cartes de visite*, small prints mounted on cardboard that were used everywhere as calling cards.

Despite the commercial success of his galleries in New York and Washington, Brady knew when the Civil War began that he had a larger mission in life—to record the faces of its combatants. He started his wartime project as he had started his photography business, by making portraits of the famous. As the war began, Americans collected, like baseball cards in a later era, the small mounted images of generals of the day. Although Brady himself was now almost blind, he worked with assistants, including Gardner and O'Sullivan, to supply photographs for the card makers. And business was still very good. But then in July 1861, Brady would do something that would begin to change the way photography was perceived by the world. He traveled with the Union army and many civilian observers from Washington to the site of the first great Civil War battle at Bull Run, some thirty miles west of Washington. Brady rode in a wagon fitted up as a photographic studio, because the wet-plate prints he would be making had to be prepared and developed on the spot. Riding with him, quite possibly, was Timothy O'Sullivan. An 1866 *Harper's New Monthly Magazine* article about O'Sullivan (likely written by O'Sullivan himself), says that "the Battle of Bull Run would have been photographed 'close-up' but for the fact that a shell from one of the Rebel field pieces took away the photographer's camera."

In any case, the photographs attributed to Brady taken on July 21 pictured men before the battle and after the Confederates routed the Union troops, and these images showed the world that battlefield photography was both possible and necessary.

Soon Alexander Gardner would set up his own business on 7th and D streets NW, not far from Brady's gallery. O'Sullivan, who had now been working with Gardner for several years in Washington, went to work for him, leaving the employ of his first teacher. But Brady, who by this time was operating as a sort of photographic news service, continued to represent Gardner and O'Sullivan in New York, crediting their work to himself—an arrangement that was apparently acceptable to all sides. Like Brady (or his assistants), Gardner and O'Sullivan would spend the war years making images that would alter forever the view of war held by those who had never fought in one. O'Sullivan spent much of his time with the Union Army of the Potomac, and saw and recorded many of the conflict's biggest battles—Fredericksburg, Second Manassas, Chancellorsville, Antietam, and the siege of Petersburg. But it was

O'Sullivan's photographs of the Gettysburg battlefield, photos attributed to Brady, that might well be the most indelible. Chief among these is his image "Harvest of Death," showing the dead members of the 24th Michigan infantry lying in a field.

Although O'Sullivan had not yet been recognized publicly for his vast and impressive body of Civil War photographs, many military men in Washington after the war knew firsthand of his skill and bravery as a photographer, and it was likely one of these officers who recommended O'Sullivan to King. The photographer would work with King on the Fortieth Parallel survey for three years, the beginning of a career in the West that would make his landscapes as celebrated as his Civil War photographs.

As they assembled their scientific corps, King and Gardner also bought the equipment they would need that could not be acquired in the West. As the *Times* reported in its May 8 article,

> The outfit of the party is excellent, including all the variety of mathematical and geodetic instruments which will be required for the nicest measurements, barometers, sextants, levels, compasses, etc., of the best construction, besides the necessary articles for the comfort and protection of the travelers.

In letters he wrote during April, King notes having purchased a six-inch theodolite, "new style gradienters," chronometers, a box of drawing supplies, field glasses, thermometers, and "one box blowpipe apparatus." O'Sullivan bought the photographic supplies he needed at about this time as well.

When everything was ready, and they were about to ship off to the West via Panama, King got sick while he was in New Haven, where the party assembled, and was in bed at William Brewer's house recovering for a week. Bailey, the Hagues, and Emmons went to visit him there, and, as Bailey recalls, "Even illness . . . could not repress his ebullient, joyous, witty, or eloquent flow of language." Bailey adds that "I never associate uproarious mirth with his unequalled talk. His humor was too subtle, too delicate, the thoughts too evanescent, or even fragile, in their butterfly-like sparkle, to be met with a vulgar guffaw." On this day, April 30, despite King's "obvious discomfort, he kept us merry." Perhaps the stress of the previous months, as he lobbied for his expedition and then prepared it, had caught up with him. The Sheffield School held a send-off dinner that night, at which both college and state officials were present, but King was too ill to attend. "The feast was emphatically a temperance one," Bailey reports, and the speeches included an explanation by Jim Gardner of the expedition's goals. Brewer displayed, Bailey reports, "the identical U.S. flag" to one King and Cotter had placed on what they believed at the time was Mount Whitney. The enthusiasm of the evening must have overcome the realization that all U.S. flags tend to be identical.

The dinner ended early so that Gardner, the Hague brothers, Samuel Emmons, and F. A. Clark could catch an overnight steamer to New York, where they boarded a Pacific Mail vessel the next day. King's group, including the Swiss topographer Custer, the young Ridgway, W. W. Bailey, and O'Sullivan, followed on May 11. King once again found himself aboard the Pacific Mail side-wheeler *Henry Chauncey,* heading for Aspinwall, where the Panama Railroad's Atlantic terminus was. The five men shared two rooms— King and Custer in one—on the hurricane deck of the vessel, where the breezes were. They could talk without leaving the deck, and King helped make the uneventful days pass quickly by telling stories. Bailey considered himself lucky to be one of King's listeners: "Truly, since Scheherazade there has been no more gifted story-teller." They steamed past Cape Hatteras and the Bahamas, and along the coast of Cuba, where a crewman fell overboard in shark-filled waters and was dramatically rescued to shouts of "hooray" from everyone on board. They reached Aspinwall on May 19, and Bailey notes that "The sight of the green trees and shrubbery was very refreshing. One easily tires of the blue meadows of the sea."

The bay at Aspinwall was thick with sharks, which ominously followed the small boats in to shore. King's group spent a few hours waiting for the train, wandering beneath the palm trees along the refuse-filled streets of the town, looking at the shops selling tropical fruit. Bailey noted that the native shopkeepers "were but half-dressed, and most of the children were costumed in a Panama hat and a cigar." If the men availed themselves of the city's many and variously hued prostitutes, Bailey doesn't note it. The town was famous for sending travelers forth with venereal keepsakes, but Bailey mentions only that they would later have malarial fevers attributable to mosquitoes. Hundreds of soldiers headed to the West, fellow passengers on the *Henry Chauncey*, first boarded a special train, traveling without firearms because of a treaty provision. Then the engine bell called King's party to the crowded cars of the next train. "Until the cars actually start," Bailey writes, "the fruit and variety vendors throng them. It is a perfect Babel, with cries of 'oranges!' 'cu-rosities!' "

One of the stories that King liked to tell about himself had its beginnings, or would have were it true, at about this moment. According to James Hague, in a memoir of King, the train did not leave once the cars were full, and the delay grew so lengthy that people got back off to wander along the station platform. Suddenly the train lurched forward, with no warning whistle, and the passengers had to scramble to get aboard. King, who was standing on the platform near the last car, was deeply surprised when a mother thrust a baby into his arms and ran down the platform to grab her other child, a little boy who was playing far enough away that she couldn't reach him in time to get them both on the departing train. King, perhaps worried that he would miss his steamer connection at the other end of the line, jumped aboard and from the rear of the last car held the baby up for the mother to see, "as a sign of accepting the charge thus thrust upon him."

On the hot and crowded train, the baby's mewling turned to something louder and more insistent as his or her diapers grew full and stomach grew empty. King went through the cars looking for a possible wet nurse or at least a nursemaid, but the sounds and smells the baby was producing did not rouse any sympathy in the

dense heat. When the train finally reached Panama City, King was
able to learn that another train from Aspinwall, presumably bearing the mother, would follow in a few hours. But what to do
with the baby until then? King wandered through the city streets
until he found a "neat and tidy cabin containing a small family of
English-speaking, 'light-complected' colored women, one of who
was the healthful-looking mother of a nursing child." We are left
to imagine what King might have done had the women been of
darker hue or the cabin untidy; given the by now dramatically
untidy aspect of the wailing child, one suspects King's standards
would have been different from those that Hague assumes the
story's listeners would have. In any case, these women took the
baby, sent King away for an hour or two, and when he returned
the child was cleaned up and sleeping contentedly with a full
stomach. King was able to meet the next train and return the baby
in perfect condition.

Bailey quotes the story at length in his own memoir of the journey, but tactfully reports first that "The critical event must have
taken place in my presence, or very near me, but Hague's record
gives me my first acquaintance with it." In other words, the story
was just that, a story.

When the nonfictional train left Aspinwall, it steamed east
toward the Pacific Coast, which is logical only if you remember the
twisting shape of the isthmus, and deposited the travelers at a
ferry dock outside Panama City. There a boat took them to another
side-wheeler, the *Constitution*, docked three miles across the shallow bay. Bailey writes that this ship was "larger, neater, and more
commodious" than the *Henry Chauncey,* and featured a "vast prom-
enade deck, covered over by canvas in the hotter hours of the day."
At night the canvas would be pulled back so the passengers could
gaze up at the Southern Cross and other glories of the tropical
night sky.

Once again King regaled them. "For him to start a story was but
a signal for a crowd to gather," Bailey writes, adding the incautious
claim that King was "one of the great raconteurs of the world." Bai-

ley allows that in King's writing "you get something of his charm, but to know King at his best you had to hear his voice, and above all his musical, infectious laugh."

The ship steamed steadily north in gorgeous weather, stopping late one night at Acapulco, where the vendors paddled out to the ship in small boats, bearing torches that glowed red on the waters of the bay. Writing more than four decades later, Bailey concludes that "No memories of my life thrill me more in the recollection than those of this sail on the Pacific."

The steamer arrived in San Francisco early on the morning of June 3, and King met Gardner at the Italianate four-story Occidental Hotel on Montgomery Street at Sutter, one of the city's best hotels and a favorite of Mark Twain. Gardner had already established a camp near Sacramento in a grove of cottonwood trees. There the group that had left New York on the earlier ship had begun to purchase animals and get the equipment ready to move into the field. In San Francisco, King and Gardner immediately began buying more equipment and hiring camp men. Among those hired was their old friend Dick Cotter. Thurman Wilkins writes that Cotter had just returned from two years in Alaska, where he had helped to lay a cable across the Bering Strait to Siberia, joining North America to Asia. Dick was recovering from a severe case of exposure that had left him addled and weakened. But as Gardner would write his mother, he and King hoped they could nurse him back to full health.

King steamed up to Sacramento with his friend the German geographer and geologist Baron Ferdinand von Richthofen on June 6, joining the growing assemblage of men, supplies, and animals. Given his keen interest in mules, King almost certainly conducted personal interviews with those essential members of the crew. The governor's office had recommended that the survey use Ben Crocker to help them buy animals and wagons; Crocker had outfitted surveying parties for the Central Pacific Railroad through the same territory where the King expedition would be working. King ended up being more than satisfied with Crocker's procurements.

While the party was camped in the relatively flat, hospitable land-scape near Sacramento, the greenhorn members of the crew got used to riding the mules and horses. Bailey wrote on June 16 that "I take a little ride every day on mule back, and am at present afflicted with a most grievous tail. What with my knife and six-shooters, canteen, spurs, etc., I am quite a knight-errant." Two weeks later Bailey, still evidently sore from riding mules, wrote his brother that "King says for my comfort there is no bum on earth but will get hardened to it."

While in camp near Sacramento the group drew a visit from the president of the Central Pacific, Leland Stanford himself. Ben Crocker almost certainly led his boss, Stanford, to King's Sacra-mento camp, but the project, with its promise of discovering coal the railroad would desperately need, must already have been known to Stanford through his contacts in Washington. King would for the rest of his life be a great hobnobber with the rich and powerful. He had seen in Washington how helpful power could be, and as his life went on and his own interests moved from science to getting rich he would need the backing of the wealthy as well as the powerful. But just as people would be drawn to King's physical beauty, ebullient personality, and glittering talk, King would be drawn to men like Stanford. Perhaps it was the lost income of his family's China trading business that made wealth so fascinating to him.

King had hoped to have his expedition under way by June 20, but he was waiting for the snows to melt in the passes of the Sierra Nevada and for a shipment of gold coins from Washington so that he could pay for necessities in the remoter parts of the West, where currency was not much good. The party finally moved out without King on July 3, heading northeast toward the Donner Pass, with its eventual destination a spot in Truckee Meadows near the present site of Reno, Nevada. At the seven-thousand-foot top of Donner Pass the snow was still eight feet deep, but Gardner managed to get through it with the party's two freight wagons and a thoroughbrace—a wagon whose undercarriage used leather straps to absorb shocks, making it desirable for transporting the expedition's delicate instruments and O'Sullivan's photographic equipment. When King caught up to his men on July 15, he found them camped by the Truckee River where the grass was green for the animals and local farmers sold fresh produce to the men. Gardner had hired a cook's helper as he passed through Alta, a young Jamaican named Jim Marryatt. Jim would remain with King for years, eventually serving as his valet—a job description that was rare if not unprecedented among American parties of western explorers before that time.

On July 17, a cavalry unit, nineteen "well mounted and well armed" men led by Sergeant W. A. Martin, arrived from Fort Churchill, forty miles to the east, swelling the expedition's head count to something just under forty men. Like other troops King had worked with in the West, these cavalrymen at times seemed more frightening than the Indians they were expected to guard the party against. Four would soon desert and others were drunks, but whether because of them or in spite of them, King's problems with Indians would be minor. Robert Ridgway would later recall that "As to protection from Indians [the soldiers] caused the only trouble we had with the latter during the three years they were with us."

A year after King and Gardner had peered out from mountain peaks across the Great Basin, they were in the field again, leading a major expedition. The light-colored canvas tents of their party were arrayed beside the fresh, cold waters of the Truckee River, in sight of the cooling shade trees that grew along its banks, if not actually under them. The men and beasts were well rested and well provisioned, and eighty thousand square miles of lonely, inhospitable desert and mountain waited to be mapped and studied. They were ready to begin.

PART FOUR

# The Fortieth Parallel

❧❧

*Near the end of the hard, cold autumn of 1871, we were heading back to
Fort Bridger. It was just after breakfast and our stomachs were full,
thank goodness, for we had been provisioned after a hungry stretch of eating only fried dough and the occasional rabbit or what little venison
remained. I looked off across the emptiness of the Badlands and saw something stir. Through the glasses I could see it was a grizzly who was probably, like us, readying himself for a winter's retreat. As I watched, he raised
himself up on two legs and his tongue lolled in his mouth. He looked big
from that distance, but I have never seen a grizzly who looked small. When
the four others caught up to me—Emmons, Wilson, Jim, and one of the soldiers—we set out after the creature. They were on horseback and I was
quite happily astride a mule, and we tracked him with no luck for several
hours before he got into a series of ravines, gullies with steep walls, and
before we could pursue the big fellow on foot we had to tie our mounts
together, since there was not even a bush anywhere in that bleak landscape.*

*I say fellow because his footsteps looked like a man's—the largest man
there ever was. We would follow the tracks up the dry bed of a gully and
then make a sudden turn where the creek had changed course, hollowing
out caves that the stream had cut through the walls—shortcuts in the
shales. The tracks led us in and out of a number of these caves when, at
the mouth of one, we saw a tuft of grizzly fur caught in a crack in the
rock. We put our heads up against the side of the bank to listen and could
hear the heavy breathing of the bear within. Someone went around to the*

*other side of the cave, perhaps fifteen yards distant, a larger opening than the one the grizzly had squeezed through, and the sound of the bear's breath was audible from that end of the cave as well. The opening at our side was very low—how the grizzly had wriggled through it I cannot say. We stationed Emmons and Jim at the far end of the cave and thought how we might get the grizzly out. Indian whoops were of no avail; nor was the soldier's rebel yell; then we gathered enough dried grasses to try to smoke him out. Also to no avail.*

*Once in California I had seen a grizzly crash through a rail fence into a small pasture where a steer was grazing. The steer fled, but the bear bounded up to it in a second, and with a swipe of a paw to the flank, broke several ribs away from the steer's spine, killing it instantly. Thus I had no great interest in testing our caved friend. But soon I got tired of waiting and inched up to the opening and looked inside. The cave was black as a pocket, and still hazy with smoke, but I thought I saw a glint, whether of the bear's eyes or its tongue I do not know. I backed out, checked the chamber of my Ballard single-shot, and looped a lasso around one leg, handing the end of it to the soldier. "If I say, 'Pull,' don't ask how hard," I told him. Leading with the carbine, I wriggled into the opening and slowly got close enough to the old monster to feel the humidity of his exhalations. Eventually, as his breathing measured the passing seconds, my eyes adjusted to the dark so that I could sight my rifle at the glint. When I fired the soldier did not wait for a command; nor did he worry about being gentle. He dragged me out of the cave and for some distance across the gravel of the stream bed, so that in the end I was about as torn and bloodied as my grizzly friend might have made me.*

*We could no longer hear the bear breathing, so Jim and Emmons entered the cave at the other end. From that angle they could see the outline of the bear, one of its paws raised as if in greeting. As they approached the paw fell to the ground with a thud and the two crab-walked quickly back out of the cave. More listening. Not a sound. Into the cave they went again and slipped a strap around the poor brute's neck. It took the five of us to drag him out. He weighed a thousand pounds if he weighed an ounce. My shot had entered through the roof of his mouth and lodged in his brain . . .*

CHAPTER TEN

# Between Missouri and Hell

*The Fortieth Parallel Survey in camp in Nevada*
*in 1867. Clarence King is in the center in front*
*of the pole, which Dick Cotter has climbed.*
*Photograph by Timothy O'Sullivan.*

Before he undertook the United States Geological Exploration of the Fortieth Parallel, Clarence King had achieved things in the West that depended largely on his physical stamina and phys-

ical courage. To go up and down uncharted mountains without anything more than a rope in the way of climbing gear and to endure
freezing temperatures without proper clothing or adequate nourishment—these required a young man's hardiness and, perhaps, a
young man's foolhardiness. But the campaign of 1867, the first season in the field for what would become known as the King Survey,
would draw on its leader for different sorts of strength. To start
with, this would be the first time King *was* the leader. As geologist
in charge of the exploration, he was responsible for his forty-man
corps of scientists, camp men, and soldiers, and he was responsible
to General Humphreys in Washington and by extension to Congress and the nation, under whose auspices he set forth. As the first
civilian to be in charge of a federal exploration devoted largely to
scientific goals, King also had a responsibility to science itself.
And certainly not least, King knew very well that his own reputation and his own future depended on how his corps performed.
Many of the leading American scientists of his day had spoken up
for him; he needed to justify their faith. This was also the ultimate
opportunity to put to rest the doubts of such men as his former boss
Josiah Whitney, who had had misgivings about him since King's
first season in the field four years earlier.

King was careful to call his expedition an exploration rather
than a survey, a distinction that might be lost on us but, according
to his friend and fellow geologist Samuel Emmons, writing after
King's death, was one that showed a touch of humility at the mag-
nitude of the task ahead of him. Emmons called King's use of the
term "exploration" a "characteristic . . . scientific thoroughness." As
it would turn out, King's would be the most justified of all the great
western surveys to make the claim to completeness that the word
"survey" implied.

The orders that General Humphreys had given King, based on
King's own recommendations, had called for the expedition to
work from west to east, starting at the 120th meridian, which
defines the border between Northern California and Nevada from
Lake Tahoe north, moving across the states of Nevada and Utah

and ending at the 105th meridian on the eastern side of the Rocky Mountains in Colorado. The three-year project would go north and south of the fortieth parallel as far as the route of the transcontinental railroad dictated, but would cover not less than five degrees of longitude a season. Thus the 1867 campaign ought to have stretched east past the Ruby Mountains of Nevada, almost to the Utah border.

Even while they were camped at Truckee Meadows, in a place known as Glendale Crossing, King, Gardner, and James Hague climbed nearby Peavine Peak, and at its 8,300-foot summit established the first point from which the first surveying triangle would be established. Because the method of triangulation builds each subsequent triangle from the one preceding it, the topographical map of the entire eighty-thousand-square-mile area they were to explore emerged from this peak. Within each large triangle that comprised the map, a second level of smaller triangles was created, and within these a third level, in all of which distances and heights were measured and measured again, and geographical features sketched by hand. Cistern barometers measured height. Jim Gardner's geological maps, unlike those of his mentor Charles Hoffmann, used contour lines rather than hachuring to represent vertical distances. The geologists then filled in behind the topographers, collecting samples of everything the earth held on or near its surface, both solid and liquid, and making meteorological observations. And as soon as they had settled at Truckee Meadows, the botanist W. W. Bailey and the zoologist Robert Ridgway had begun to gather specimens of flora and fauna.

The survey party broke camp at Glendale Crossing, and King divided it into two main teams, one ranging to the north and one to the east. A small party consisting of Bailey, Ridgway, and the photographer Timothy O'Sullivan had decided to join the local Indian agent, H. G. Parker, in sailing his boat the *Nettie* down the Truckee to Pyramid Lake. To O'Sullivan's eye, the sailboat "was the handiwork of an artisan who had built boats for New London fishermen. She was a perfect model of her class." No boat of its size, it was believed, had yet managed to pass through the Truckee's boiling rapids, and the four men would have a harrowing time trying to make the *Nettie* the first. Much of the river was deep and calm, and the boat slipped along under sail or propelled by oars made of ash. But then the river widened and flattened and the rapids came up. A large tree shot ahead of them into the swirling waters and was chewed to splinters. As the *Nettie* itself tumbled into the "mad velocity" of the rapids, it avoided the fate of the tree trunk by lodging up against two rocks. But now they were stuck in the rushing stream. O'Sullivan, believing he was the strongest swimmer of the four, offered to make for the riverbank forty yards away. As he plunged into the water he was swept downstream. By the time he got to the bank he was a hundred yards below his comrades and had to walk through brambles along the riverbank to get back even with the *Nettie*.

*Dome and pyramid-shaped tufa rocks in Pyramid Lake, Nevada.*
*Photograph by Timothy O'Sullivan, 1867.*

The men in the boat tried to throw a rope to O'Sullivan on land, but it was too far without something to weight its end. Unluckily for O'Sullivan, the closest thing at hand in the boat was his "pocket-book, freighted with three hundred dollars in twenty-dollar gold pieces." The rope made it to him but, predictably, the purse did not, landing in the river. "That was rough," the photographer said, "for I never found that 'dust' again, though I prospected a long time, barefooted, for it." Before looking for his gold, though, he tied off the rope and pulled the boat and his comrades to the river-bank. They camped among the brambles that night, and the next morning they managed to maneuver the *Nettie* with ropes through the rapids and sailed on to Pyramid Lake.

The clear salty waters of the lake held a variety of fish, which they caught with artificial flies as they sailed toward the feature of the lake that gave it its name, a volcanic island, shaped very much like a pyramid. It rose five hundred feet above the water's edge, and was made of a fluffy volcanic rock formation called tufa, which looked a bit like giant coral, except that it was gray. As they approached the island, "from every crevice there seemed to come a hiss. The rattling, too, was sharp and long and continued. The whole rock was evidently alive with rattlesnakes." O'Sullivan notes that in every western party there are those who react to the presence of rattlers by madly trying to kill every single one. But at the pyramid rock it soon became obvious that this would not be possible. Later, they sailed farther on the lake to Anaho Island, where their approach scattered so many white pelicans that the sounds of their beating wings made it impossible to hear each other's words.

O'Sullivan, Bailey, and Ridgway went by foot to rejoin the others, and the team headed northeast toward the Humboldt Valley. The landscape they passed through was inhabited by Indians and by the occasional white squatter who had followed the emigrant trail west this far and for some reason stopped. They lived, if you could call it that, by cutting wild hay and selling it to the mining companies in the vicinity. One such squatter, undoubtedly noting how well equipped King's party was, and hoping that the freshness of their

outfit suggested a corresponding naïveté about the ways of the
West, tried to present King with a bill for $260 for the grass his ani-
mals had eaten and the driftwood his men had gathered for campfires. King just laughed at the bill, given that the squatter did not
own the land any more than King did, but as he went away the man
threatened what he might do to King if the two of them found
themselves alone apart from King's comrades. King claims that he
did indeed run into the squatter again, quite alone, but the man beat
his "retreat into the sandhills."

Another scruffy-looking white man approached the party one
day at about this time, and he, too, wanted something from King.
His name was Sereno Watson and, like King and Gardner before
him, he had come west with a degree from the Sheffield School in
order to join a survey. But Watson was twenty years older than Clare
and Jim had been when they went west, and his bedraggled look
came from walking alone across the Sierras in boots that hurt so
much he had ended up going barefoot. Watson had graduated
from Yale in 1841 and had studied medicine, taught school, done
some editing, worked for an insurance company run by his brother,
and eventually returned to the college in 1866 to study chemistry
and mineralogy at Sheffield. After finishing up in 1867, he had gone
to California with a letter of introduction for King from a mutual
friend in Hartford. King had no position to offer Watson but,
undoubtedly remembering his own first meeting with William
Brewer on the Sacramento River paddlewheel, agreed to take him
on as a volunteer. Within a month, Watson, whose broad experience
made him useful in ways that were immediately apparent, was
drawing a modest wage. By the beginning of the 1868 season,
when Bailey's health required him to go back east, Watson would
replace him as botanist. He would go on to write the botany volume
of the King Survey report, and its glowing reception landed him a
job with Asa Gray at the Gray Herbarium at Harvard, where he
eventually became curator, a job Watson held for the rest of his life.

As they made their way to the northeast, following the stagecoach
route, beside which the Central Pacific Railroad was taking shape,

they approached the Humboldt Sink, an area known locally as "the worst place between Missouri and Hell," and characterized either by rotting marshes or white alkali flats. But getting to it was almost worse than being there, because they had to climb over volcanic debris piles of shifting rocks, which made the mules ever more mulish and made it dangerous for those climbing below as they were pelted by small rocks dislodged by those above them. As for the sink itself, Robert Ridgway wrote in his report for the expedition:

> Upon the whole, the entire region was one of the most desolate and forbidding that could be imagined, and in these respects is probably not surpassed by any other portion of the land of "alkali" and the "everlasting sage-brush." The effluvium from the putrid water and decaying vegetation of the marshes was at times sickening, while at night the torments of millions of the most voracious mosquitoes added to the horrors of the place.

The mosquitoes drove them across the sink as quickly as possible, but it wasn't quick enough. They had barely emerged from it when young Ridgway was struck down by malaria. King would claim that the disease that would take down almost everyone in his expedition could be traced back to the jungles of Panama, but those Humboldt Sink mosquitoes are the likelier cause. Ridgway felt "sick and 'queer,' " got off his mule and lay in its shadow, and the next thing he knew he awoke in a new camp, with no memory of being put into O'Sullivan's wagon and of bouncing along until they got to the stopping place. Soon virtually everyone in the party grew malarial, and even King, evidently weakened by the disease but insisting upon making a side trip, was felled by sunstroke and went blind for several days. Meanwhile, his party moved up the Humboldt River to Oreana, and they camped in a nearby field of sunflowers. In early September, King writes to General Humphreys, he moved his corps across the Humboldt Range to Unionville, "in order to place sick men, who at this time numbered about three-fourths of our whole party, under shelter, for the barometer had indicated the approach of a great storm." Unionville was a silver-mining town that had seen better days. Many buildings had been abandoned and even the jail was empty except for one convicted killer in chains in the basement, and King was able to rent the jail building for his men. Before the malaria ran its course that fall it had made all but three members of the survey too ill to work.

King remained well enough, though, and a growing anxiety about what the survey was supposed to accomplish in that season drove him to do the work of several men, according to Bailey. Later in September, King went south to the Stillwater Mountains with F. A. Clark, the topographical assistant who had manned the chains at Yosemite, accompanied by a soldier and a Paiute guide. On September 22, King had another death-defying experience that would enhance his legend. That day the four men climbed a mountain sacred to the Paiutes, which the Indians believed to be the *axis mundi,* and which whites called Job's Peak. While they were on the summit taking measurements, a thunderstorm approached. The men could feel the atmosphere charging with electricity, tickling their scalps and, as Thurman Wilkins writes, "Soon the air sizzled like bacon in a pan, and as the cloud rolled near, the rocks sang like a plague of mosquitoes." A flash of lightning far enough away not to cause alarm drained the electrical charge from the air around them, but soon they could feel the atmosphere recharge. The tripod for the theodolite began to dance at this point, but whether out of foolishness or bravado (imagine the discomfort of the Paiute guide) King continued to take his readings. He was bent over the theodolite when there came a terrible explosion. Suddenly the theodolite was yards away and King was on his back, his arm and side singed by the lightning strike. The others helped their scrambled leader back to camp, where his side turned black and the skin peeled off. It took a week for his nerves to settle down, and he would have circulation problems on that side for more weeks to come. In spite of this, he and Clark continued to survey the Stillwater Range and what is now called the East Range, directly east of Unionville.

This would be as far as the survey would reach in its first season, just beyond the 117th meridian and far short of its 115th meridian goal. But now that King's men were getting healthy again he felt it wiser to deploy them back across the landscape through terrain that they had been too ill or too shorthanded from illness to study properly. Half the team, under Samuel Emmons, went north and west to the Black Rock Desert region and beyond until they reached the California line. The other team went back through the sinks and across the ranges of the Humboldt and Carson rivers. Meanwhile, King and Hague would go north into Idaho to check out a rumored gold and silver strike, and return to California by way of Oregon. The whole corps would meet in late November in Truckee Meadows at the Glendale Crossing.

In the end, King would write Humphreys that, in spite of the illness that had racked his corps, the season had been a success. If they hadn't achieved the five degrees of meridian goal, they had surveyed a smaller section that, King wrote, "is in every way the most difficult and dangerous country to campaign in I know of on the continent." They had completed the triangulation of the entire area, and done the two more detailed levels of triangulation, making three hundred barometric readings and more than two thousand meteorological ones. They had collected several thousand geological samples. Although King was clearly trying to put things in the best possible light for his boss, it was not much of an exaggeration when he concluded that "the few of us who kept our health have, by great effort, turned a threatened failure into a very complete success." King would always have the capacity to drift and become distracted, but he also had the ability to pour it on when necessary, to do an almost superhuman amount of work when the need was great enough.

King settled his men for the winter of 1867 and '68 in Carson City in a residence known as the White House. The mules and horses were let out to pasture for the winter to regain weight and recover their strength. As the rest of the corps went to work on their field notes and maps, and on organizing and cataloguing the specimens they had gathered, King took the geologists to the slightly ritzier town of Virginia City, where he, the Hague brothers, and Emmons stayed at the Ophir House hotel. They would spend the winter doing a vertical survey of the Comstock Lode, whose mines were going through an especially productive period, making Virginia City itself—built haphazardly on the barren flanks of Mount Davidson— a place crazed with industry, commerce, speculation, and the attendant inklings of civilization typical of boom times in mining towns. The weather was terrible that winter. Rains swelled the Carson River, creating down in Carson City a separate stream that flowed between the White House and a smaller house nearby where the men ate. "We settled down to the prospect," Bailey writes in a letter to the editor of the *Providence Journal,* "of swimming for our meals." Higher up in Virginia City the weather brought snow and an especially chilling version of the Washoe Zephyr that had almost killed King and Gardner in the fire four years before.

The surface weather did not slow the geologists' study of the silver mines, and it didn't hinder their social lives either. As educated men from the East, King and his friends were in demand among what passed for the social elite in the brawling, vulgar town. King, who was always drawn to costume, reinforced his special status in Virginia City by dressing foppishly. As Thurman Wilkins describes the spectacle, "He wore tight-fitting trousers of light-colored doeskin with a stripe down the side. The tone of his vest was more subdued, but a gold watch chain flashed across it; his coat was darker still, but against it pale violet or lemon-colored gloves made a jaunty contrast." He affected a cane and wore a hat Wilkins calls a "low-crowned wide-awake," a wide-brimmed affair also known as a Quaker hat. His men started to call him "Kingy."

Soon King met a schoolteacher whose given name is lost to history. Her last name was Dean and when she and King began to spend time together, the men quickly began to call her "Deany." Before long the two were inseparable, attending dances, sharing meals, skating, sleigh-riding (in a mule-drawn contraption that King had improvised), and bathing at the nearby Hot Springs Bath

House. In a private journal King kept at the time, he mused on the power of love and the necessity to love and marriage of "physical mergence." One guesses that Deany knew enough not to make available for free what most of the town's women were busy retailing. Little else is known about King's relationship with Miss Dean, about which King was mostly silent throughout his life except to make a few dark, oblique statements about romantic obligations. But one other important thing is known. As Emmons noted in his diary, Kingy and Deany became engaged at Easter time, when King brought a diamond ring back from a trip to San Francisco to buy provisions. Thurman Wilkins believes that King was in love, and if he was it was the only time in his life that he would fall in love with a woman of his own race and of something approaching his own class. And yet all that's really known about Miss Dean is that she was relatively better educated and of relatively higher moral status than the average woman in Virginia City at the time. That still leaves room for her to have been almost a different species from women of his mother's class; Deany might have been more like Susan Newty, the buxom, athletic (and fictional) daughter of the Newtys of Pike, than the neurasthenic drawing-room ladies of the East for whom King would develop such an aversion. Given the activities King and Miss Dean shared, she was certainly comfortable in the outdoors.

In "So Deep a Trail," the unpublished and often unreliable biography of King by Harry Crosby, it is said that the engagement lasted a year and a half, until the fall of 1869, when King took Deany home to Newport to meet his mother. Wilkins interprets a letter from King to James Hague referring to "private reasons which you can guess" for not wanting to commit to work that fall as meaning King intended to marry Deany then. But the marriage never took place, and soon after the supposed meeting with King's mother King told his men that Deany had gone back west alone. The story feels metaphorically true, at least. Florence Howland exerted a power over her son that complicated his relationships with women throughout his life. Many years later King would say to Henry Adams in

Samuel Emmons's presence that family obligations had made him "refrain from marrying the woman" he had once wanted to marry. But that, too, could be one of King's fictions.

In February of 1868, the survey's photographer, Timothy O'Sullivan, joined the geologists in their study of the Comstock Lode mining operations. O'Sullivan had taken photographs in 1867 of the town of Virginia City and of the aboveground mining buildings of the Gould & Curry Mine and other mining outfits in the vicinity. Now O'Sullivan would become the first photographer to go down a mine shaft hundreds of feet below the earth and, by the light of burning magnesium wire, take photographs of miners at work. Underground photographs had been made using various methods for several years, and a well-known photographer from Cincinnati named Charles Waldack had just published a series of stereograph photos of Mammoth Cave in Kentucky. O'Sullivan's photographs were of particular interest, though, not only because they took viewers farther below the earth's surface than anyone had before, but like his Civil War images these shots introduced the public to a purgatorial reality that they had never before seen up close. And just as with the Civil War images, these were taken at some risk to the photographer himself.

As Alan Trachtenberg points out in *Reading American Photographs,* O'Sullivan's proximity to miners at work told a different story than the one that King, James Hague, and the other geologists would tell in the first volume of the King Survey report, *Mining Industry,* which would be published in 1870. Because the principal justification for the King Survey and best argument for its continued funding was its potential to encourage the commercial exploitation of the West's mineral resources, the point of view of the geologists, when it ranged beyond the purely scientific, was very much that of mine operators and investors, and would ignore questions of mining conditions or the workers themselves. This was not only good politics; it was probably instinctive with King, the Hagues, and Emmons, all of whom came from privileged families in the East. O'Sullivan, the Irish immigrant who went to work in his early teens and who was still dazed from what he had witnessed and photographed in the Civil War, saw something very different in the mines than King and his aristocratic brethren did. He showed men working in claustrophobic spaces with bad air and little light; one of his photographs shows a mine cave-in. His sympathy is clearly with the workers themselves and with the appalling and dangerous conditions under which they worked.

Still, as Trachtenberg also points out, the issue is a little more complicated when it comes to King's own perspective on the mines. *Mining Industry* did use a lithograph of one of O'Sullivan's photographs as a frontispiece, a beautifully composed image of miners getting ready to descend into the mines. What does the photograph say? Does it suggest these are men going about their business, however risky, in a calm and orderly way? Is it an image that reassures the reader, at the beginning of *Mining Industry*, that there's no reason to be too concerned about the workers themselves in what

*Cars coming out of the mine shaft, Virginia City, Nevada.*
*Photograph by Timothy O'Sullivan, 1867–68.*

follows? Or does the image, of men standing at the top of lighted shafts surrounded by darkness—the rectangular outlines of the shafts around the men's torsos suggesting men lying in their coffins—undercut the study that follows, or warn the reader of its inadequacies?

King's Romantic side was always at war with his scientific side. Before the publication of *Mining Industry,* King had created a portfolio of O'Sullivan's photographs in which the mining photographs are collected between clusters of images from the field, first of Shoshone Falls, which would come later chronologically than the mining photos, and then of the Carson Desert. One of the most deeply characteristic aspects of O'Sullivan's photography during his years with the King Survey was his tendency to include a person or a sign of human activity in any photograph he took of a natural scene. Photographs of Shoshone Falls have the tiny figure of a man perched on its brink; one of O'Sullivan's most famous photographs, of a sand dune in the Carson Desert, places his mule-drawn photography wagon in what would otherwise be an empty waste of sand. We even see the photographer's own footsteps leading from the wagon to the top of the dune from which the photograph was taken. Many of his images show photographic equipment at the edge of the composition. In a practical sense, O'Sullivan was helping King put the best possible face on the work his survey was doing, by showing the members of the survey at work. And the men and equipment help give a sense of scale to the often vast scenes he was photographing. But it's hard not to think that, either consciously or unconsciously, O'Sullivan found these prospects to need the reassuring presence of man. Perhaps O'Sullivan, like Ruskin and like King, could hardly comprehend the idea of nature unmitigated by man. Mining is the perfect human activity for King to be drawn to, not only because of his scientific training but because of its metaphorical force. For King, those miners standing at the top of the mine shaft in O'Sullivan's photograph were doing just what he was doing as a scientist and an explorer, heading directly into the hellish heart of nature itself.

♦   ♦   ♦

The fieldwork resumed on May 8, 1868, with teams traveling due east to Austin, Nevada, and northeast to the region beyond Unionville, picking up where King had left off the previous fall. King remained in Virginia City to finish up his Comstock Lode work, making a side trip back to Pyramid Lake with Robert Ridgway at a time when the pelicans of Anaho Island were roosting; Ridgway gathered more than a hundred eggs as specimens to send back east. While King was working up his Comstock studies he learned of a mineralogist who had been mine superintendent for the Comstock region and was interested in selling his field notes from the early 1860s, soon after the excavation of the Comstock Lode had begun in earnest. King snatched up the notes and, using them together with his own studies, he would write "the most thorough account of any great silver mining district in the world." That was his modest assessment, at any rate. In *Mining Industry,* where his Comstock report appeared, he would challenge the general belief that the region was just about played out, predicting instead that more rich veins of silver could be found at greater depths. A major strike in 1874, the richest of the whole lode, proved King right. King's geological team also discovered that the chemical process for smelting the ore was inefficient and worked out a new formula that increased by half the amount of metal that could be extracted from a given amount of ore, which hugely increased the profitability of the mines.

Meanwhile, King's men began to fill in the rest of the map of Nevada. As they moved across the state they found themselves crossing a number of north-south divides, or small mountain ranges, with narrow valleys between them. Even in summer these ranges had deep snow at the top, which the parties soon learned made them impassable by day, when the snow crust was too thin to support the men and heavily packed animals, who would fall into drifts as deep as forty feet. They took to traveling after midnight, when the cold would harden and thicken the crust and they could proceed on top of the snow instead of laboring through it. O'Sullivan, who describes this strategy for crossing the divides, was especially taken by the beauty of the Ruby Range, whose canyons were spotted with small, clear lakes of snowmelt surrounded by massive pines, whose nuts the local Paiutes used as a staple.

On June 18, King went into the field himself, traveling east to join the rest of his men in Austin, where the team that had been surveying farther north rejoined them. King divided his party into three parts now and took one team west of Austin to the Shoshone Mountains, while Gardner went alone back to Job's Peak, where he spent the rest of the summer reworking the figures from the year before and presumably avoiding thunderstorms if at all possible. King's men were accompanied by a small detail of cavalrymen led by a sergeant. Desertions had been a constant and annoying if understandable problem in a West where luck still doled out fortunes to men of as little learning and talent as the average soldier. An incident occurred at about this time that put an end to the survey's desertion problem, while adding another chapter to the myth of Clarence King. One cavalryman, a "bad man . . . known as a desperate character," stole some equipment from the survey while King and his men were in the field. The trooper headed north and had half a day's head start before King realized what had happened. King and the sergeant set out immediately, "trailing him like a bloodhound" all one day through the Nevada desert. Near sunset on the second day, about a hundred miles to the north in the Sonoma Range close to the present city of Winnemucca, they saw the man's trail lead into the eastern opening of a pass through the mountains. Rather than follow him, King and the sergeant rode all night over the mountains so they could literally head their man off at the other end of the pass. They reached the western opening at sunrise, and there King saw the man's horse tied in a grove of willows near a spring. The deserter was nearby making breakfast over a campfire. The situation took all King's nerve, he remembered later.

> I captured him in a hand to hand struggle in which I nearly lost
> my life, and only saved myself by dodging his shot and cramming

my pistol in his ear in the nick of time. I lodged him in the Austin jail, and the fact of his capture forever reduced the soldiers and the working men of the survey to obedience.

By August, King's teams met up east of the Ruby Mountains at Fort Ruby, which would be decommissioned the next year when the transcontinental railroad went through. As James D. Horan writes in *Timothy O'Sullivan: America's Forgotten Photographer,* "The fort itself was far from luxurious. There were split-pine bunks and fleas. Wind moaned through the chinked log walls, and the food was crude and rough. Days never seemed to end. The monotony was maddening." The U.S. Army itself rated Fort Ruby as "the worst post in the West." O'Sullivan took a number of pictures at and around the fort and, as Horan writes, "not even a century can dispel the stark loneliness of the crude log huts, the barren, windswept parade, and the morose privates of the Indian fighting army." Here King once again divided his party to survey the length of the Ruby Mountains, the rest of northeast Nevada, and northwest Utah. Besides covering huge stretches of the fortieth-parallel territory, the most significant accomplishment of the late summer and early fall of 1868 was mineralogical. Several places in the two states where people believed there were coal deposits in the desert turned out instead, upon inspection by King or his team, to be deposits of black volcanic rock, news of which Leland Stanford and others no doubt took badly.

In October, as his men finished up along the northern border of Nevada and Utah, King, O'Sullivan, and one other person went with a contingent of soldiers into southern Idaho, crossed over the Goose Creek Mountains, and, as he writes in *Mountaineering in the Sierra Nevada,* "descended by the old Fort Boise road to the level of the Snake plain." For several days the weather was hazy, limiting their views, and "the monotony of sage-desert was overpowering." They camped on Rock Creek the night of the third day, and an all-night windstorm cleared away the mists, so they awoke to a dazzlingly clear, cold morning. "The remotest mountain-peaks upon the horizon could be distinctly seen, and the forlorn details of their brown slopes stared at us as through a vacuum." So much for being cheered up by the view. But they were headed to the canyon of the Snake River, and pretty soon they could not only see "a ragged, zigzag line of black, which marked the further wall of the Snake Cañon," but they began to hear a dull throbbing sound. "Its pulsations were deep," King writes, "and seemed to proceed from the ground beneath our feet." He knew the sound belonged to Shoshone Falls, which, with Niagara and Yosemite, was considered to be one of America's three greatest waterfalls. King and his two companions left O'Sullivan's photography wagon for the cavalry escort to bring along, and galloped up to the canyon's edge.

"We looked down into a broad, circular excavation," King writes, "three-quarters of a mile in diameter, and nearly seven hundred feet deep. . . . The wall of the gorge opposite us, like the cliff at our feet,

*The southern half of Shoshone Falls on the Snake River.*
*Photograph by Timothy O'Sullivan, 1868.*

sank in perpendicular bluffs nearly to the river." What a scene. What exultation King and his men must have felt at first seeing it. The river ran placidly through an absolutely flat plain that in some directions stretched all the way to the horizon and in others was stopped by a distant blue line of mountains. Then the river plunged in a series of falls, "tumbling over a precipice two hundred feet high." And yet King remembers it, in a piece first written for Bret Harte's *Overland Monthly* two years later, as

> a strange, savage scene: a monotony of pale blue sky, olive and gray stretches of desert, frowning walls of jetty lava, deep beryl-green of river-stretches, reflecting, here and there, the intense solemnity of the cliffs, and in the centre a dazzling sheet of foam.

Just in case the reader doesn't get it, King reinforces his own unlikely response: "Dead barrenness is the whole sentiment of the scene. The mere suggestion of trees clinging here and there along the walls serves rather to heighten than to relieve the forbidding gloom of the place."

Consider, by contrast, the response of Timothy O'Sullivan, standing beside him on this bright, clear, crisp day, a man who as it happened possessed one of the most celebrated eyes in American photography. For him, "Standing upon the craggy rocks that jut out from and form the walls of the tableland below the falls, one may obtain a bird's-eye view of one of the most sublime of Rocky Mountain scenes." Where King saw gloom and monotony, O'Sullivan saw this:

> From the position on the crags you have also a grand sight of the different falls, of which the main one seems but the culmination. Each small fall is in itself a perfect gem with a setting of grandeur in the glorious masses of rock.

Unlike King, O'Sullivan takes from the scene as a whole a sense of awe expressed in the illusion we sometimes have in nature that nobody else could have preceded us to this place, or have felt as deeply about it as we have felt. It's a feeling comparable to one King mocks when describing the first visitors to Yosemite, who reach a certain point in the approach to the great valley and "burst into rhetoric." But O'Sullivan's response, if more uncomplicated than King's, seems more pure, as he predicts that others following him will "feel sensible of the fact that you are in the presence of one of Nature's greatest spectacles as you listen to the roar of falling water and gaze down the stream over the fall at the wild scene beyond."

Here again, as he had on the peak of Mount Tyndall or after he had passed through the endless desert on his return with Jim from Arizona, King Ruskinizes. Nature this raw appears to King's Romantic side as hellishly overwhelming. Later the three men worked their way some four hundred feet down to the top of the largest of the falls, and camped beside it. King reports that he lay awake for hours that night, watching the moonlight come and go between swiftly moving clouds, illuminating the gorge below them intermittently. "A moment of this strange picture," he writes, "and then a rush of black shadow, when nothing could be seen but the breaks in the clouds, the basin-rim, and a vague white centre in the general darkness." You can feel King's excitement in his words and deduce it from his wakefulness, but he concludes that "After sleeping on the nightmarish brink of the falls, it was no small satisfaction to climb out of this Dantean gulf and find myself once more upon a pleasantly prosaic foreground of sage." They spent ten days in the vicinity of Shoshone Falls, and when they climbed onto their mounts and headed south King believed that even those "sensitively organized creatures," the mules pulling the wagons, were relieved "at their escape from the cañons" and stepped lightly. As for himself, "You turn from the brink as from a frightful glimpse of the Inferno, and when you have gone a mile the earth seems to have closed again; every trace of cañon has vanished, and the stillness of the desert reigns."

However much Ruskin guided his hand as he wrote about Shoshone Falls two years later, the scientist and the writer in him sought to analyze and compare what he saw, putting what he'd learned in context:

> The three great falls of America,—Niagara, Shoshone, and Yosemite,—all happily bearing Indian names, are as characteristically different as possible. There seems little left for a cataract to express. Niagara rushes forward with something like the inexorable will of a natural law. It is force, power; forever banishing before its irresistible rush all ideas of restraint.

Shoshone, we know, he sees as a Dantean abyss, a frightening black gash in the earth. Yosemite is the antithesis of each of the other two falls, light to Shoshone's dark, fragile to Niagara's strength:

> From the far summit of a wall of pearly granite, over stains of purple and yellow,—leaping, as it were, from the very cloud,— falls a silver scarf, light, lacelike, graceful, luminous, swayed by the wind. . . . The Yosemite is a grace. It is an adornment. It is a ray of light on the solid front of the precipice.

Within King himself there was something of Yosemite and something of Niagara. His witty, foppish storytelling side, the side that drew others to him, was as luminous as Yosemite. Henry Adams would call him "a bird of paradise . . . rising in the sagebrush." But as he had proven again and again on the California survey and was proving with the new survey that bore his name, he had a force of personality and a mental strength to match his physical strength—a Niagara-like inexorableness. Shoshone, the dark side of his personality, would come later.

## CHAPTER ELEVEN

# Rising in the Sagebrush

*Henry Adams in the early 1870s.*

A fter two seasons in the West, King and his fellow scientists
went east in October 1868, boarding the train in Green River,
Wyoming Territory, where the Union Pacific tracks had been laid
only a couple of weeks before their departure. King gave the men a
month off and then most of them met him in Washington, where
fifty large trunks of samples had been shipped, ranging from Sereno
Watson's flora to Robert Ridgway's fauna to the rocks and fossils
that King and the other geologists had gathered. They unpacked
and began to organize this vast miscellany at their offices in a

brick building at 294 H Street. Jim Gardner, who in September had married his own Nevada schoolteacher, Josephine Rogers, was in charge of the winter work, while King applied himself to the political problem of getting an appropriation for what was supposed to be their third and final season in the field. Among the luminaries King lobbied were President-elect Grant, who visited the survey's offices and declared himself impressed. But it was one of Grant's detractors, another former Civil War general and now a U.S. representative from Massachusetts, Benjamin Butler (who had earned the nickname "Beast" for his treatment of civilians in New Orleans during the war), who led the fight for a bill supporting the survey. Butler, who had been appointed a general rather than moving through the ranks, hated regular army officers and especially West Pointers such as Grant. When King told him that his survey team was made up only of civilians, even though he reported to General Humphreys, the chief of army engineers, Butler said, "You mean to tell me there're no West Pointers in the outfit?" That was enough to put Butler in King's camp, and by March the congressman had helped push through an appropriation for the survey that included a raise for King to $360 a month, the equivalent of a colonel's salary.

King took the train back to Utah in May, arriving in Salt Lake City five days after the ceremonial completion of the transcontinental railroad on May 10 at Promontory Summit. By the end of the month he had three teams in action, one led by Samuel Emmons surveying south of the Great Salt Lake, one led by King surveying to the north, and the third plying the lake itself in a rented boat called the *Eureka*, which included topographers as well as Watson and Ridgway. The lake team had drawn the hardest duty, given the swarms of flies and the revolting odor of decomposing grasshoppers along the shore; plus, the boat capsized twice in storms and once the men nearly drowned, swallowing the salty lake water, which made them crazy with thirst as they held on to the overturned boat overnight while waiting for rescue. But they were able to complete their study, discovering that the lake had risen by about ten feet and grown in area by 660 square miles since its first survey only twenty years before by Captain Howard Stansbury. By midsummer all three teams had moved to northeast Utah, concentrating on what they believed would be the last portion of their exploration, a triangle defined by the Wasatch Mountains to the west, the Uinta Mountains to the south, and the Green River to the east. There King and his men found evidence of the coal that so many commercial interests hoped his survey would discover, what King understatedly called "a most satisfactory estimate of the *unopened fields.*"

King adored the Uintas, a sawed-off mountain range running 150 miles west to east, which he decided had been formed at the same time as the Alps and had at first been taller than the Himalayas, but had been sheared and worn to their present height of about 11,000 feet by glaciers and erosion. Among the three tallest mountains in the Uintas are Mount Agassiz, which King named for his teacher and was the first to climb, at about 12,500 feet; Mount Emmons at 13,400 feet; and Kings Peak, at more than 13,500 feet, the tallest mountain in Utah. It's generally agreed that Kings Peak was named for Clarence King after his death. Two photographs taken at about this time suggest what a satisfactory period of his life King was passing through. In one by Timothy O'Sullivan, he is seated on a large rock by Lake Uinta, one of the range's many picturesque alpine settings, his barometer slung over his back, wearing leather leggings, pants, and coat, his hat at a jaunty angle and the sun on his face. He sports a full blond beard and looks fit, confident, and serene. The photograph so perfectly represents King in the field that Thurman Wilkins used it on the cover of his biography. King wears the same clothing, the same beard, and appears to be carrying the same barometer in another photograph in which he is posed, stagily resting in the crevice of a rock face and holding a rope as though lowering himself down the side of a cliff. Here again he looks relaxed and even a bit amused. He was twenty-seven years old, nearing the midpoint of his life. Having already accomplished so much, could he have had an inkling that things would rarely be this good again?

♦　　♦　　♦

By the late summer of 1869, the Fortieth Parallel Survey had only gone as far east as the 110th meridian, five degrees short of its original goal. But the King team's three years were just about up, and another great survey, that of Ferdinand V. Hayden, had completed work in Nebraska and by this time had moved into Wyoming and would eventually undertake Colorado, and so would cover much of the territory that King had originally planned to explore. In August, King sent some of his men east to continue working on the huge amount of data and samples they had collected, and the rest went west, checking and elaborating their observations between the Green River and the Great Salt Lake. King, who was always restless, was ready for the field studies to be over, and went to San Francisco to work more on his Comstock report for the *Mining Industry* volume, which would be the survey's first published report. He stayed in San Francisco until November, and fell in with a group that was more literary than scientific, even throwing a breakfast at the Union Club for Bret Harte, who was editor of the *Overland Monthly*, where some of Harte's best stories and sketches of the West had begun to appear.

King returned to the East hoping that all the reports growing out of the field studies could be finished in two years. He first rented rooms in Washington to work both on the Comstock report and on another chapter for *Mining Industry* about the coal deposits in the Green River area. But soon he moved to New Haven, where the laboratories and intellectual resources of the Sheffield Scientific School outstripped anything available in the nation's capital. The Hagues, Emmons, and King would finish *Mining Industry* that winter, Watson's botanical studies were moving forward, and Ridgway would complete the ornithological part of his work in the spring, classifying a total of 262 bird species. Things were going so smoothly that King accepted an invitation from Spencer Baird of the Smithsonian to join him and his wife in Woods Hole, Massachusetts, for a summer vacation.

But without any prodding from King, his forces on Capitol

Hill made money available for a fourth season in the field. The word from General Humphreys came so late in 1870, and so much progress was being made on the reports, that King asked to put off a trip to the West until the following spring. But a canny military bureaucrat like Humphreys knew that not using a spending authorization in a given year was a good way to get your future budgets cut, so he insisted that King go. The compromise King proposed was that he take a small team west while the rest of his men worked under Jim Gardner on their reports. Although the short season's goal would only be to study the volcanoes of the West Coast, from which "lava flows . . . have poured eastward from the Sierra Nevada and the Cascades Ranges into the Great Basin," King would stumble upon one of his most important discoveries. When General Humphreys agreed to the abbreviated plan, King wrote the Bairds a doggerel explanation for missing out on Woods Hole: "Mappin' up wat's called out West / Bustin' rocks for Uncle Sam / Tearin' holes in pants and vest / Eatin' semi-fossil ham— / That's wat fell ter this child's lot."

King, Emmons, Arnold Hague, and the topographers Frederick Clark and A. D. Wilson accompanied him, as did Jim the cook, who had begun to go everywhere with King as a sort of personal manservant. They reached San Francisco on August 12 and hurriedly pulled together mounts and supplies with the help of a general at the Presidio. Because O'Sullivan was taking photos for an expedition in Panama, King contracted with the San Francisco photographer Carleton E. Watkins, famous for his pictures of Yosemite, to join them. The painter Gilbert Munger volunteered to go along, as he had in the previous season. By the end of August, the party made its way up the hazy Sacramento Valley, headed for Shasta, the mountain that had drawn King to California at Professor Brush's house eight years earlier. They stopped in Chico, and here King picks up the story in an article that would appear in the *Atlantic Monthly* in December 1871. He writes that the fields of the valley had already been cut, and as they headed north, "Miles of harvested plain lay close shaven in monotonous Naples yellow, stretching on, soft and vague, losing itself in a gray, half-luminous haze."

As they moved into the foothills, King's pulse began to quicken as it always did at the prospect of mountains. The air became crisper, the streams clearer, the green of the pines brighter, and eventually the snow-capped pyramid of Shasta began to dominate both the view and King's imagination, just as it had on that first trip into the field with William Brewer in 1863. They made their way to Sisson's, south and west of Shasta, and set up camp. Sisson himself, "the pioneer guide of the region," would lead them up what is now called Shastina, a "large and perfect crater whose rim reaches about twelve thousand feet altitude" just west of Shasta itself. Four of them set out on mules with Sisson and two muleteers on September 11 and went above the tree line before they had to go on by foot. When they got to the top of the southwestern side of Shastina, they looked across a "round crater-bowl, about a mile in diameter and a thousand feet deep." They made their way clockwise around the top of the cone, "and came to a place where for a thousand feet it was a mere blade of ice, sharpened by the snow into a thin, frail edge, upon which we walked in cautious balance, a misstep likely to hurl us down into the chaos of lava blocks in the crater."

But it was not the climb itself that would make this day spectacular. Rather it was the glacier they would see when they got to the north edge of Shastina and could look straight down into a gorge that separated the two peaks.

There, winding its huge body along, lay a glacier, riven with sharp, deep crevasses yawning fifty or sixty feet wide, the blue hollows of their shadowed depth contrasting with the brilliant surfaces of ice.

He also wrote about this moment in an article for James Dwight Dana's *American Journal of Science and Arts* the next spring, calling what he saw "a fine glacier, which started almost at the very crest of the main mountain, flowing toward us and curving around the circular base of our cone." He knew immediately that what he saw presented "all the characteristic features of glaciers everywhere." This moment was credited in scientific circles as the first discovery of an active glacier anywhere in the United States.

The next day, after spending the night on the rim of Shastina, they climbed Shasta itself. Even the King of *Mountaineering,* so adept at creating drama where later mountaineers would note a leisurely climb, admitted that "The fact that two young girls have made the ascent proves it a comparatively easy one." But now that he knew to look for glaciers he saw three active ones in all, and long broad moraines dug by ancient glaciers proved that Shasta had once been wreathed in them. (The U.S. Geological Survey today says that Shasta has seven active glaciers.) As ever, King could take a prospect from a mountaintop and turn it into a brief but emphatic narrative. "What volumes of geographical history lay in view!" King expostulated. "Old mountain uplift; volcanoes built upon the plain of fiery lava; the chill of ice and wearing force of torrent, written in glacier-gorge and water-curved cañon!"

But it was the glaciers themselves, as he wrote to General Humphreys a few weeks later, that he found a "somewhat startling discovery," considering that "Whitney, Brewer, Dana, and Frémont, all visited the Peak without observing them; and that Whitney, Dana, and Agassiz have all published statements that no true glaciers exist in the United States." Brewer recalls in *Clarence King Memoirs* that when he and King had skirted Shasta in 1863 they had seen a muddy trickle coming off the mountain that Brewer said exactly resembled glacier-fed streams in the Alps. "Why is it not?" Brewer remembers King arguing, but Brewer had seen no evidence of glaciers when he had been atop Shasta the year before. Two years after his own discovery, King told Brewer, "That stream haunted me for years, until I got on Mount Shasta and found the glaciers!"

King had sent Arnold Hague to Oregon to study Mount Hood and would now send Samuel Emmons to Washington Territory to do the same at Mount Rainier, and they both returned with reports of active glaciers. King was so excited by all of their discoveries that he asked General Humphreys to keep the news quiet until he could return to the East to report it himself at Yale and Harvard. What had begun as a scramble to fill a square for Humphreys was now looking very much like a triumph. King would write to Humphreys that winter, looking back on the findings of the fall, that "The discovery of active glaciers and the knowledge we have gotten of the volcanic period are among the most important late additions to American geology."

After he made his presentations to the scientific community in the East, King became so celebrated in Boston that the famous Saturday Club invited him for a visit on the last Saturday of December 1870. His former teacher Agassiz was ill and could not attend, but when King went to the Parker House hotel with the *Atlantic Monthly* editor James T. Fields (for whom King had written a second piece about the discovery of glaciers), those who were there included Oliver Wendell Holmes Sr., Ralph Waldo Emerson, and Henry Wadsworth Longfellow. The members of the club were more interested in King's acquaintance with Bret Harte than in glaciers, as it turned out, and Longfellow inquired of Harte, "Is he a *gen-i-us?*" To which King unthinkingly replied, "Why as to that, Mr. Longfellow, everybody knows that the country possesses no *three-syllabled genius* outside of Massachusetts." King had meant to be witty not cruel, but Longfellow took offense and the rest of the morning did not go well.

But it was another Boston resident whom King had most hoped to impress with his discovery, his first boss Josiah Whitney, who now taught at Harvard. King's disagreement with Whitney about glaciers in Yosemite had been a sore point between them, and Whitney had often wavered in his loyalty to King over other matters as well. Whitney and Brewer had had their chance to find glaciers at Shasta, but because they had ascended the mountain from the south side rather than the west, they were blocked from seeing what King saw so plainly. And perhaps Whitney's firm convictions as a catastrophist had made him blind to the existence of glaciers at

Shasta in 1862 as he would be in Yosemite three years later. Now King's name would forever be connected to the discovery of active glaciers in the United States. But thanks to King, so would Whitney's. That first stream of ancient ice he saw when looking down from Shastina King named the Whitney Glacier.

King had also named Mount Whitney, of course, during his years with the California survey, and his relationship with that peak—at 14,494 feet the highest in the continental United States—was as troubled as his relationship with the man himself. The same summer he had named Mount Whitney, in 1864, he had tried a solo ascent of it from the south but for some reason had stopped well short of the top. In the summer of 1871, he would find an excuse to make another attempt on "the sharp terrible crest of Whitney . . . bright and glorious above the whole Sierra." This ascent, which would turn out to be the sort of fiasco from which a lesser man than King might not recover, also became a chapter in his book *Mountaineering in the Sierra Nevada,* finding its way into print before it became clear that King had managed to climb the *wrong* mountain.

But the year 1871 would turn out to be trouble from beginning to end. Once Dana published King's claims for the discovery of live glaciers, a number of counterclaims arose from others who had noticed active glaciers in the United States going back as far as 1833. Even on Shasta itself there were at least two earlier sightings, one described in the *Yreka Journal* in 1866. But credit for a scientific discovery—including Darwin's theory of natural selection, the tenets of which had been in the air for some time—is often a matter of being in the right place at the right time and ultimately of who you know. King's status in the scientific community helped elevate his observations to the level of a discovery. Glaciers were popping up everywhere at about the time King's article came out. John Muir was even then hurrying to get credit for discovering them in the Sierra Nevada. Still, the controversy over King's claim had one implication for the Fortieth Parallel Exploration. King now wanted to continue his investigations of glaciers and volcanoes, and he argued against pushing farther east along the Fortieth Parallel to the 105th meridian, claiming that the Hayden Survey had "skimmed the cream" from the region. But the public nature of the claims against King discouraged General Humphreys from allowing him to build on his glacier studies. He ordered King back to Wyoming to complete the job at hand.

For the fifth year, then, King went west with his men, and this time established one camp near Cheyenne, right on the 105th meridian, and one near Fort Bridger in western Wyoming. Gardner would lead a party working west from Cheyenne, and Emmons would lead a party that would work its way across the Continental Divide. King went on to San Francisco to buy supplies and hire mule packers for Emmons's work in the Rockies. On the way back to join his men from San Francisco, King took a hard right after crossing the Sierras, riding a stagecoach from Carson City south along the eastern side of the Sierras into the Owens Valley to the town of Lone Pine, which was due east of Mount Whitney. Imagine the satisfaction he must have felt looking out the right window of the coach as the peaks went by: "I recognized the old familiar summits: Mount Ritter, Lyell, Dana . . . Conness." And as he got closer to Whitney he could see Mount Brewer, Mount Tyndall, Mount Williamson, and perhaps before that the triangle of peaks Mount Gardner, Mount Cotter, and Mount Clarence King. When he got to Lone Pine the weather was stormy in the mountains for two days, but at the end of the third day the storminess broke so that, as he looked west, the mountaintops were outlined by the golden rays of the setting sun. The blue shadows crept up the peaks as the sun went down, at last leaving only Whitney haloed, a very painterly and a very Clarence King moment.

Just as he had seven years earlier, King had come alone to climb Whitney, but in Lone Pine he met a French climber named Paul Pinson, who agreed to go with him up to the top of the whole country. King and Pinson rode horses into the foothills of the Sierra, and "Directly in front of us," King writes in *Mountaineering*, "rose the rugged form of Mount Whitney spur, a single mass of granite, rough-hewn, and darkened with coniferous groves. The summits were lost in a cloud of almost indigo hue." Soon they left their horses with a Mexican boy who had accompanied them that far, and began to climb with their heavy packs. Their destination was a grove of pines at about ten thousand feet, but one ascent they tried became impassable, and when they climbed back down to find a new way up a great storm struck, drenching them and making their next hours of climbing "not noticeable for their cheerfulness." But by nightfall they reached the grove and were able to gather wood and start a fire under an outcropping of rock, so they could warm and dry themselves and have hot beef and toast and tea. Overnight the weather cleared and next morning after breakfast they climbed above the tree line and into the summer-softened snows. King only notes one characteristic moment of danger before they made it to the summit:

> within a hundred feet of the top I suddenly fell through, but, supporting myself with my arms, looked down into a grotto of rock and ice, and out through a sort of window, over the western bluffs, and down thousands of feet to the far away valley of the Kern.

When they reached the top they found evidence that they were not the first to be there: a pile of rocks with an Indian arrow pointing out of it to the west. As they ate their lunch King took out a silver half-dollar and engraved his name and Pinson's on it, leaving it as proof that they had at least been the first white men to climb what they still believed was Whitney. King took a barometric reading, having engaged someone to make comparative readings on an identical barometer back in Lone Pine. Scattered clouds had begun to develop as they climbed and while they were atop the peak the weather worsened. During a break in the clouds while they were at the top King probably saw Mount Whitney to the north, but since he thought he was on Whitney he mistook it for Mount Tyndall. As they made their descent the visibility worsened to less than a hundred feet, and they became disoriented by the terrain. But they found their way down and King headed back to his men in Wyoming not knowing of his mistake. As it happened, the peak he had climbed was one he had already named from afar in 1864, Sheep's Rock, which is today called Mount Langley; it is several miles south of Whitney, and at 14,042 feet, about 450 feet shorter.

In an addendum in 1873 to his 1871 account of the ascent, King reports that his first suspicion that he had climbed the wrong mountain came when he sent his barometric readings to Josiah Whitney, who had the best available data for converting barometric pressure to altitude. When the computation came back, the mountain was shorter than King had expected, but "Realizing at once that this must be an error, I attributed it to some great oscillation of pressure due to storm." Still, he was worried enough about it to consult the best existing map of the Sierras, Charles Hoffmann's for the California Geological Survey. The map reassured him at the time, but it would turn out that the map was wrong, too. When it was proven definitively in 1873 that King had climbed Sheep's Rock, he immediately admitted his mistake and also blamed the error in Hoffmann's map on a faulty reading King himself had taken on Mount Tyndall in 1864.

W. A. Goodyear, the man who uncovered King's goof in a paper for the California Academy of Sciences, was also a graduate of the Sheffield School and didn't much like King. In his addendum, King notes that Goodyear's "paper shows such evident relish at my mistake," and he pretends to be glad for Goodyear's sake to have missed his mountain because "One has in this dark world so few chances of conferring innocent, pure delight." In September 1873, the very month that he read Goodyear's report, King hurried back to Whitney to see if he might yet be the first person to climb it, but when he reached the top at last on September 19 he found evidence of two of the three climbing parties that had beaten him there by only a matter of days. John Muir would climb Whitney a month later and find a note from King that said "All honor to those who came before me." In his addendum, however, King was careful to mitigate that honor by suggesting that Indian hunters had probably been to the mountaintop long before any of the rest of them had.

King returned to Fort Bridger on June 27, but he was only with the Emmons party for a short time before he went back to the East, in part to look at proofs for an atlas, but also to tend to his budding literary career. His article on glaciers in the United States had appeared in the *Atlantic Monthly* in March, and articles that would form the bulk of *Mountaineering in the Sierra Nevada* had appeared in the May, June, and July issues, and would appear in every month except September for the rest of 1871. Not only was *Atlantic* editor James Fields obviously a fan of King's work, but so was an assistant editor of the magazine, William Dean Howells, who would soon be editor of the magazine himself and later become one of the great men of American letters. King met Howells in Cambridge that summer, and Howells would remember that "I regarded the brilliant and beaming creature before me simply as a promise of more and more literature of the vivid and graphic kind," and after King's death Howells would write of the sketches in *Mountaineering,* "He has brilliantly fixed forever a phase of the Great West already vanished from actuality."

When King returned to his men in early August, he would have a chance meeting that would do more to vouchsafe a place for him in American literature than all of his own literary endeavors combined. King went south from Cheyenne to check in with Arnold Hague, who was camped on Longs Peak on the eastern slope of the Rockies. Because it was late in the day when King reached Estes Park by buggy from the town of Greeley, he found a cabin where he could spend the night, planning to push on to Hague's camp the next morning. Several hours after dark, a mule arrived at the door of the cabin, and atop the mule was the unlikely person of Henry Adams. Adams had just finished his first year as an assistant professor of history at Harvard and as editor of the *North American Review.* Having written an article about the British geologist Charles Lyell, Adams was growing more and more interested in things geological, which was one reason he accepted an invitation from his friend Samuel Emmons to observe their fieldwork in the West. While Emmons was off working in the Uintas, Adams had run into Arnold Hague, another Boston acquaintance, who "took charge" of him for a while. On the day in question, Adams had wandered off on muleback from Hague's camp in order to do some fishing and when night fell had realized that he was utterly lost. Wisely, he had allowed the mule to follow its nose back to civilization, or to the cabin in the park that turned out to be the closest thing to it, which also happened to be the place where King was staying. Adams describes their meeting in *The Education of Henry Adams,* employing a flair for the dramatic that rivaled King's own. When he first saw the light in the distance that came from the cabin, Adams was certainly tired and hungry, and possibly a little scared. But in his telling, he fell into King's arms at the cabin door, and their friendship began at that instant, "never a matter of growth or doubt." Inside the cabin there was only one room for guests and that room had only one bed. "They shared the room and the bed," Adams writes in the third person about King and himself, "and talked till far towards dawn."

Adams goes on to lavish praise upon King that was less informed by what he knew of him at that moment than by the decades of friendship that would ensue before King's death in 1901, several years before Adams wrote *The Education.* Adams and King had met before, while attending a lecture in Washington in 1870 at which John Wesley Powell reported on his trip down the Colorado River into the Grand Canyon. They had also met briefly in Cheyenne in July as King was heading east. But in retrospect this meeting at Estes Park with King was for Adams almost like falling in love, as "The one, coming from the west, saturated with the sunshine of the Sierras, met the other, drifting from the east, drenched in the fogs of London." He writes that "a new friend is always a miracle, but at thirty-three years old [Adams's age; King was twenty-nine], such a bird of paradise rising in the sage-brush was an avatar." The praise goes on for several pages of what is arguably the most influential work of American nonfiction, building on the general notion that "None of [King's] contemporary's had done so much, singlehanded, or were likely to leave so deep a trail."

Henry Adams's biographer Ernest Samuels notes that in the winter following the meeting at Estes Park, Adams would write a review in the *North American Review* of *Mountaineering in the Sierra Nevada* in which Adams says that the book, "though agreeable reading enough, is but a trifle." To Samuels, the review's "impersonality comes as a shock in view of Adams's dramatic recollection of their meeting." But it seems likelier that the reticence of the review reflected Adams's feelings when he wrote it, just as the lavishness of the praise for King in *The Education* reflected Adams's feelings not only of love for his longtime friend but of loss and nostalgia after his death. To overpraise a friend at one's own expense also fits into the general rhetoric of *The Education,* just as Adams's description of King as the man most perfectly educated to succeed in their time meets the thematic needs of the book when King ends up not fulfilling that expectation. Yet there those adoring words are in Adams's famous book, and both Adams and Hay are unstinting in their affection for King in letters and elsewhere as well. Samuels even suggests that the warmth of King's personality affected the relationship between Adams and Hay, deepening their own friendship.

King and Adams would remain together for several days, but then the latter went off with Emmons to the Green River and the former went up to Cheyenne, where he and N. R. Davis, who had worked on the survey the year before, began the first of many cattle operations that they would undertake together during the next decade. Davis bought a ranch a dozen miles south of Cheyenne and, staked by King, bought their first cattle, which could graze for free on the open range, making them a very good investment. This was the first time that King would indirectly use the knowledge he had gained as a government servant for his own financial gain. But it would not be the last.

## CHAPTER TWELVE

# Pretty Crystals

*In camp, from left to right: Jim Gardner,
Clarence King, and Dick Cotter.*

The rush for gold in California at the end of the 1840s and for
silver in Nevada at the end of the 1850s filled the West with
people hooked on the Next Big Thing. Smaller finds and rumors of
larger ones fed the addiction, not only among the grubby prospectors washing dirt in a thousand western streams, but also among
bankers in San Francisco and speculators in New York and London
who had either already made a fortune or only missed out on one so
far. Nobody doubted that the mountains and riverbeds of the West
held an abundance of mineral wealth, and such was the irrational
exuberance of the time that everyone expected to get a piece of it.

By the end of the 1860s, with the completion of the transcontinental railroad, San Francisco was a city of 150,000 souls, and its daily papers, such as the *Alta,* the *Bulletin,* and the *Chronicle,* kept their readers well supplied with news and gossip about where the next Sutter's Mill or Comstock Lode might be found. An announcement in the Tucson *Arizonian* in April of 1870 catches the mood: "We have found it! The greatest treasures ever discovered on the continent, and doubtless the greatest treasures ever witnessed by the eyes of man." Located in the Pyramid Mountains of New Mexico, the new mine was dubbed the Mountains of Silver. Bankers were brought in, stakes claimed, capital sought in London, towns laid out nearby. But in the end, the silver mountains did not yield enough of the stuff for a single belt buckle.

At about the same time, the papers were also full of stories about a diamond rush in South Africa, at the third major diamond field known to the world after one in India near the city of Golconda and an eighteenth-century site discovered by the Portuguese in Brazil. Before long avaricious dreamers were looking for diamonds in Arizona and New Mexico, where the terrain was said to be similar to that where the South African diamonds were found. Early nineteenth-century trapper-guides like Jim Bridger and Kit Carson had told tall tales about diamonds, rubies, and other precious gems that could be scooped right off the ground in Colorado, Arizona, and New Mexico. The odd diamond had turned up now and then during the Gold Rush, especially near Placerville, California. In a report on the phenomenon, a state geologist had helpfully recommended that, "though it may not pay to hunt for diamonds, yet it always pays to pick them up when you do happen to see them."

So the papers began to focus less on the latest gold or silver prospects and more on diamonds and other gems. As the *San Francisco Chronicle* puckishly put it in 1872, "The intelligent prospector nowadays finds rubies in rivulets, sapphires in sand dunes, emeralds in ant hills, and jewels in everything. Since . . . last Summer, diamonds have been found in profusion in every known quarter of the great West. At the rate things are going on we shall soon have the whole of North America ablaze with brilliants." Diamonds, then, would be that Next Big Thing.

The demand for a big diamond find in the West at last became so great that someone had to supply it. The someone turned out to be Philip Arnold, a Kentuckian born in the same county as Lincoln, a poorly educated former hatter's apprentice, Mexican War veteran, and forty-niner. By the early 1870s, Arnold had spent two decades working in mining operations in the West, making enough money at times to pay periodic visits back to Kentucky, where he bought a farm, married, started a family, and perhaps stashed a little cash. He was the superintendent of mining—a hollow title, given that no mining was ever done—in the Mountains of Silver scheme while also working as an assistant bookkeeper for the Diamond Drill Company, a San Francisco drilling operation that used diamond-headed bits. For a bookkeeper, Arnold, now just past forty, showed a surprising interest in the industrial-grade diamonds that kept the drills running. He even plowed through technical books on the subject.

Soon he acquired a bag of uncut diamonds, presumably borrowed from his employer, mixed with garnets, rubies, and sapphires that Arnold likely bought from Indians in Arizona. He also picked up a partner, an older cousin from Kentucky who had, like him, fought in the Mexican War, gone after gold in 1849, and was now employed by the Mountains of Silver venture. This fellow went by the Dickensian name of John Slack, and indeed in the months ahead, as the two men hatched and unfolded their scheme, Slack played the listless, taciturn foil to the voluble and cunning Arnold. Nobody ever learned how far beyond these two the conspiracy went, but soon others from the Mountains of Silver operation were drawn in, wittingly or not, by the bag of diamonds.

One of these men was George D. Roberts, the sort of business-man described in the papers as prominent, but his was a prominence earned by moving fast and not asking too many questions. Arnold and Slack turned up one night at Roberts's San Francisco office, so the story goes, looking "weather-beaten" and clutching the fateful bag. Inside was something of great value, they said, which they would have deposited in the Bank of California except for the late hour. The two men feigned a reluctance to talk about what was in the sack until Arnold allowed himself to let slip the words "rough diamonds." But Arnold and Slack were more circumspect about where they'd found the jewels, mumbling something about Indian territory, an answer that might have been the truth, but not in the way Roberts took it.

Arnold would say later that he'd approached Roberts quite openly to become an investor in the diamond fields that he and Slack purported to have discovered, but much of the romance of the hoax depends upon the idea that two plain men—rural Southerners, no less—had by playing the rube to perfection drawn in the likes of Roberts and then a gaggle of his prominent, greedy friends. However the hoax got rolling, it is hard not to enjoy in what came next how richly the swindled deserved their swindlers.

The mineral deposits of the West had drawn Clarence King, too. He had not gone west in the first place to get rich, and certainly the failed gold and silver mining towns he saw throughout the Sierra Nevada in his first years in California gave him a clear picture of where the fever for precious metals could lead. But as he learned the many skills that would make his Fortieth Parallel Exploration so successful, he was also learning from the experience of Josiah Whitney with the California legislature and from his own time in political circles in Washington that like everything else in the Gilded Age, Congress ran on money, and so ambitious undertakings like his ran on money, too. That was why the first of the seven survey reports, *Mining Industry,* included Arnold Hague's chemical analysis of the smelting process, which led to efficiencies that would save mining operators many millions of dollars. In the same report, King's own optimistic study of the Comstock Lode's future yields, as well as his study of the coal-mining potential of the Uinta foothills, would eventually make more millions for commercial interests. Whitney and others praised the book as a work of science, but King was in no particular hurry for that sort of validation—his own volume for the survey, *Systematic Geology,* which would be his magnum opus, would not appear until 1878. With *Mining Industry* he wanted to prove the commercial value of what his scientists did, and he succeeded.

The hardships of the campaign in the fall of 1871 had affected King's health. He stayed in the West trying to recover from the onset of a rheumatism that would dog him intermittently for the rest of his life, but when his thirtieth birthday came on January 6, 1872, and he was no better, he and Arnold Hague determined to go to the Sandwich Islands, as Hawaii was then known, for a more extended period of recuperation. They returned to San Francisco by the end of March and were ready for what would be the survey's sixth and last season in the field. Before November of that year, King's men would retrace the whole area of the survey and would do some new work north of the Humboldt River in Nevada. King himself continued to work on glaciers and volcanoes, concentrating on the High Sierras southeast of Yosemite. But his health continued to be a problem, and he sometimes returned to the survey's headquarters in the Montgomery Block building in San Francisco, where Whitney had had his offices for his California survey. Indeed, as Thurman Wilkins writes, Montgomery Block, "with its interior jungles of palms, its lobby and billiard room as hazy as Indian summer with the smoke of cigars . . . was the haunt of engineers and mining men, and there one heard sub rosa news from all the mining districts of the West." Clearly King would have been aware of the rising diamond fever, but it probably did not begin to alarm him until Samuel Emmons was riding west on the train, destined for San Francisco, when as his diary for October 6 notes, another passenger, a well-respected mine expert named Henry Janin, met up with a group of what looked like prospectors.

"Find that suspicious looking characters on the train are returning diamond hunters," Emmons writes. "Henry shows me some of the diamonds—pretty crystals." Most of the rumors about diamond finds had focused on Arizona and New Mexico, which were not within their purview, but as the Arnold and Slack hoax began to gather steam, King's men picked up professionally disquieting hints of a vast diamond field somewhere on the very lands that they had now gone over more than once. King would later claim that he had been too busy with his survey to give diamonds much thought, but he knew that if diamonds were discovered by someone other than his men within the bounds of their survey, it could undermine all of the work they had done so far. Like Emmons on the train, King's men recorded their potential clues, and once the survey's work for the season was done, King gathered them together, heard the evidence, and quickly decided to find the secret diamond fields himself.

Whether Philip Arnold and John Slack approached George Roberts openly or coyly, their bag of diamonds sank the hook in deep. "Roberts was very much elated by our discovery," Arnold would tell the *Louisville Courier-Journal* in December 1872, soon after their scheme had been exposed, "and promised Slack and myself to keep it a profound secret until we could explore the country further and ascertain more fully the extent of our discoveries." Like many able liars, Arnold had a good intuitive sense of how others would react to his fictions. What better way to get Roberts to spread the word, thus increasing the potential value of their claim, than to make him swear a profound oath of silence?

Almost before his office door banged shut behind the two miners, Roberts broke his promise—twice. First he told the founder of the Bank of California, William C. Ralston, a legendary financier who was a central figure in the development of San Francisco. Ralston had built hotels and mills, and invested in almost everything else, including the Comstock Lode. He had even helped fund the completion of the transcontinental railroad when the Big Four— Collis Huntington, Leland Stanford, Mark Hopkins, and Charles Crocker—came up a little short. The banker had put money into the Mountains of Silver venture, and in return the nearby town of Grant had been courteously renamed Ralston, Arizona.

The second person Roberts told about the diamond find was one

Asbury Harpending, who was in London trying to float a stock offering for the Mountains of Silver. Forty-five years later, Harpending would publish a colorful account of his life, as readable as it was mendaciously self-serving, and modestly title it *The Great Diamond Hoax and Other Stirring Incidents in the Life of Asbury Harpending*. Harpending remembered in the book that he had been drawn into the scheme by the big shot Ralston rather than by his own partner, the relative nobody Roberts. "The impression began to grow on me," Harpending wrote, "that Ralston had actually captured a fifty-million-dollar financial circus and that I was badly needed as ringmaster."

But more than one person remembered at the time that Harpending heard about the diamond find from Roberts and swallowed the bait as hungrily as Roberts had. Harpending told a friend in London that he must hurry home, that "they had got something that would astonish the world." He made his way to San Francisco "as fast as steamships and railroads would carry us," arriving in May 1871. In the meantime, Arnold and Slack had claimed to have made another visit to the diamond fields and, according to Roberts, had returned with sixty pounds of diamonds and rubies said to be worth $600,000. Roberts drew others into the trap with this bigger bag of jewels, which he said a local jeweler had authenticated. All along, the cagey businessmen—Roberts, Ralston, Harpending, and now mining entrepreneurs William Lent and General George S. Dodge—had wanted to get Arnold and Slack out of the picture as soon as possible by buying out their interests. But the two prospectors had never revealed the location of the diamonds, of course, and at first resisted the quick payday. But now Slack asked for $100,000 for his share, $50,000 now and $50,000 after the two made what they promised would be a third visit to the diamond field.

Once they got Slack's fifty grand, the two headed for London to buy uncut gems. Under assumed names—Arnold was Aundel and Slack used his middle name, Burcham—they bought rough diamonds and rubies from a London diamond merchant named

Leopold Keller, visiting him three times during July 1871, paying in banknotes on the spot for a total of almost twenty thousand dollars' worth of gems of different sizes, thousands of stones in all, including some rubies that Keller had to order for them from Paris. "I asked them where they were going to have the diamonds cut," Keller later testified in a London court, but of course they didn't intend to cut the stones at all. Some of the gems would go straight to San Francisco as further evidence of the richness of their find, and some they would plant for others to discover.

Now rolling in rough gems, Arnold and Slack offered to make one more trip to the diamond fields to allay any doubts the potential investors still harbored by returning with "a couple of million dollars worth of stones," which they would allow the businessmen to hold as a guarantee for their investment. Off the two swindlers went, and when they returned Harpending met their train at Lathrop, California, a junction east of San Francisco. "Both were travel stained and weather beaten," Harpending wrote, "and had the general look of having gone through much hardship and privation." Slack was asleep but "Arnold sat grimly erect like a vigilant old soldier with a rifle by his side, also a bulky looking buckskin package." The two men claimed that they had managed to find a spot that conveniently yielded the promised two million dollars' worth of diamonds, which they had put in two packs. But while they were crossing a river in a raft they had built, one pack was lost, leaving only the one Harpending now observed.

At Oakland, the swindlers handed the pack to Harpending, who gave them a receipt and manhandled it onto the ferry to cross the bay. "Arrived at San Francisco," he wrote, "my carriage was waiting and drove me swiftly to my home," where the other investors were assembled. "We did not waste time on ceremonies. A sheet was spread on my billiard table; I cut the elaborate fastenings of the sack and, taking hold of the lower corners, dumped the contents. It seemed," Harpending wrote, "like a dazzling, many-colored cataract of light."

William Ralston was no fool, but finance was at best an imperfect art in those freewheeling years when California was growing at an incredible clip. The Big Four had repaid Ralston's assistance on the transcontinental railway by stabbing him in the back, and he had of course lost money in the Mountains of Silver project. But as Harpending put it, "Nothing seemed to disturb his imperturbable good humor. He was at once the best winner or loser in the world—could pick up or drop a million with equal gaiety and nonchalance." Perhaps Harpending, who put Ralston's good humor to the test more than once, is not entirely reliable on this count. When a run on the Bank of California in 1875 caused its temporary closure, the supposedly unflappable Ralston died of an apparent stroke while swimming in San Francisco Bay. But before Ralston and the others involved would risk more than the fifty thousand dollars already paid to Slack, they decided to send 10 percent of the latest bag of gems to Tiffany's in New York for appraisal and to hire a reputable mining engineer to check out the diamond fields. Because the diamonds were presumably on federal land, an act of Congress was required to permit them to purchase the property once it was identified. Passing special legislation might seem daunting, but all that was needed was to buy a congressman to introduce the bill and push it through. Within a day or two the business partners allowed a generous sampling of the stones to go on display in open trays in the window of San Francisco jeweler William Willis, thus feeding the diamond fever in the city—and potentially increasing the value of their future investments.

Arnold and Slack did not blink at the idea of sending the diamonds off to Tiffany's or of leading a mining engineer to the diamond fields, but they must have believed that their hoax would blow up before very long. Slack took the second fifty thousand dollars and was out of it, but Arnold held firm. Harpending, Lent, and Dodge went to New York with the diamonds and hired a pricey New York corporate lawyer, Samuel Barlow, who was a friend of Ralston. Sometime in August 1871, an unlikely mix of men met at Barlow's house on the corner of Twenty-third Street and Madison Avenue for the appraisal. In addition to Barlow and the three businessmen from the West were Charles Lewis Tiffany and two Civil War generals, one famous and one infamous—George B. McClellan, who had commanded the Union army and run against Lincoln for president, and Benjamin "Beast" Butler, the U.S. representative from Massachusetts who had helped King with an appropriation. Butler turned out to be the very congressman whom Barlow recommended that they buy for their mining bill. Also present was Horace Greeley, the legendary editor of the *New York Tribune,* who was about to run for president himself. His death fifteen months later would come just as news of the diamond hoax was made public.

Imagine the theatrical flourish with which Harpending must have opened the bag of diamonds before this august group. Tiffany fussily sorted the stones, which also included some rubies, emeralds, and sapphires, "viewed them gravely," Harpending writes, and "held them up to the light, looking every whit the part of a great connoisseur." Once he finished his inspection, Tiffany delivered his preliminary verdict. "Gentlemen, these are beyond question precious stones of enormous value." How valuable he could not say until he had taken them back to the shop and let his lapidary have a look. Two days later he reported that the stones were worth $150,000. Harpending did a little multiplication and, since this was only 10 percent of the whole, concluded that Arnold's million-dollar sack was worth $1.5 million.

Arnold couldn't believe his good luck. His little scheme now had the imprimatur of the country's most famous jeweler. After the hoax was revealed, Tiffany would sheepishly admit that neither he nor his lapidary had had much experience with uncut stones. Arnold quickly extracted another hundred thousand dollars from the investors and scurried back to London, where he spent eight thousand dollars on more uncut gems from Leopold Keller, the better to prepare the fields for Henry Janin, the mining engineer the Californians had selected. Janin had a sterling reputation, one that he had acquired, according to Samuel Emmons, by "condemning most every new scheme he was called to report on." In more ways than one, it would turn out, Janin was the Tiffany of mining engineers.

Because of cold weather, the Janin inspection trip to the fields did not take place until the following June. Arnold and Slack, a hired hand now that he had sold his share, met Janin, Dodge, Harpending, and an English crony of Harpending's named Alfred Rubery in Denver, where they took a train to Rawlins, Wyoming. The location of the fields was still a secret. In truth, the spot that Arnold had picked and salted was only forty-five miles from the Black Buttes Station, also in Wyoming, but the swindler led them on a confusing four-day journey, often pretending to be lost and climbing hills to get his bearings. With uncharacteristic understatement, Harpending noted that "the party became cross and quarrelsome." They finally reached the salted mesa at about four o'clock on the afternoon of June 4, 1872, and eagerly began looking for diamonds. Like a mother coaxing her children at a back-yard Easter egg hunt, Arnold was extraordinarily solicitous about showing them where to dig. "After a few minutes," Harpending wrote, "Rubery gave a yell. He held up something glittering in his hand. . . . For more than an hour, diamonds were being found in profusion, together with occasional rubies, emeralds, and sapphires. Why a few pearls were not thrown in for good luck I have never been able to tell. Probably it was an oversight."

Within two days, even Janin was "wildly enthusiastic." He got busy staking out three thousand acres of surrounding land, although the area where the diamonds were salted was less than two acres. As it turned out, his time would have been better spent looking carefully just beyond the mesa itself. But in addition to his $2,500 fee, Janin had been promised a thousand shares of stock at ten dollars a share. He was no longer thinking as an inspector but as a stockholder. When he returned to New York his report would conclude that the proposed one hundred thousand shares of stock were easily worth forty dollars each, and he soon sold his shares at that price, netting an extra thirty thousand dollars, making him the only non-swindler to profit from the scam. When the rest of the party finished up at the mesa, Slack and Rubery were left behind to guard the site. But the two men did not like each other, and within a couple of days they took off. Nobody ever heard from Slack again. When Arnold got back to New York, he collected another $150,000 that had been promised him after the Janin inspection, and then quickly sold $300,000 more in stock to Harpending, making his total take $550,000, less expenses, worth about $8 million today. He had more shares coming to him, but he must have sensed that his luck would only take him so far. In the spring of 1872, he moved his family back to Kentucky from San Francisco, and by the time the affair was exposed, he was gone, too.

The diamond hunters that Samuel Emmons saw on the train in October 1872 were part of a large group sent to survey the three thousand acres Janin had staked out. On the strength of Janin's report, the California businessmen had established the San Francisco and New York Mining and Commercial Company, which would offer a hundred thousand shares of stock at a hundred dollars a share to a limited number of investors, including General McClellan and the attorney Samuel Barlow in New York, both of whom were among the new company's directors. The company opened fancy offices in the formidable Harpending Building on Market Street in San Francisco, where they displayed the best of the diamonds found so far and a large map of the three-thousand-acre claim, marking such colorfully named spots in the grim landscape as Diamond Flat, Ruby Gulch, and Sapphire Hollow. The surveying expedition had been something of a farce. For one thing, the directors had chosen the British hanger-on Rubery as guide, and it had taken him a month to find the mesa, whose location was still a closely guarded secret, apparently even from Rubery himself.

Among the returning diamond hunters was one who "was desirous of getting some information from us with regard to the boundary lines of Colorado, Utah, and Wyoming," Emmons wrote in a report. The spot where those boundaries met was of course not far from where Emmons had been doing fieldwork the year before, and he had followed up in the same area again in the present season. By the time King joined Emmons, Gardner, and a few others in San

Francisco on October 19, his men had gathered enough hints from Janin and others to make an educated guess where the find was located: in the remote northwest corner of Colorado, not far from the Wyoming state line, just northeast of an unusual flat-topped mountain that would later be called Diamond Peak. When they explained their reasoning to King, he said that his own investigations had led him to a similar conclusion. The next morning, Emmons and the topographer A. D. Wilson took the train east to Fort Bridger, where the survey team had left some of its mules for the winter. King followed them the next day.

As they gathered supplies at the fort for the 150-mile overland trip to the suspected site, Emmons's diary shows a preoccupation with the weather: "Spits snow all day . . . Temp: 11 degrees at 8 p.m.—I slept warm except my feet . . . All hands jumping with cold. . . . King gets scarfs for the party—Have on 4 shirts 2 pairs of socks, & top boots I bought from soldier." They left on October 29 and after several days of crossing small streams, their mules' legs "became encased in balls of ice, which rattled as they went like crude castanets." When they reached the general vicinity of the site on the fifth day, they camped and began to look around. Before long they saw one of Janin's claim notices and by following the notices soon saw the mesa to which all the tracks in the area led. They "came upon a bare iron-stained bit of coarse sandstone rock about a hundred feet long," Emmons reported, "just jutting out above the level of the mesa. . . . Throwing down our bridle reins we began examining the rock on our hands and knees, and in another instant I had found a small ruby."

They had discovered the secret diamond field, and caught their own nearly fatal case of diamond fever. "While daylight lasted," Emmons wrote, "we continued in this position picking up precious stones . . . and when a diamond was found it was quite a time before our benumbed fingers could succeed in grasping the tiny stone." When they went to bed that night, they "dreamed of the untold wealth that might be gathered."

By the next day they had regained a bit of their scientific composure. King noticed that wherever he found a diamond he would also find a dozen rubies. Then his men realized that they weren't finding stones at all except in places where the ground had been tampered with in some way. In anthills where they found rubies, for instance, "beside the top hole by which the ants made their exit, there was visible in the side another small break in the crust." These hills always had footsteps nearby, but at the anthills with no footsteps and no second small hole, there were no rubies. "Our explanation," Emmons wrote, "was that some one must have pushed in a ruby or two on the end of a stick." Now that they believed there had been a fraud, they spent the next two days doing more tests, which included digging a trench three feet long and ten feet deep in a gulch where the diamonds should have been distributed well below the surface. Nothing.

On their fourth day at the site, they were astonished to be approached by a man on a horse, "a stout party, city dressed, and looking very much out of keeping with the surroundings," Emmons wrote. His first words were, "Have you found any carats around here?" King and his men were so shocked by the sudden appearance in the empty landscape of this comic figure that they told him about the fraud. "What a chance to sell short on the stock" was his immediate reply. He introduced himself as J. F. Berry, a New York diamond dealer who had followed them from Fort Bridger and had been watching them with a spyglass from the top of a nearby butte.

In camp that evening, they could see Berry's campfire in the distance. Later, King would write a high-minded letter to General Humphreys saying that "because the fact of fraud was placed beyond any question" he had decided that night "to go at once to San Francisco, and find out the status of the Company, and prevent if possible further transactions in the stock." He would also claim that he hurried off in order to prevent the irritatingly brash Berry from getting rich on the inside knowledge his party had incautiously given him. But a good bet would be that King simply didn't want this fat little fellow from New York revealing the fraud before he could. In any event, King and Wilson left camp well before dawn, riding as the crow flies for Black Buttes Station, "across a pathless reach of desert and mountain," finding their destination in the middle of the next night only when they saw the light of a locomotive in the distance. They put their mules on a freight train heading west and themselves jumped on the next passenger train, reaching San Francisco on November 10. King didn't know any of the principals of the mining company, so he went to Janin's hotel and "through nearly all that night I detailed to him my discovery, and at last convinced him of its correctness."

The next morning King and Janin met the directors of the company at Ralston's office at the Bank of California, where King read a letter saying that the diamond fields were "utterly valueless" and that the directors had been the victims of an "unparalleled fraud." The letter spelled out the tests they had made on the site. "They were astonished," King would write, "and thrown into utter consternation." Emmons in a later report writes that one of the directors, no doubt hoping to sell short himself, suggested that King might benefit financially if he were to sit on the news for a few days, to which King supposedly responded, "There is not enough money in the Bank of California to make me delay publication a single hour." The board agreed to stop the planned sale of a hundred thousand shares of stock at a hundred dollars a share. They then persuaded King to lead another party, including Janin and other representatives of the company, back to the spot.

The group set out the next day and made its investigations in weather so cold that whiskey was said to have frozen in a bottle. One member of the party, General David Colton, who had become general manager of the company just three weeks before, reported back to the directors that he had seen rubies scattered on a bare rock, where "it would have been as impossible for Nature to have distributed them as for a person standing in San Francisco to toss a marble in the air and have it fall on Bunker Hill Monument." Upon receiving the reports from this latest inspection on November 25, including Janin's lame attempt to explain his failure, the directors voted to publish King's letter and dissolve the company. Diamonds would not, after all, be the Next Big Thing.

The newspapers went wild. The *San Francisco Evening Bulletin* called it "one of the most remarkable swindles ever perpetrated," and that being the case, the affair required its villains and heroes. Because Arnold and Slack were long gone, and despite the initial glee in the *Chronicle* at "How the millionaires were victimized," the principals were criticized for being duped, as was Henry Janin. Harpending, especially, came under suspicion because he was reported to have been in London at the time of one of Arnold's diamond-buying sprees. The helpful U.S. congressman, General Butler, was shown to have received a thousand shares of stock for hustling a mining act through Congress that had enabled the company to buy the federal land that held the bogus diamond field. William Lent claimed in a lawsuit that he lost some $350,000 in the hoax, and it was widely reported that Ralston lost $250,000.

Because nobody touched by the great diamond hoax ever heard of John Slack again it was generally assumed that he had either left the country or died soon after leaving the diamond fields with Rubery. But in 1967 a Denver accountant named Bruce A. Woodard, who had become obsessed with the hoax, published a book called *Diamonds in the Salt*, which showed that Slack had ridden the Union Pacific train east to St. Louis and taken a job building caskets. Eventually he moved to White Oaks, New Mexico, where he became an undertaker and lived alone until he died at the age of seventy-six in 1896. After his death his total wealth was reported in the local paper to be $1,600.

But crime paid for Philip Arnold. He bought a two-story brick house in Elizabethtown, Kentucky, in July 1872, according to court papers quoted by Woodard, and lived there with his family. After acquiring some five hundred acres of nearby land—all of the property was put in the name of his wife, Mary—he bred horses and raised sheep and pigs. The Civil War was still fresh enough in the minds of local people that they admired him for having gotten the best of the big-city financiers. A grand jury in San Francisco returned indictments for Arnold's crimes, but the contents of the indictments were never revealed, and Woodard speculates that they were quashed by the investors to avoid more bad publicity. In any case, the charges were never pursued. Arnold answered the news of the indictments by telling the Louisville paper that "I have employed counsel myself—a good Henry rifle." But eventually he did settle with William Lent out of court to the tune of $150,000, Arnold's only acknowledgment, though tacit, that the diamonds had been planted. In 1873, Arnold became a banker himself by investing in an Elizabethtown bank that had temporarily closed its doors. In 1878, he got into a quarrel with another banker in the town and the two of them shot the place up, hitting several bystanders. Arnold took a shotgun blast in the shoulder but was recovering nicely when, in early 1879, he contracted pneumonia and, at age forty-nine, died. Although he left his family comfortably off, several hundred thousand dollars have never been accounted for.

King's role in the Great Diamond Hoax made him the man of the hour. The *Chronicle* editorialized that "We have escaped, thanks to God and CLARENCE KING, a great financial calamity." In the *Bulletin,* an editorial writer wrote, "Fortunately for the good name of San Francisco and the State . . . there was one cool-headed man of scientific education who esteemed it a duty to investigate the matter in the only right way." Both the *Bulletin* and *The Nation* said that the incident showed the value of governmental surveys such as King's. *The New York Times* and the *Times* of London also covered the episode and its exposure in detail.

The diamond hoax made King an international celebrity for a good many years, and he dined out on his role in it for the rest of his life. He was also the toast of San Francisco, where he remained both to bask in the glory of the publicity and to field the lucrative offers from mining companies that started to come his way. King had not yet turned thirty-one when the swindle was revealed. It came at almost the precise midpoint of his life and represented a turning point in his career as well. Although for many people he now represented the power of science and knowledge to stand up against the unbridled greed of the age, he soon enough began to seek a Gilded Age fortune for himself, taking mine inspection jobs like the one Henry Janin had done, receiving as payment for his work stock options that might make him rich.

But King's scientific career was far from over. He would oversee the publication of the other volumes reporting the findings of the U.S. Exploration of the Fortieth Parallel, which reached its high point with the appearance in 1878 of *Systematic Geology*. In that book King attempted to give a complete history of the geology of the West that would also explain the laws of geology itself. The book was received as a brilliant synthesis of observation, knowledge, and creative scientific thought, and as a model of what a government-sponsored report could be. One critic called it "the most important single contribution made to the scientific knowledge of the continent." On the strength of its reception in the scientific community, added to the overall success of the Fortieth Parallel Exploration itself, he was in 1879 appointed by President Rutherford B. Hayes as the first director of the U. S. Geological Survey.

But even if he still had intellectual and bureaucratic achievements ahead of him, the Great Diamond Hoax marked the end of his career as an explorer for science. He would make the trip up Whitney the next year, but by 1874 he would write in a preface to the fourth edition of *Mountaineering* that "there are turning points in men's lives . . . the pass which divides youth from manhood is traversed" and so, for him, he was through with climbing mountains, at least. His health would remain a problem for the rest of his days, but when he was well he could still be admirably robust, once even riding a mule for several hundred miles in remote parts of Mexico while working for mining investors.

Perhaps it should be said only what King himself admitted, that his youth was over. He had come to California exactly a decade ago at the age of twenty-one, and he had spent the years of his youth well, achieving as H. H. Bancroft would later put it, "a reputation and a position second to no scientist in America." Thurman Wilkins scoffs at the overstatement of that claim, suggesting that the famous historian's "judgment was warped by the magnetism of King's personality." So perhaps were the judgments of all of the people who came within his sphere for the rest of his days. Few of those who gathered their thoughts about him after his death in 1901 would admit what at this distance seems clear, that King lived the better half of his life first, that what came later was a disappointment if not an outright failure. But King deserves to be remembered as he was in the weeks after the Diamond Hoax exposure, as what Josiah Whitney called "the King of Diamonds." His life had reached its highest peak, and although there would be other peaks not quite so high, everything from then on would be some form of descent.

# Change or Die

*Mount Clarence King.*
*Photograph by Ansel Adams.*

When Clarence King died of tuberculosis in a new brick cottage in Phoenix, Arizona, on the day before Christmas in 1901, he was alone except for his brother-in-law, who had hurried west by train to be at his bedside. He died not only far away from the people who loved him, but also deep in debt, especially to his wealthy friend John Hay. As his life drained away in spite of the

supposedly healing climate, he had finally disclosed his true identity to Ada, the black nursemaid he had taken as his wife thirteen
years earlier, who had known him until then by the name James
Todd. King assured Ada in a letter just weeks before his death that
she and the five children she had borne him would be taken care of,
and urged them to move to Toronto, where the racial prejudice that
had driven him to keep her existence secret from all but his closest
friends would be less burdensome. Despite the difficulties their
unlikely marriage had had to endure, difficulties of separation and
of a secrecy that Ada only now understood, they remained passion-
ately in love. So she trusted him enough to move her family north,
at least until after King's death, when they returned to Queens.

But King had not provided for them adequately. After his death,
Jim Gardiner (he had added the "i" to the spelling of his name)
would sell off King's one asset, paintings that he had collected in
Europe and America when he was flush, to help pay his debt to
Hay. Hay bought Ada a small house in Flushing and he and his
heirs would anonymously provide her a modest monthly stipend for
the next thirty years. But this was done out of Hay's love for King,
not because King had set up a trust fund as he had promised he
would do.

Of the many disappointing things in the second half of King's
life, this is the one that smells the worst. Even keeping the secret of
his identity from Ada, while far from admirable, can at least be
understood in light of the racial attitudes of his day. But to intend
to leave her and their children secure and then fail to do so was inex-
cusable. Although King never made his vast fortune, and although
the depression of 1897 had hit him hard, he retained his good reputation as a consultant in mining matters, and he could always make
a pretty penny as an expert witness in a mining legal dispute. As late
in his life as February of 1900, he was a witness in the "War of the
Copper Kings" lawsuit in Butte, Montana, pitting Anaconda against
former Senator William A. Clark. If he was saving his handsome
payment from that testimony to support Ada, it did not prevent him
from taking his black valet along with him to Butte; each day as

King went to inspect the copper mines in order to form his testimony, he did so in freshly pressed trousers.

His other failings are more forgivable because they did not hurt anyone as this one did. Borrowing tens of thousands of dollars from a close friend is not a particularly good thing to do, nor is drawing your friends and acquaintances into mining investments that rarely paid off. But however willing he was to employ his abundant charm with such people, they had the money to lose and made their own decisions. In the end, his friends seemed to be more disappointed by his failure to make further contributions to science or to write a remarkable work of fiction than by his bad luck or ineptitude, or both, in business. They were bothered most, perhaps, by his betrayal of the myth of Clarence King that those stories of his youth had created, a myth that they eagerly accepted and abetted. To read *Clarence King Memoirs,* the volume of tributes that his friend and colleague James D. Hague put together after his death, is to sense in King's friends—among them John Hay, Henry Adams, William Dean Howells, and William H. Brewer—a propensity for overstatement that feels as if they are protesting too much. To adumbrate what King became they eagerly adorned the youth he once was, or at least what he once represented to them in their own youths. The second half of his life embarrassed them, and they hid their embarrassment behind their enthusiasm for him as a young man.

And yet, and yet. King was a brilliant scientist, and that brilliance never left him. The very qualities that made his friends expect him to write great works of fiction—his imagination, his self-confidence, and his intellectual boldness—flared up from time to time throughout his life. He once told his mother that to be a good geologist required the imagination of a novelist. How else could you deduce from the surface what lay beneath it? Those powers of imaginative deduction served him well in the employ of mining interests, as he predicted where the seams of gold or silver or lead might run, and it was not for a lack of these powers that he failed to become rich in his own mining ventures, but for more mundane miscalculations like the costs of labor or the difficulties of extracting the precious metals from the ore and getting them to market.

But there is one great feat of scientific deduction for which King gets too little credit, a burst of prescience that only a once-in-a-generation scientific mind could have produced. It happened at the Sheffield School at Yale, where his scientific career had begun.

Clarence King returned to New Haven in glory in 1877 to speak at the graduation ceremonies for Sheffield on June 26. His former professor George Jarvis Brush, still only in his midforties, had been named director of the school in 1872, and the author of the letter to Brush that had inspired King's whole career, William Brewer, remained on the Sheffield faculty. Both men were undoubtedly present at the commencement, which was also the thirty-first anniversary of the school's founding, and many other alumni returned for the speech. Brush would one day refer to King as Sheffield's "greatest graduate," and this was undoubtedly King's greatest moment at his old college.

The Fortieth Parallel Survey had first gone into the field exactly a decade before King gave his speech, and because he had a tendency not to reveal his scientific thinking piecemeal, the speech was, as Henry Adams would write of it in *The Nation* two months later, King's "first expression of opinion as to the bearings of his survey on the theory of his science." The next winter King would sit down and write, or more accurately dictate, *Systematic Geology*, the synthesis of his findings from all those years in the West with his theories about how the landscape beyond the plains was formed. It would be received by some as "the most masterly summary of a great piece of geological field-work that has ever been written," as his colleague Samuel Emmons asserted soon after King's death, and was still used at that time "by university professors of geology as a model for their advanced students."

The excitement in the hall must have been palpable. King always had a penchant for the dramatic, and because of the Great Diamond Hoax exposé he would be, upon returning to his alma mater, what is jokingly called in geological circles today a rock star. Perhaps the graduation robe he wore hid the fact that he had lost the athletic physique of his young manhood; his hair was cut short because of a growing baldness. If he was no longer the dazzling boy he had for so long been, he was nonetheless basking in the warm presence of some of his closest friends, people who had worked with him and who remained under the considerable sway of his charm. Many of them also happened to be among the most important scientists of the day.

Unless Josiah Whitney journeyed down from Cambridge for the event, probably almost nobody in the audience would call himself a catastrophist. Catastrophism was by then the old-fashioned geological attempt to reconcile the changes that could be observed on the earth's surface and in the fossil record with the biblical story of creation and the belief of biblical interpreters that the earth was four thousand years old at the birth of Christ. In the nearly two decades since Darwin's *On the Origin of Species* had appeared, most modern scientists had accepted the gradualist or uniformitarian principles of Charles Lyell that, as Adams puts it in his article in *The Nation*, "all changes, whether in the earth's crust or in the nature of species, have been the result of still existing forces acting through indefinite time by continuous but not violent modifications." If the geological or fossil record suggested that the process had not been continuous and gradual, if it were to "show a violent interruption of continuity," then such an upheaval did not prove the position of catastrophists but simply showed an inadequacy in the far-from-complete record that the earth had so far yielded. Rigorous catastrophists clung to the pre-Darwinian view that science could be reconciled with a literal interpretation of the Bible, and the orthodoxy of the uniformitarians was just as uncompromising. These competing theories of how the earth's surface had formed and how species developed addressed the most important scientific questions of the day, questions whose answers had implications far beyond science. The biggest question of all was whether the findings of science had undermined the dogmas of religion. In the end it was a crucial question for all people of faith, which was just about everyone, because if people did not have faith in the old-time religion then they believed in the new secular religion, science. Almost nobody took a middle position, and the catastrophists and the uniformitarians emphatically did not.

What King would say that day was, as Adams put it, "certainly calculated to rouse curiosity." In the same short unsigned *Nation* piece, Adams would prophetically suggest that "the speaker has hardly taken care enough to guard against misconstruction." What King said was brash: he took a middle position, but with special prejudice against the uniformitarians, meaning almost everyone in his audience.

In his speech, which he called "Catastrophism and the Evolution of Environment," King began by considering the geological questions of how the earth's crust was formed and concluded with the biological questions of how species developed. Along the way he managed to take on two of the most important scientific figures of his century, Charles Lyell and Charles Darwin. First he asserted that "a theory of the destructive in nature is an early, deeply rooted archaic belief," based on the human experience of catastrophes and on the effect that passed-down stories of such disasters have on the human imagination. Added to this was what King called "a very early piece of pure scientific induction," the observation by the ancients of marine fossils on land, which suggested an environmental change catastrophic enough to dry up a sea. Then he chided the uniformitarians for projecting the present era of geological calmness into the infinite past, and said of those who do so that "They lack the very mechanism of imagination." But he followed with a sort of reconciliation, admitting that "The facts of one school are the facts of the other"; both sides would agree that the present and the recent past were times of relatively gradual geological processes, but that the effects of dramatic changes were there to be read on the landscape. If they agreed on effects they could also agree on causes, given that the amount of energy needed to cause a slow change or a fast change would be equal. He offered as proof the analogy of two trains that stop in different ways: one has its power cut and comes slowly and evenly to a stop; the other runs into a bridge abutment and stops immediately. "Precisely equal resistance has been expended in bringing them to a stop," King said. The question in dispute, then, was only how fast those changes that they all could observe had happened.

He turned to what he knew best, what the geological facts of the North American continent said about the different rates of geological processes. As he was able to do more than once in *Mountaineering in the Sierra Nevada,* while describing the view from a lofty mountain peak, King in effect made a brief narrative out of unimaginable aeons of geologic time. Much of his story had to do with depths of sedimentation, instances of subsidence, and other matters likely to make his listeners' eyes grow heavy. But in sum, he described the great American ocean that once existed between the mountain ranges of the East and those of the West, and how the eastern half of that ocean's bottom sank at a "difference of rate" from the western half that "was simply immense." In effect the eastern half of the United States subsided in ways that could be called uniformitarian and the western half "was distinctly catastrophic in the widest dynamic sense."

Later, the bed of the ocean rose, creating the American continent, and later still freshwater lakes covered the West. A series of minor catastrophes followed, raising mountains, draining lakes. The most recent catastrophe, King said, occurred when the floor of a lake covering the area that is now the Great Plains suddenly tilted, "causing a difference in height of 7,000 feet between the south and west shores." He went on to talk about the effects of volcanoes and glaciers, two subjects on which his studies in the West made him a formidable authority. The creation of a volcanic cone, where spilled lava gradually builds up, might be uniformitarian, but even Vesuvius seemed puny, he suggested, compared with the volcanic activity of an earlier age, whose violent effects would have been felt across the globe. As for glaciers, their work, so clearly marked on the landscape of the West, dealt uniformitarianism a "fatal blow," he claimed. Only the mighty deluges caused by glacial melting could have cut the dramatic canyons of the West. "Uniformitarians are fond of saying that give our present rivers time, plenty of time, and they can perform the feats of the past," King said. But the western canyons "could never have been carved by the pigmy rivers of this climate to the end of infinite time."

King's studies proved to him, then, that strict uniformitarianism could not have created the American West. But he conceded that "the ages have had their periods of geological serenity" and suggested that "geological history seems to be a dovetailing of the two ideas," what he called "modified catastrophism." He admitted, however, that his middle course was a "downright rejection of strict uniformitarianism" and "nothing less than an ignited bomb-shell thrown into the camp of the biologists, who have tranquilly built upon uniformitarianism."

King's biographer Thurman Wilkins found a letter from a man present that day in New Haven who said that the famous Yale paleontologist O. C. Marsh, who would later work for King on the U.S. Geological Survey, attended the speech and "got very warm before King finished and used his fan vigorously." This was undoubtedly one of those hot-flash moments in the speech for Marsh. King was now taking on the orthodoxy of the life scientists just as he had taken on that of the earth scientists, claiming that "biologists have signally failed to study the power and influence of the inorganic or geologic environment." The ability of species to adapt, King continued, was not simply a matter of interspecies warfare, of fitter species surviving at the expense of weaker ones, but also of how they reacted to environment, ranging from climate to catastrophe. In times of catastrophic changes, what "sounded in the ear of every living thing [were] the words 'change or die.'" At such times, "plasticity," not fitness, "became the sole principle of salvation." King predicted that once the scientific record was complete, the periods when species were discovered to have changed most rapidly would coincide with the periods of catastrophic change. Thus catastrophe was not simply something for species to survive, it was the primary engine of evolution. He concluded his speech by saying:

> Moments of great catastrophe, thus translated into the language of life, become moments of creation, when out of plastic organisms something newer and nobler is called into being.

Charles Peirce at Harvard, one of the founders of the Metaphysical Club, ranked King's idea of how catastrophe effects the development of species as "a third theory of evolution," comparable to Darwin's and to Jean-Baptiste Lamarck's 1809 theory of progressive adaptation, adding that King's theory was "the most efficient." But the tenor of King's speech, in which he accused his audience of ignoring scientific facts and of being members of "the army of scientific fashion followers who would gladly die rather than be caught wearing an obsolete mode or believing in any penultimate thing," was not calculated to change the minds of those whose faces flushed with anger on that June day in New Haven. The text of the speech, which was printed in both the *New York Tribune* and the *American Naturalist,* led to a few denunciations and defenses elsewhere, but it did not have an appreciable effect on the scientific community, which would continue for decades to be unwaveringly uniformitarian. Even *Systematic Geology,* which appeared the next year, would be admired more widely than it was read; its methods would be more influential than its conclusions.

But a century later, Niles Eldredge of the American Museum of Natural History and Stephen Jay Gould of Harvard began to put forth a series of theories collectively called punctuated equilibria, which said that geological time passed in a sequence of "rapid flips between stable states." They suggested that the gaps in the fossil record do in fact punch holes in the theory of uniformitarianism, that "the modern theory of evolution does not require gradual change," as Gould writes in his book *The Panda's Thumb.* "It is gradualism that we must reject," he wrote, "not Darwinism." As for King's own theory of evolution, that species are created and changed more by catastrophe than by gradual adaptation, Gould's conclusions sound quite similar: "Lineages change little during most of their history, but events of rapid speciation occasionally punctuate this tranquility. Evolution is the differential survival and deployment of these punctuations." Gould elsewhere describes modern geology "as a blend of Lyell and the catastrophists," what King had clearly called modified catastrophism. Gould and Eldredge never mention Clarence King in their discussions of punctuated equilibria, which shows just how invisible, seventy-five years after his death, he had become.

But think about it. In his Sheffield speech King had stood up to the best scientific minds of his day and looked a hundred years into the future. It was not geological or paleontological data that had made him conclude that species were created in bunches at times of greatest geological change, and that it was not the fittest species that survived such disastrous times but what he called the most plastic, meaning those species that happened to be able to survive the particular disaster of the moment. Today we would call this chance or contingency. If his conclusions were not based on data, what were they based on? I suggest they were based on the same qualities that allowed him to see below the surface of the earth and predict where a seam of gold would run. Call it intuition. Call it imagination.

# BIBLIOGRAPHY

Because my book is more a work of synthesis than of scholarship I am deeply indebted to the scholars and writers listed below. First among them, by quite a distance, is Thurman Wilkins, whose *Clarence King: A Biography,* is not only a model of patient, thorough scholarship, but also a book that is well written, carefully imagined, and generously felt. Like Clarence King himself, *Clarence King* deserves to be much better known. Although I relied on it less, Richard A. Bartlett's *Great Surveys of the American West* also proved to be utterly reliable; I'd like to acknowledge my particular admiration for it as well.

My thanks for research assistance to the staffs of the Huntington Library Department of Manuscripts, the Manuscript Division of the Library of Congress, and the National Archives.

Online and periodicals sources appear in the endnotes.

—ROBERT WILSON

Adams, Henry. *Henry Adams: Democracy, Esther, Mont Saint Michel and Chartres, The Education of Henry Adams.* New York: The Library of America, 1983.

Ambrose, Stephen E. *Undaunted Courage: Meriwether Lewis, Thomas Jefferson, and the Opening of the American West.* New York: Simon & Schuster, 1996.

Bartlett, Richard A. *Great Surveys of the American West.* Norman: University of Oklahoma Press, 1962.

Bowles, Samuel. *Across the Continent: A Summer's Journey.* Springfield, MA: Samuel Bowles & Co.; New York: Hurd & Houghton, 1866.

Brewer, William H. *Up and Down California in 1860–1864.* Francis P. Farquhar (ed). Berkeley: University of California Press, 1966.

Bronson, Edgar Beecher. *Reminiscences of a Ranchman.* Lincoln: University of Nebraska Press, 1962.

Brooks, Van Wyck. *New England: Indian Summer 1865–1915.* Chicago: University of Chicago Press, 1984.

Browne, Janet. *Charles Darwin: Voyaging, Volume I of a Biography.* New York: Alfred A. Knopf, 1995.

Cater, Harold Dean. *Henry Adams and His Friends: A Collection of His Unpublished Letters.* New York: Octagon, 1970.

Chaffin, Tom. *Pathfinder: John Charles Frémont and the Course of American Empire.* New York: Hill and Wang, 2002.

Crosby, Harry H. "So Deep a Trail: A Biography of Clarence King." Unpublished dissertation manuscript, submitted to the committee of graduate study at Stanford University in 1953. Published on demand by University Microfilms International, Ann Arbor, 1985.

Cunliffe, Marcus. *The Literature of the United States, Fourth Edition.* New York: Penguin, 1986.

Dickason, David H. *The Daring Young Men: The Story of the American Pre-Raphaelites.* Bloomington: Indiana University Press, 1953.

Dowdey, Clifford. *The Seven Days: The Emergence of Lee.* Boston: Little, Brown, 1964.

Edel, Leon. *Henry James: A Life.* New York: Harper & Row, 1985.

Farquhar, Francis P. *History of the Sierra Nevada.* Berkeley: University of California Press, 1965.

Fenton, Carroll Lane, and Mildred Adams Fenton. *Giants of Geology.* Garden City, NY: Doubleday and Co., 1945.

Finch, Robert, and John Elder, editors. *The Norton Book of Nature Writing.* New York: W. W. Norton, 1990.

Friedrich, Otto. *Clover.* New York: Simon & Schuster, 1979.

Goetzmann, William H. *Exploration and Empire: The Explorer and the Scientist in the Winning of the American West.* New York: Alfred A. Knopf, 1966.

Gould, Stephen Jay. *The Panda's Thumb: More Reflections in Natural History.* New York: W. W. Norton, 1980.

Grove, Noel, and Phil Schermeister. *Range of Light: The Sierra Nevada.* Washington, D.C.: National Geographic, 1999.

Hague, James D., editor. *Clarence King Memoirs.* Published for the King Memorial Committee of The Century Association. New York: G. P. Putnam's Sons, 1904.

Harpending, Asbury. *The Great Diamond Hoax and Other Stirring Incidents in the Life of Asbury Harpending.* James H. Wilkins (ed.). Norman: University of Oklahoma Press, 1958.

Horan, James D. *Timothy O'Sullivan: America's Forgotten Photographer.* New York: Bonanza Books, 1966.

James, Henry. *Collected Travel Writings: Great Britain and America.* New York: The Library of America, 1993.

Kaplan, Justin. *Mr. Clemens and Mark Twain: A Biography.* New York: Simon & Schuster, 1966.

King, Clarence R. *Mountaineering in the Sierra Nevada.* Francis P. Farquhar (ed). Lincoln: University of Nebraska Press, 1997.

Leech, Margaret. *Reveille in Washington.* New York: Harper & Row, 1941.

McPhee, John. *Annals of the Former World.* New York: Farrar, Straus and Giroux, 1998.

McPherson, James M. *Battle Cry of Freedom: The Civil War Era.* New York: Oxford University Press, 1988.

Menand, Louis. *The Metaphysical Club.* New York: Farrar, Straus and Giroux, 2001.

Muir, John. *The Mountains of California.* Introduction by Edward Hoagland. New York: Penguin, 1985.

O'Toole, Patricia. *The Five of Hearts: An Intimate Portrait of Henry Adams and His Friends.* New York: Clarkson N. Potter, 1990.

Roosevelt, Theodore. *The Wilderness Hunter.* The Works of Theodore Roosevelt, Vol. II. New York: Charles Scribner's Sons, 1926.

Ruskin, John. *Modern Painters.* Edited and abridged by David Barrie. New York: Alfred A. Knopf, 1987.

Rybczynski, Witold. *A Clearing in the Distance: Frederick Law Olmsted and America in the 19th Century.* New York: Scribner, 1999.

Samuels, Ernest. *Henry Adams: The Middle Years.* Cambridge: Harvard University Press, 1958.

———, ed. *Henry Adams: Selected Letters.* Cambridge: Belknap Press, Harvard University Press, 1992.

———. *Henry Adams* (one-volume edition). Boston: Belknap Press, Harvard University Press, 1989.

Sandweiss, Martha A. *Print the Legend: Photography and the American West.* New Haven: Yale University Press, 2002.

Smith, Michael L. *Pacific Visions: California Scientists and the Environment, 1850–1915.* New Haven: Yale University Press, 1987.

Spence, Jonathan D. *The Search for Modern China.* New York: W. W. Norton, 1990.

Starr, Kevin. *Americans and the California Dream, 1850–1915.* New York: Oxford University Press, 1973.

Stegner, Wallace. *Beyond the Hundredth Meridian: John Wesley Powell and the Second Opening of the West.* Boston: Houghton Mifflin, 1954.

Trachtenberg, Alan, introduction. *The American Image: Photographs from the National Archives, 1860–1960.* New York. Pantheon Books, 1979.

———, editor and introduction. *Democratic Vistas, 1860–1880.* New York: George Braziller, 1970.

———. *The Incorporation of America: Culture and Society in the Gilded Age.* New York: Hill and Wang, 1982.

———. *Reading American Photographs: Images as History, Mathew Brady to Walker Evans.* New York: Hill and Wang, 1989.

Twain, Mark. *The Innocents Abroad* and *Roughing It.* New York: The Library of America, 1984.

Van Noy, Rick. *Surveying the Interior: Literary Cartographers and the Sense of Place.* Reno: University of Nevada Press, 2003.

Ward, Geoffrey C. *The Civil War: An Illustrated History.* New York: Alfred A. Knopf, 1990.

Whitney, J. D. *Geology of California, Vol. I: Report of Progress and Synopsis of the Field-Work from 1860 to 1864.* Published by authority of the Legislature of California. Philadelphia: Sherman and Co., 1865.

Wilkins, Thurman, with the help of Caroline Lawson Hinkley. *Clarence King: A Biography, Revised and Enlarged Edition.* Albuquerque: University of New Mexico Press, 1988.

Woodard, Bruce A. *Diamonds in the Salt: The First Authentic Account of the Sensational Diamond Hoax Chicanery.* Boulder: Pruett Press, 1967.

Worster, Donald. *A River Running West: The Life of John Wesley Powell.* New York: Oxford University Press, 2001.

Wyatt, David. *The Fall into Eden: Landscape and Imagination in California.* Cambridge: Cambridge University Press, 1986.

Young, Bob, and Jan Young. *Frontier Scientist: Clarence King.* New York: Julian Messner, 1968.

# NOTES

## Introduction: The Little White House

2   "let us invite the President": "Pandora," in *The Novels and Tales of Henry James,* vol. 18, p. 128. From Ernest Samuels, *Henry Adams: The Middle Years,* p. 168.

2   "enemies or friends": Samuels, *Henry Adams,* p. 149.

3   "in that room": George F. Becker, *Transactions of the American Institute of Mining Engineers,* 42: 648. From Thurman Wilkins, *Clarence King: A Biography,* p. 470n.

3   "as good company": Clover Adams in a letter to her father. From Otto Friedrich, *Clover,* p. 242.

3   "scientific renaissance": Samuels, *Henry Adams,* p. 135.

3   "best of the 19th century": Clarence King to John Hay, Aug. 12, 1888. From Patricia O'Toole, *The Five of Hearts,* p. 65.

4   "intimacy of sorts": Samuels, *Henry Adams,* p. 134.

5   " 'couldn't please him' ": Friedrich, *Clover,* p. 261.

6   "toffy all over him": John Hay, in *Clarence King Memoirs,* ed. James D. Hague, p. 130.

7   "axioms of physics": Henry Adams, *Esther,* in *Henry Adams* (Library of America), pp. 284–85.

8   "naturally sympathetic": Ibid., p. 296.

8   "nursery tales!": Ibid., p. 319.

8   "without fear": Wilkins, *Clarence King,* p. 27n.

8   "his generation": Quoted in *The Education of Henry Adams* in *Henry Adams* (Library of America), p. 1005.

8   "wanted to be": Ibid.

10  "private fortune in the west": Ibid., p. 1014.

10  "his life underground": Ibid., p. 1020.

11  "Mexican gold mines": Wallace Stegner, *Beyond the Hundredth Meridian: John Wesley Powell and the Second Opening of the West,* p. 246.

11  "wanted to be rich": Ibid.

11  "ambitious course": Adams, *The Education of Henry Adams,* p. 1020.

12  Edward VII: Wilkins, *Clarence King,* pp. 321–22.

12  "madness": Van Wyck Brooks, *New England: Indian Summer, 1865–1915,* p. 192.

14    "our Byron": Quoted in Samuels, *Henry Adams: The Middle Years,* p. 31.
15    "delightful man in the world": Quoted in Leon Edel, *Henry James: A Life,* p. 473.


## Part One: Going West


17    General sources for fictional passage: Wilkins, *Clarence King*; Hague, *Clarence King Memoirs*; Samuel Bowles, *Across the Continent*; Theodore Roosevelt, *The Wilderness Hunter*; and J. T. Redman, "Reminiscences and Experiences on My Trip across the Plains" (HM 20462, Huntington Library).


## Chapter One: Alone Together


23    "would-be investors": William H. Goetzmann, *Exploration and Empire: The Explorer and the Scientist in the Winning of the American West,* p. 355.
24    "given moment": John Ruskin, *Modern Painters,* p. 470.
25    "to the subject": Florence K. Howland to S. F. Emmons, Feb. 24, 1903, Box 29, Emmons Papers, Manuscript Division, Library of Congress. From Wilkins, *Clarence King,* p. 444n.
26    "scents of the Far East": Edgar Beecher Bronson, *Reminiscences of a Ranchman,* p. 5.
26    "her own name": Wilkins, *Clarence King,* p. 10.
26    Background about Canton, the Treaty of Nanjing, and the Taiping Rebellion, from Jonathan D. Spence, *The Search for Modern China,* p. 165–84.
27    "her father's death": Florence K. Howland to S. F. Emmons, Jan. 17 [1902], Emmons Papers. From Wilkins, *Clarence King,* p. 445n.
28    Old Town Newport: Henry James, "The Sense of Newport," in *Henry James: Collected Travel Writings* (Library of America), p. 532.
28    "to a lady": Ibid., p. 533.
28    "almost to squalor": Henry James, "Portraits of Places," in *Henry James: Collected Travel Writings,* p. 345.
29    "stony shoulder": Ibid.
29    "any of his friends": Harry H. Crosby, "So Deep a Trail."
29    "boating oracle": King to Gardner, Jan. 30, 1862, King Papers, Huntington Library, San Marino, California. From Wilkins, *Clarence King,* p. 447n.
30    "omnipotent Author": *Pantology; or, a Systematic Survey of Human Knowledge,* p. 401. From Wilkins, *Clarence King,* p. 445n.
30    "my ignorance": Florence K. Howland to S. F. Emmons, Feb. 24, 1903, Emmons Papers. From Wilkins, *Clarence King,* p. 445n.
30    "veritable museum": Ibid.
30    "hunting and botanizing": *Clarence King Memoirs,* p. 259.
31    "powers of observation": "C.K.'s notes for [Hague's] biographical notice of him," King Papers. From Wilkins, *Clarence King,* p. 445n.
32    "in later life": *Clarence King Memoirs,* p. 297.
33    "attacking tutors": "Artium Magister," *North American Review* 147 (October 1888), 377.

33 "badgering grammarians": Ibid., p. 377–78. From Wilkins, *Clarence King*, p. 447n.

33 "natural womanhood": King to John Hay, August 12 [1888?], Hay Papers, Brown University Library. From Wilkins, *Clarence King*, p. 446n.

33 "inspire enthusiasm": *Clarence King Memoirs*, pp. 307–8.

34 "rambled": Ibid., p. 307.

34 "fifteen as at fifty": Ibid.

34 "most brothers": *Surveys West of the Mississippi*, House Report 612 (ser. 1626), 43rd Cong., 1st sess., 70. From Wilkins, *Clarence King*, p. 446n.

34 "brothers in Christ": Wilkins, *Clarence King*, p. 24.

34 "happy boyhood together": Dewey to King, quoted in [Lloyd], *Memorial*, p. 25. From Wilkins, *Clarence King*, p. 446n

35 " 'modesty is the best policy.' " Bronson, *Reminiscences of a Ranchman*, pp. 329–30.

36 "jet-black hair": Harry H. Crosby, "So Deep a Trail," p. 38.

36 "a close intellectual companionship": *Clarence King Memoirs*, p. 259.

36 "mind and soul": Florence K. Howland to J. D. Hague, July 27, [1904], King Papers. From Wilkins, *Clarence King*, p. 445.

36 "sweetness of our relation": Florence K. Howland to C. W. Howard, January 17, 1902, J. D. Hague Collection, Huntington Library, San Marino, California. From Wilkins, *Clarence King*, pp. 18–19n.

36 "because of illness": Letter from Thomas J. Quirk, Principal, November 8, 1949 (information from school records). From Wilkins, *Clarence King*, p. 446n.

36 "father of the fatherless": King to Gardner, October 2, 1859 (HM 27809, Huntington Library). From Wilkins, *Clarence King*, p. 446n.

37 "govern myself": Ibid.

37 "to blame": King to Gardner, January 4, 1860 (HM 27810, Huntington Library). From Wilkins, *Clarence King*, p. 446n.

37 "perfectly fagged out": King to Gardner, January 4, 1860 (HM 27810, Huntington Library). From Wilkins, *Clarence King*, p. 446n.

38 "camphor": Wilkins, *Clarence King*, p. 12.

38 "mighty inflaming": King to Gardner, January 4, 1860 (HM 27810, Huntington Library). From Wilkins, *Clarence King*, p. 446n.

38 "eradicating the melancholy": King to Gardner, May 20 [1860] (HM 27813, Huntington Library). From Wilkins, *Clarence King*, p. 446n.

38 "not impossible": Ibid.

## Chapter Two: A Scientific Education

41 Early history of the Yale Scientific School. Yale University Faculty of Engineering. (Last updated November 2000.) *History of Sheffield Scientific School.* From http://www.eng.yale.edu/history/sheffield.htm

42 "nonexistent institution": Ibid.

43 "test tubes": A. D. White, in Fabian Franklin, *Life of Daniel Coit Gilman*, p. 324. From Wilkins, *Clarence King*, p. 447n.

43 "courses of study": Quoted by R. Chittenden. Quoted in Yale University Faculty of Engineering. From http://www.eng.yale.edu/history/sheffield.htm

43 "same planet": Loomis Havemeyer, quoted by W. J. Cunningham. Quoted in Yale University Faculty of Engineering. From http://www.eng.yale.edu/history/sheffield.htm

43 "'scientifics'": *North American Review*, 147 (October 1888), 370. From Wilkins, *Clarence King*, p. 447n.

43 "Switzerland": King to Gardner, October 10, 1861 (HM 27821, Huntington Library) From Wilkins, *Clarence King*, p. 447n.

44 "in my studies": Ibid.

44 transfer to Yale: Wilkins, *Clarence King*, p. 33.

44 "purposes of life": Stephen Van Rensselaer, 1824. Quoted by Shirley Jackson, "President's View," *Rensselaer Alumni Magazine* (March 2002).

44 "conversion": Crosby, "So Deep a Trail," p. 47.

44 "sunshine": King to James T. Gardner, June 9, 1861. Francis Farquhar Collection, Berkeley, California. From Crosby, "So Deep a Trail," p. 52n.

45 "clearer to me now": King to James T. Gardner, January 30, 1862. Farquhar Collection. From Crosby, ibid.

45 Wilkes's United States Exploring Expedition: Details in Goetzmann, *Exploration and Empire*, pp. 235–38. See also Nathaniel Philbrick, *Sea of Glory: America's Voyage of Discovery, the U.S. Exploring Expedition, 1838–1842* (New York: Viking, 2003).

45 "bloody Tarawa": Goetzmann, *Exploration and Empire*, p. 236.

46 along with him: Ibid., p. 235.

46 "geological synthesis": James H. Natland, "James Dwight Dana: Mineralogist, Zoologist, Geologist, Explorer," *GSA Today* (February 2003).

46 "in geology": Gardner to his mother, June 14, 1862, Gardiner Papers. From Wilkins, *Clarence King*, p. 447n.

46 "did nothing": Carroll Lane Fenton and Mildred Adams Fenton, *Giants of Geology*, p. 230.

46 "his travels": Gardner to his mother, June 14, 1862, Gardiner Papers. From Wilkins, *Clarence King*, p. 447n.

46 "the Shasty peak": James Dwight Dana, "Notes on Upper California," *American Journal of Science and Arts*, 2nd ser., 7 (1894).

47 "'if found out.'" James D. Hague, *Clarence King Memoirs*, pp. 377–78.

47 "with honor": Letter signed by eleven Yale professors to President Hayes, January 10, 1879, Hayes Collection, Rutherford B. Hayes Presidential Center, Fremont, Ohio. From Wilkins, *Clarence King*, p. 447n.

49 written a novel: Wilkins, *Clarence King*, p. 22.

49 "than thou art?": Sophia Robbins Little, *Thrice Through the Furnace: A Tale of the Times of the Iron Hoof* (Pawtucket, RI: A. W. Pearce, 1852), p. 31.

49 "philanthropic radicals": King to Gardner, March 28 [1860] (HM 27811, Huntington Library). From Wilkins, *Clarence King*, p. 447n.

49 "knight-errant of unfriended truth": Geoffrey C. Ward, *The Civil War: An Illustrated History*, p. 16.

49 Moravian faith: Wilkins, *Clarence King*, p. 9.

49    "militarism overnight": Louis Menand, *The Metaphysical Club*, pp. 31–32.

49    "smells good": Ibid., pp. 31–32.

49    "tearing my soul in two": King to Gardner, March 18, 1862 (HM 27824, Huntington Library). From Wilkins, *Clarence King*, p. 447n.

50    "keep in trim": Dewey to King, n.d., quoted in [Lloyd], *Memorial*, p. 28.

50    " 'freedom' ": King to Gardner, March 18, 1862 (HM 27824, Huntington Library). From Wilkins, *Clarence King*, p. 447n.

51    "from the draft": Gardner to his mother, August 14, 1862, Gardiner Papers, New York State Library, Albany. From Wilkins, *Clarence King*, p. 447n.

53    "by that light": Brewer to Brush, October 1, 1862, ed. F. P. Farquhar, *California Historical Society Quarterly*, 7 (1928), p. 125. From Wilkins, *Clarence King*, p. 448n.

53    "That settles it": Ibid., p. 125.

54    "in that direction": King to Brush, January 30, 1863, Brush Papers, Yale Library. From Wilkins, *Clarence King*, p. 448n.

54    "study under him": Menand, *The Metaphysical Club*, p. 117.

54    "possible hardness": Fenton and Fenton, *Giants of Geology*, p. 117.

54    "of an idea": Menand, *The Metaphysical Club*, p. 121.

55    "individual living forms": Louis Agassiz, *Contributions to the Natural History of the United States of America* (Boston: Little, Brown, 1857–62), vol. 3, 88. From Menand, *The Metaphysical Club*, p. 128.

55    "of a mind": Menand, *The Metaphysical Club*, p. 127.

55    "scientific mistake": Louis Agassiz, "Prof. Agassiz on the Origin of Species," *American Journal of Science and Arts*, 2nd ser. 30 (1860): 154. From Menand, *The Metaphysical Club*, p. 127.

55    "were not elsewhere": "Journal of Trip to Northern Sierras" (D23), entry for September 10, 1863, King Papers. From Wilkins, *Clarence King*, p. 448n.

56    "their every undulation": John Ruskin, *Modern Painters*, p. 114.

57    "modern thought": Clarence Rivers King, *Mountaineering in the Sierra Nevada*, pp. 305–6.

57    "good as sunshine": Gardner to his mother, January 31, 1863, Gardiner Papers. From Wilkins, *Clarence King*, p. 448n.

57    "of the city": Ibid.

57    "Society for the Advancement of Truth in Art": David H. Dickason, *The Daring Young Men: The Story of the American Pre-Raphaelites*.

58    "holds sway": Wilkins, *Clarence King*, p. 43.

58    "almost singlehanded": Dickason, *Daring Young Men*, p. 73.

59    "capable of": Private Notes, 1863 (A2), King Papers. From Wilkins, *Clarence King*, p. 448n.

59    "mule driver": King to George J. Brush, January 30, 1863, Brush Papers. From Wilkins, *Clarence King*, p. 448n.

59    contributions to Yale: Ibid.

59    "greatest graduate": Quoted in A. Phelps Stokes, *Memorials of Eminent Yale Men*, vol. 2, 82. From Wilkins, *Clarence King*, p. 447n.

## Chapter Three: Crossing the Continent

62 "some excitement": Samuel Bowles, *Across the Continent,* pp. 6–7.

63 "terrible massacres": Ibid., p. 10.

64 "what it may": Thomas Carney, 1863 inaugural address as governor of Kansas. Kansas State Library, *Kansas Governors' Messages.* (Last updated 2002.) www.kslib.info/ref/message/carney/1863

64 "quagmire court": Wilkins, *Clarence King,* p. 45.

64 "Missouri emigrant": Notes on King for Raymond, King Papers. From Wilkins, *Clarence King,* p. 448n.

65 "satisfies the eye": Bowles, *Across the Continent,* pp. 12–13.

65 buffalo-hunting accident: Wilkins, *Clarence King,* p. 46.

67 astonished with: Mark Twain, *Roughing It* (Library of America), p. 569.

67 had mended: Wilkins, *Clarence King,* p. 46.

68 "over the whole": Twain, *Roughing It,* p. 605.

68 "a biscuit instead of a bullet": Redman MS (HM 20462, Huntington Library).

68 "death in every canyon": Fitz Hugh Ludlow, *The Heart of the Continent,* p. 282. From Wilkins, *Clarence King,* p. 449n.

68 "same road": Gardner to his mother, September 11, 1863, Farquhar Collection. From Wilkins, *Clarence King,* p. 449n.

69 "above the valley": Bowles, *Across the Continent,* pp. 75–76.

69 "human hands": D. A. Shaw. *Eldorado; or, California as Seen by a Pioneer, 1850–1900,* p. 31.

69 "culminating point": John C. Frémont, *Report of the Exploring Expedition to the Rocky Mountains in the Year 1842,* pp. 57–60. From Chaffin, *Pathfinder: John Charles Frémont and the Course of American Empire,* p. 116.

69 "gleaming like silver": Ibid., p. 117.

70 "dark green pines": Clarence King, from James D. Hague, *Mining Industry,* p. 12.

70 "jackass rabbits": Twain to Mrs. Jane Clemens, September or October 1861. Mark Twain, *The Letters of Mark Twain,* Volume 1, 1853–1866.

71 "spills the passengers": Twain, *Roughing It,* p. 643.

73 "wolves' clothing": Bronson, *Reminiscences of a Ranchman,* p. 341.

73 "read aloud from a Bible": Wilkins, *Clarence King,* p. 51.

73 "fascinating individual": Quoted by F. P. Farquhar in William H. Brewer, *Up and Down California in 1860–1864,* p. 469n. From Wilkins, *Clarence King,* p. 449n.

74 "evening together": *Clarence King Memoirs,* pp. 311–12.

74 "in San Francisco": Ibid., p. 315.

74 "Shasta valley": Ibid., pp. 310–11.

76 "to engage him": Ibid., p. 316.


## Chapter Four: Into the Field

78 "spirit it fostered": Entry on Josiah D. Whitney. *Dictionary of American Biography,* 4: 273.

79 "gold in the soil": Josiah D. Whitney to William D. Whitney, December 11,

1848, Whitney Family Papers, Yale University Library. From Goetzmann, *Exploration and Empire*, p. 357.

79 "zoological productions": Francis P. Farquhar in Brewer, *Up and Down California*, p. x.

79 "perfectly heavenly": Brewer, *Up and Down California*, p. 9.

81 "much whiskey": Ibid., p. 12.

81 "spring and summer": Ibid., p. 13.

81 "in our tents": Ibid., p. 15.

81 "another rainy Sunday": Ibid., p. 19.

81 "without cessation": Ibid., p. 25.

81 "we feel much": Ibid., p. 24.

81 "not favored": Ibid., p. 38.

82 "over me": Ibid., pp. 46–47.

82 "corner of the sack": Ibid., p. 32.

83 "in my command": Ibid., p. 63.

83 whaling industry: Ibid., p. 105.

83 Brewer's accomplishments with first year of Whitney survey: Ibid., p. 296.

83 "economically": Ibid.

84 "mountain climbing": Ibid., pp. 235–36.

84 "starving and drowning": Ibid., p. 242.

85 "a jolly time": Ibid., p. 267.

85 "restore the strength": Ibid., p. 314.

86 "on the rocks": Ibid., p. 315.

86 "as is common": Ibid.

86 "so many nights": King, "Journal of Trip in Northern Sierras" (D23), entry for September 6, 1863, King Papers.

87 "work being good": Ibid.

87 "realm of sentiment": King, *Mountaineering in the Sierra Nevada*, p. 292.

88 "fair gelding": Quoted in Wilkins, *Clarence King*, p. 53.

88 "picturesquely located": Brewer, *Up and Down California*, p. 455.

88 "houses of all kinds": King, "Journal of Trip in Northern Sierras" (D23), entry for September 12, 1863, King Papers.

88 "important matter geologically": Brewer, *Up and Down California*, pp. 456–57.

89 "Ruskin and Tyndall": *Clarence King Memoirs*, p. 317.

89 "great plains": Ibid., p. 318.

89 "are past": Brewer, *Up and Down California*, p. 457.

89 "snow and rocks": Ibid., p. 458.

89 "in the hills": Ibid., p. 459.

90 "obliged to retreat": King, "Journal of Trip in Northern Sierras" (D23), entry for September 26, 1863, King Papers.

90 "intensely blue sky": *Clarence King Memoirs*, pp. 318–19.

90 "the Pacific coast": Ibid., p. 313.

90 "had seen *this*!" Ibid., p. 319.

91 "unimportant bruises": Ibid.

91 "drink you know": King, "Journal of Trip in Northern Sierras" (D23), entry for September 27, 1863.

91 "greet the day": Ibid., entry for September 29, 1863.

91    "terrestrial object": *Clarence King Memoirs,* p. 320.

91    "the sun": Brewer, *Up and Down California,* p. 463.

91    "without much pain": King, "Journal of Trip in Northern Sierras" (D23), entry for September 29, 1863.

92    "of my life": *Clarence King Memoirs,* p. 320.

92    "dismal place": John Muir, *Steep Trails.* From www.sierraclub.org/john_muir_exhibit/writings

92    "take home": Brewer, *Up and Down California,* p. 468.

93    "fantastic shapes": Ibid., p. 473.

93    "silent black darkness": King, "Journal of Trip in Northern Sierras" (D23), entry for October 10, 1863.

93    "beyond the animal": Ibid., entry for October 8, 1863.

93    "make alone": Brewer, *Up and Down California,* p. 477.

93    "entirely dead": Ibid., p. 476.


PART TWO: THE HIGHEST PEAKS

Chapter Five: Man of Action

95    Direct quotation of King on his love of geology. From Bronson, *Reminiscences of a Ranchman,* pp. 3–4.

100   "honestly paying expenses": Witold Rybczynski, *A Clearing in the Distance: Frederick Law Olmsted and America in the 19th Century,* p. 231.

101   "deep and savage": King, *Mountaineering,* p. 196.

101   "metamorphic Sierra": Ibid., p. 193.

101   "little 'blow-hard'": Ashburner to Brewer, January 22, 1865, Ashburner Letters, Bancroft Library, Berkeley, California. From Wilkins, *Clarence King,* p. 449n.

101   "mere nature-lover": King, *Mountaineering,* p. 193.

102   "Stockton to Hornitas": Ibid., p. 192.

102   "jolly of heart": Ibid., pp. 193–94.

102   "flat acceptance": *Clarence King Memoirs,* p. 410.

104   "the gold-belt was discovered": King, *Mountaineering,* p. 194.

104   "I was fully persuaded": Ibid., p. 45.

105   "some important explorations": *American Journal of Science,* 2nd ser., 38 (1864), 260; also Whitney to Brewer, July 10, 1864 (C-B 312: 100, Bancroft Library, University of California, Berkeley). From Wilkins, *Clarence King,* p. 450n.

105   "the map of California": Whitney, *Geology,* vol. 1, p. 224.

105   "as to the result": King, *Mountaineering,* p. 45.

105   "with great cordiality": Ibid., p. 46.

106   "nothing about packing": Brewer, *Up and Down California,* p. 505.

106   "his own astonishment": King, *Mountaineering,* p. 47.

107   "pollutes the air": Brewer, *Up and Down California,* p. 509.

107   "old mule": Ibid., p. 512.

107   "dark eye": King, *Mountaineering,* p. 47.

108   "about the neighborhood": Brewer, *Up and Down California,* p. 514.

108   "wonderful ride": Ibid., p. 515.

108    "reproduced on the other": King, *Mountaineering*, p. 52.
109    "points of view": Ibid., p. 53.
109    "impressive gloom": Ibid., p. 54.
109    "in camp": Ibid., p. 55.
110    "rest of the day": Ibid., p. 64.
110    "wet and numb with cold": Brewer, *Up and Down California*, p. 519.
110    "the Snow Group": King, *Mountaineering*, p. 66.
111    "ornamental finish": Ibid., pp. 67–68.
111    "be the first": Ibid., p. 65.
111    "in lieu of buttons": Ibid., p. 64.


## Chapter Six: The Top of California

114    "disappearing altogether": King, *Mountaineering*, p. 69.
114    "privileged to behold": Brewer, *Up and Down California*, pp. 524–25.
115    "terrible fatigue": King, *Mountaineering*, p. 69.
115    "points in California": Ibid., p. 70.
116    "forty pounds apiece": Ibid., p. 71.
117    "might not go": Ibid., pp. 74–75.
117    "highest peak in the range": Ibid., p. 75.
117    "microscopic forms": Ibid., p. 76.
118    "precipitous slope": Ibid., pp. 76–77.
118    "amphitheater": Ibid., p. 77.
118    "miserably tepid tea": Ibid., p. 78.
118    "many tons": Ibid., p. 79.
118    "thawed them out together!": Ibid., pp. 79–80.
119    "soundness until four": Ibid., p. 80.
119    "more than ordinary courage": Farquhar, *History of the Sierra Nevada*, p. 145.
120    "led to rather deeper steps": King, *Mountaineering*, p. 81.
120    "up the smooth cliff": Ibid., pp. 81–82.
121    "without once stopping to rest": Ibid., p. 83.
121    "almost Yosemite cliff": Whitney, *Geology*, p. 385.
122    "many accordant bells": King, *Mountaineering*, p. 84.
122    "seemed untraversable": Ibid., p. 85.
123    "all the help in his power": Ibid., p. 86.
124    "took quite coolly": Ibid., p. 87.
124    "strain upon any point": Ibid., p. 88.
125    "walking was a delicious rest": Ibid., p. 89.
125    "quintessence of gastronomy": Ibid., p. 90.
126    "cobalt-blue penetrated": Ibid., pp. 92–93.
127    "MOUNT TYNDALL": Ibid., p. 94.
127    "glorious, but inaccessible": Ibid., p. 95.
127    "grand old glacier": Whitney, *Geology*, p. 386.
128    "watery expanse": King, *Mountaineering*, pp. 95–96.
128    "Ruskin's sublime": Michael L. Smith, *Pacific Visions: California Scientists and the Environment, 1850–1915*, p. 88.

129  "a great Alp": Ruskin, *Modern Painters*, p. 470.
129  "no shadow cools the glare": King, *Mountaineering*, p. 96.
129  "empty and dark": Ibid., p. 97.
129  "desolation, desolation!": Ibid., p. 98.
130  "snow-ridge": Ibid., p. 100.
130  "rough-hewn walls of rocks and snow": Ibid.
131  "constant victory": Ibid., p. 102.
131  "sharp and rugged": Ibid., p. 103.
132  "held us": Ibid., p. 104.
132  "gymnastics I ever witnessed": Ibid., p. 108.
133  "courage as this of Cotter's": Ibid., p. 109.
134  "It becomes my painful duty to inform you": Ibid., p. 111.
134  "performed on the Survey": Brewer, *Up and Down California*, p. 527.

## Chapter Seven: Tall Tales

136  "beans to eat": Brewer, *Up and Down California*, p. 527.
136  "jerked bear meat": Whitney, *Geology*, p. 388.
136  "indescribably funny": King, *Mountaineering*, p. 112.
137  "eye and the compass": Whitney, *Geology*, p. 389.
137  "in the midst of every difficulty": Ibid., p. 390.
138  "returned to the plains": King, *Mountaineering*, p. 129.
138  "beyond the animal": King, "Journal of Trip in Northern Sierras," (D23), entry for October 10, 1863.
139  "is not wit": E. C. Stedman, quoted in Marcus Cunliffe, *The Literature of the United States*, p. 188.
139  "a single bombshell": King, *Mountaineering*, p. 113.
140  "then again they's better": Ibid., p. 114.
140  "city of York": Ibid., p. 116.
140  "pootiest band of hogs in Tulare County!": Ibid., p. 117.
141  "queenly poise of her head": Ibid., p. 121.
141  "start for Montana": Ibid., p. 124.
141  "won't you, say?" Ibid., p. 127.
141  "hard, repulsive figures": Ibid., p. 128.
141  "flitted about during the day": Ibid., p. 129.
142  "stolidity and utter cruelty": Ibid., p. 130.
142  "lonely sort of landscape": Ibid., p. 131.
142  "half-dollar ferriage": Ibid., p. 133.
143  "Hold on, you—!": Ibid., p. 135.
143  "deep-heaving breath": Ibid., p. 136.
143  "shocks from a battery": Ibid., p. 137.
144  "a sort of pleasantry": Ibid., p. 140.
144  "wonder and sympathy": Ibid., p. 142.
145  "even in California": Wilkins, *Clarence King*, p. 73.
145  "nothing of interest": "Notes on Mount Whitney Trip," July 1864 (B1), King Papers. From Wilkins, *Clarence King*, p. 451n.

146    "sublimity": Brewer, *Up and Down California*, p. 531.
146    Attempt to reach Mount Goddard: Whitney, *Geology*, p. 399.
147    "eight to do": Brewer, *Up and Down California*, p. 543.
147    "horses poor": Ibid., p. 547.
148    "Switzerland": Edwin T. Brewster, *Josiah Dwight Whitney*, pp. 237–38. From Goetzmann, *Exploration and Empire*, p. 374.
148    "a significant way": Goetzmann, *Exploration and Empire*, p. 377.
148    "Olmsted and others": Wilkins, *Clarence King*, p. 75.
148    "inalienable for all time": Rybczynski, *A Clearing in the Distance*, p. 238.
149    "eight-man commission": Wilkins, *Clarence King*, p. 75.
149    "use, resort, and recreation": Quoted in Farquhar *History of the Sierra Nevada*, p. 123, from Raymond to Conness (February 20, 1864). The Act of June 30, 1864, is given in full in *Laws and Regulations Relating to the Yosemite National Park, California*, 1908.
149    "mountain trails": King, *Mountaineering*, p. 152.
150    "with emotion": Lafayette Bunnell, *Discovery of the Yosemite and the Indian War of 1851, Which Led to That Event*, p. 63; see also pp. 78–79. From Goetzmann, *Exploration and Empire*, p. 369.
151    "dismount and inflate": King, *Mountaineering*, pp. 165–66.
152    "cannot have been very long": Whitney, *Geology*, p. 423.
153    "attempt it at all hazards": King, *Mountaineering*, pp. 167–68.
153    "rain of sparks": Ibid., p. 177.
153    "long parabolic curve": Ibid., p. 172.
154    "geological Micawber": Ibid., p. 174.
154    "refused to go on": Ibid., p. 175.
155    "beating them constantly with clubs": Ibid., p. 176.
155    "thick coating": Ibid., p. 177.
155    "shot off their loads": Ibid., p. 179.
155    "monotonous roar": Ibid., p. 182.
156    "at all costs": Ibid., p. 186.
157    "labor on": Ibid., p. 187.
157    "first-class hotel prices": Ibid., p. 191.
158    "chill in our bones": Ibid.

## Part Three: Geologist in Charge

159    General sources for fictional passage: King, *Mountaineering*; Wilkins, *Clarence King*; *Clarence King Memoirs*; Goetzmann, *Exploration and Empire*; Richard A. Bartlett, *Great Surveys of the American West*.

## Chapter Eight: Making the Leap

164    "suspended life": "The Biographers of Lincoln," *Century Magazine*, 32 (October 1886), p. 864.
164    "see him": W. D. Whitney to J. D. Whitney, February 26, 1865, W. D. Whitney

Collection of Whitney Family Papers, Yale Univiversity Library. From Wilkins, *Clarence King*, p. 452n.

165 "parts of Arizona": King, "Report on Arizona Reconnaissance," 1866 (B11), King Papers. From Wilkins, *Clarence King*, p. 452n.

165 "get their scalps": J. D. Whitney to W. D. Whitney, December 24, 1865, W. D. Whitney Collection of Whitney Family Papers, Yale University Library. From Wilkins, *Clarence King*, p. 452n.

166 "this Christian century": King, *Mountaineering*, p. 59.

167 "fit to be exterminated": Ibid., p. 60.

167 "satisfaction of loneliness": Ibid., p. 33.

168 "obsolete upon the ground": Ibid., p. 34.

168 "green grove": Ibid., p. 35.

168 "wall of the Sierra": Ibid., p. 36.

168 "blood-warm": Ibid., p. 38.

168 "in a long sleep": Ibid., p. 41.

168 "unfolding of plant life": Ibid., p. 42.

168 "distant lowing of cattle": Ibid.

169 "epaulets": J. D. Whitney to Brewer, April 25, 1866 (C-B 312: 208, Bancroft Library, University of California, Berkeley). From Wilkins, *Clarence King*, p. 452n.

170 "open granite country": Ibid., p. 213.

170 "sapphire zenith": Ibid., p. 214.

171 "utterly inaccessible": Ibid., p. 215.

171 "a hundred feet above": Ibid., p. 216.

171 "to the edge": Farquhar, *History of the Sierra Nevada*, p. 150.

171 "dashed to atoms": King, *Mountaineering*, p. 217.

171 "Clark is inaccessible": Farquhar, *History of the Sierra Nevada*, pp. 150–51.

172 "the narrow pedestal": King, *Mountaineering*, p. 218.

172 "my Sunday mountain": Ibid.

172 "southern group": Gardner's journal, 1866. From Farquhar, *History of the Sierra Nevada*, p. 151.

172 "Minarets": Ibid.

172 "aptness": Wilkins, *Clarence King*, p. 87.

172 "had not vanquished us": King, *Mountaineering*, p. 218.

172 "duplicate his perils": Wilkins, *Clarence King*, p. 87.

173 "rare and singular feature": Chaffin, *Pathfinder*, p. 327.

174 "ought to be done": *Clarence King Memoirs*, p. 334.

175 "c. r. king, supt.": Yosemite Notebook, 1864, back flap, King Papers. From Wilkins, *Clarence King*, p. 452n.

176 "on me alone": King to Henry Adams, September 25, 1889 (Emmons transcript), Emmons Papers, Manuscript Division, Library of Congress. From Wilkins, *Clarence King*, p. 453n.

## Chapter Nine: Strong Men

178 "easy thing to get": Bartlett, *Great Surveys,* p. 144.

179 "to do so": Quoted in Bartlett, *Great Surveys,* p. 143.

179 "good fellow": "New Haven Memoranda" (A2), King Papers. From Wilkins, *Clarence King,* p. 453n.

179 "their mere merits": Notes on King for Rossiter W. Raymond, King Papers. From Wilkins, *Clarence King,* p. 453n.

179 "Fortieth Parallel Survey": Ibid.

180 "gold mine": *New York Times,* May 8, 1867.

180 "United States Geologist": *Clarence King Memoirs,* p. 382.

181 "modern act of legislation": Adams, *Education,* p. 1005.

181 in Adams's estimation, modern: Wilkins, *Clarence King,* p. 102.

182 "plants and animals": Humphreys to King, March 21, 1867, King Survey Letters Rec'd (R.G. 57, Washington, D.C., National Archives). From Wilkins, *Clarence King,* p. 454n.

182 "satisfy me": King to Spencer Baird, March 28, 1867, Smithsonian Institution Letters Rec'd 1867. From Wilkins, *Clarence King,* p. 454n.

182 "your place": *Clarence King Memoirs,* p. 385.

183 "my tortured body": William Whitney Bailey, "To California" (HM 39965, Huntington Library, San Marino, California).

184 "expenses necessary": Quoted in James D. Horan, *Timothy O'Sullivan: America's Forgotten Photographer,* p. 156.

186 "photographer's camera": Ibid., p. 34.

187 "protection of the travelers": Ibid., p. 152.

187 "blowpipe apparatus": Bartlett, *Great Surveys,* p. 154.

187 "flow of language": Bailey, "To California."

188 "vulgar guffaw": Ibid.

188 "temperance one": Ibid.

188 "identical U.S. flag": Ibid.

188 "meadows of the sea": Ibid.

189 "Panama hat and a cigar": Ibid.

189 " 'cu-rosities!' ": Ibid.

189 "thrust upon him": *Clarence King Memoirs,* p. 387.

190 "nursing child": Ibid., p. 389.

190 "acquaintance with it": Bailey, "To California."

190 "more commodious": Ibid.

190 "hours of the day": Ibid.

191 "infectious laugh": Ibid.

191 "sail on the Pacific": Ibid.

192 "hardened to it": Goetzmann, *Exploration and Empire,* p. 438.

193 "well mounted and well armed": King, August 3, 1867, "Copy Book of Letters" (Washington, D.C., National Archives, R.G. 57).

193 "were with us": Robert Ridgway. Quoted in Harry Harris, "Robert Ridgway," *The Condor* 30, no. 1 ( January-February 1928), p. 22.

## Part Four: The Fortieth Parallel

195     General sources for fictional passage: Wilkins, *Clarence King*; Roosevelt, *The Wilderness Hunter*; Bronson, *Reminiscences of a Ranchman*; *Clarence King Memoirs*; Goetzmann, *Exploration and Empire*; Bartlett, *Great Surveys*.

## Chapter Ten: Between Missouri and Hell

198     "scientific thoroughness": *The Engineering and Mining Journal,* January 4, 1902, p. 4.

199     "model of her class": Quoted in John Sampson's "Photographs from the High Rockies," *Harper's New Monthly Magazine* 39 (September 1869), pp. 469–70.

200     "mad velocity": Ibid.

200      O'Sullivan's rescue of the *Nettie*: Ibid.

201     "twenty-dollar gold pieces": Ibid.

201     "barefooted, for it": Ibid. (See also Harris, *The Condor,* p. 24.)

201     "alive with rattlesnakes": Sampson, "Photographs from the High Rockies," p. 468.

202     "the sandhills": King to Humphreys, June 4, 1868, King Survey Letter Book. From Wilkins, *Clarence King,* p. 454n.

203     "Missouri and Hell": Quoted in Goetzmann, *Exploration and Empire,* p. 440.

203     "horrors of the place": Quoted in Horan, *Timothy O'Sullivan,* pp. 163–64. See also "Ornithology," *Report of the Geological Exploration of the Fortieth Parallel* 4, p. 3, p. 353, and Harris, *The Condor,* p. 25.

203     "sick and 'queer' ": Harris, *The Condor,* p. 25.

204     "a great storm": King to Humphreys, December 18, 1867, "Copy Book of Letters" (Washington, D.C., National Archives, R.G. 57). From Bartlett, *Great Surveys,* p. 168.

204     "plague of mosquitoes": Wilkins, *Clarence King,* p. 115.

205     "on the continent": King to Humphreys, December 18, 1867, King Survey Letter Book. From Wilkins, *Clarence King,* p. 455n.

205     "complete success": Ibid.

206     "our meals": Bailey to editor, *Providence Journal,* January 26, 1868 (published Feb. 28, 1868, p. 1, col. 8). From Wilkins, *Clarence King,* p. 455n.

206     "a jaunty contrast": Wilkins, *Clarence King,* p. 120.

206     "Kingy" and "Deany": Ibid.

207     "physical mergence": "Private Notes," 1867–68 (D12), King Papers. From Wilkins, *Clarence King,* p. 455n.

207     "private reasons which you can guess": King to Hague, April 6 [1869], J. D. Hague Collection. From Wilkins, *Clarence King,* p. 457n.

207     intended to marry Deany then: Wilkins, *Clarence King,* p. 137.

208     "refrain from marrying the woman": King to Adams, September 25, 1889, Emmons transcript, Emmons Papers. From Wilkins, *Clarence King,* p. 457n.

211     "in the world": King to Humphreys, July 10, 1868, King Survey Letter Book. From Wilkins, *Clarence King,* p. 455n.

212 "like a bloodhound": "C.K.'s notes for [Hague's] biographical notice of him." From Wilkins, *Clarence King*, p. 456n.

213 "to obedience": Ibid. See also "Deserter Arrested," *Daily Reese River Reveille*, July 23, 1868. From Wilkins, *Clarence King*, p. 456n.

213 "Indian fighting army": Horan, *Timothy O'Sullivan*, p. 167.

214 "beneath our feet": King, *Mountaineering*, p. 202.

215 "nearly to the river": Ibid., p. 203.

215 "gloom of the place": Ibid.

215 "Rocky Mountain scenes": Sampson, "Photographs from the High Rockies," p. 472.

215 "masses of rock": Ibid.

216 "burst into rhetoric": King, *Mountaineering*, p. 165.

216 "wild scene beyond": Sampson, "Photographs from the High Rockies," p. 472.

216 "foreground of sage": King, *Mountaineering*, p. 207.

217 "ideas of restraint": Ibid., p. 210.

217 "precipice": Ibid., p. 211.

217 "sagebrush": Adams, *The Education of Henry Adams*, pp. 311–12.

## Chapter Eleven: Rising in the Sagebrush

220 "West Pointers in the outfit?": *Clarence King Memoirs*, p. 384.

221 "*unopened fields*": King to Humphreys, August 26, 1869, R.G. 57, Washington, D.C., National Archives.

223 "Great Basin": Bartlett, *Great Surveys*, p. 179.

223 "this child's lot": King, "Miscellaneous notes . . . 1870" (D19), King Papers. From Wilkins, *Clarence King*, p. 457n.

224 "half-luminous haze": King, *Mountaineering*, p. 197.

224 "the pioneer guide of the region": Ibid., 241.

224 "twelve thousand feet altitude": Ibid., p. 240.

224 "a thousand feet deep": Ibid., p. 242.

224 "blocks in the crater": Ibid.

224 "surfaces of ice": Ibid., pp. 242-43.

225 "glaciers everywhere": King, *American Journal of Science*, 3rd ser., 1 (1871).

225 "comparatively easy one": King, *Mountaineering*, p. 247.

225 "water-curved cañon": Ibid., p. 249.

225 "exist in the United States": King to Humphreys, October 10, 1870, King Survey Letter Book. From Wilkins, *Clarence King*, p. 457n.

225 "found the glaciers!": *Clarence King Memoirs*, p. 323.

226 "American geology": King to Humphreys, January 23, 1871, King Survey Letter Book. From Wilkins, *Clarence King*, p. 458n.

226 "Massachusetts": John Jay Chapman, *Memories and Milestones*, pp. 241–42. See also M. A. DeWolfe Howe, ed., *John Jay Chapman and His Letters*, pp. 121–22. From Wilkins, *Clarence King*, p. 458n.

227 "above the whole Sierra": King, *Mountaineering*, p. 282.

228 "Conness": Ibid., p. 277.

229 "almost indigo hue": Ibid., p. 284.

229  "not noticeable for their cheerfulness": Ibid., p. 285.

229  "valley of the Kern": Ibid., p. 286.

230  "pressure due to storm": Ibid., p. 291.

230  "pure delight": Ibid., p. 292.

230  "those who came before me": Quoted in W. F. Bade, *Life and Letters of John Muir*, vol. 1, p. 396. From Wilkins, *Clarence King*, p. 459n.

231  "vivid and graphic kind": *Clarence King Memoirs*, p. 139.

231  "vanished from actuality": Ibid., p. 155.

232  "took charge": Adams, *The Education of Henry Adams*, p. 1003.

232  "never a matter of growth or doubt": Ibid., p. 1004.

232  "far towards dawn": Ibid.

232  "fogs of London": Ibid., pp. 1004–5.

233  "so deep a trail": Ibid., p. 1005.

233  "a trifle": Henry Adams, *North American Review* 114 (April 1872), pp. 445–48.

233  "their meeting": Samuels, *Henry Adams*, p. 97.

233  King's effect on the friendship of Hay and Adams. Ibid., pp. 176–77.

## Chapter Twelve: Pretty Crystals

236  "eyes of man": *Tucson Arizonian*, April 9, 1870. Quoted in Bruce A. Woodard, *Diamonds in the Salt*, p. 11.

236  "see them": *Statistics of Mines and Mining in the States and Territories West of the Rocky Mountains*, 42nd Cong., 2nd sess., 1872, House Executive Document 211, p. 27. Quoted in Woodard, *Diamonds in the Salt*, p. 18.

237  "ablaze with brilliants": *San Francisco Chronicle*, November 14, 1872.

237  "weather-beaten": Asbury Harpending, *The Great Diamond Hoax and Other Stirring Incidents in the Life of Asbury Harpending*, p. 146.

238  "rough diamonds": Ibid.

239  "districts of the West": Wilkins, *Clarence King*, p. 171.

239  "pretty crystals": Samuel Emmons, unpublished diary, October 6, 1872, Box 32, Emmons Papers, Manuscript Division, Library of Congress.

240  "our discoveries": *Louisville Courier-Journal*, December 16, 1872. Quoted in Woodard, *Diamonds in the Salt*, p. 22.

241  "needed as ringmaster": Harpending, *The Great Diamond Hoax*, p. 143.

241  "carry us": Ibid., p. 144.

242  "diamonds cut": Leopold Keller, *Times* (London), December 24, 1874.

242  "to my home": Harpending, *The Great Diamond Hoax*, p. 148.

242  "cataract of light": Ibid., p. 149.

243  "nonchalance": Ibid., p. 87.

244  "enormous value": Ibid., p. 152.

244  "report on": Samuel Emmons, "The Diamond Discovery of 1872," Box 32, Emmons Papers.

245  "cross and quarrelsome": Harpending, *The Great Diamond Hoax*, p. 156.

245  "an oversight": Ibid., p. 157.

246  "Utah, and Wyoming": Emmons, "Diamond Discovery of 1872."

247 "bought from soldier": Emmons, unpublished diary, October 29, 1872, Box 32, Emmons Papers.

247 "crude castanets": Emmons, "Diamond Discovery of 1872."

247 "found a small ruby": Ibid.

247 "might be gathered": Ibid.

248 "in the crust": Ibid.

248 "end of a stick": Ibid.

248 "with the surroundings": Ibid.

248 "carats around here?" Ibid.

248 "sell short": Ibid.

248 "in the stock": King to Humphreys, November 27, 1872, R.G. 77, Washington, D.C., National Archives.

249 "desert and mountain": Ibid.

249 "its correctness": Ibid.

249 "utter consternation": Ibid.

249 "a single hour": Emmons, "Diamond Discovery of 1872."

249 "Bunker Hill Monument": David Colton, Report, *San Francisco Evening Bulletin,* November 25, 1872.

250 "swindles ever perpetuated": *San Francisco Evening Bulletin,* November 26, 1872.

250 "how the millionaires were victimized": *San Francisco Chronicle,* November 26, 1872.

251 "a good Henry rifle": *Louisville Courier-Journal,* December 16, 1872. From Woodard, *Diamonds in the Salt,* p. 123.

251 Arnold's fate: Ibid., pp. 166–67.

251 "God and CLARENCE KING": *San Francisco Chronicle,* editorial, November 28, 1872.

251 "the only right way": *San Francisco Evening Bulletin,* editorial, November 27, 1872.

252 "knowledge of the continent": *Clarence King Memoirs,* pp. 240–41.

252 "manhood is traversed," King, *Mountaineering,* p. iv.

253 "scientist in America": H. H. Bancroft, *Literary Industries,* p. 178. From Wilkins, *Clarence King,* p. 461n.

253 "King's personality": Wilkins, *Clarence King,* p. 186.

253 "King of Diamonds": J. D. Whitney to Brewer, January 5, 1873, Farquhar transcript, present whereabouts unknown. From Wilkins, *Clarence King,* p. 462n.

## Epilogue: Change or Die

258 "greatest graduate": Quoted in A. Phelps Stokes, *Memorials of Eminent Yale Men,* vol. 2, p. 82. From Wilkins, *Clarence King,* p. 447n.

258 "his science": *The Nation,* August 30, 1877, p. 137.

258 "advanced students": *Clarence King Memoirs,* p. 271.

259 "violent modifications": *The Nation,* August 30, 1877, p. 137.

260 "rouse curiosity": Ibid.

260 "misconstruction": Ibid.

260    "archaic belief": *The American Naturalist* 11, no. 8 (August 1877), p. 451.
260    "scientific induction": Ibid.
260    "mechanism of imagination": Ibid.
260    "facts of the other": Ibid., p. 452.
261    "bringing them to a stop": Ibid., p. 454.
261    "widest dynamic sense": Ibid., p. 457.
261    "south and west shores": Ibid., p. 459.
262    "fatal blow": Ibid., p. 460.
262    "infinite time": Ibid., p. 461.
262    "the two ideas": Ibid., p. 463.
262    "built upon uniformitarianism": Ibid., pp. 464–65.
262    "used his fan vigorously": George F. Becker to Henry Draper, July 2, 1877. Draper Papers, New York Public Library. From Wilkins, *Clarence King*, p. 465n.
262    "geologic environment": *The American Naturalist* 11, no. 8 (August 1877), p. 467.
262    "salvation": Ibid., p. 469.
263    "called into being": Ibid., p. 470.
263    "the most efficient": Wilkins, *Clarence King*, p. 223.
263    "not Darwinism": Gould, *The Panda's Thumb*, p. 182.
264    "these punctuations": Ibid., p. 184.

# PHOTO CREDITS

Page ii. Courtesy of the U.S. Geological Survey Library, Reston, Virginia

Page 1. Courtesy of the U.S. Geological Survey Library

Page 21. A Stanhope photograph from the Wilfred Warren Collection. Courtesy of the Providence Public Library, Providence, Rhode Island.

Page 41. Courtesy of the Library of Congress, Washington, D.C.

Page 61. Courtesy of the Library of Congress. Photograph by John C. H. Grabill, circa 1887.

Page 77. Courtesy of the Bancroft Library, University of California, Berkeley

Page 97. Courtesy of the U.S. Geological Survey Library. Photograph by F. E. Matthes, July 1935.

Page 113. Courtesy of the Bancroft Library, University of California, Berkeley

Page 135. Courtesy of the Library of Congress

Page 163. *Clarence King Memoirs* (1904), Courtesy of the U.S. Geological Survey Library

Page 177. Courtesy of the Library of Congress

Page 197. Courtesy of the U.S. Geological Survey, Courtesy of the Library of Congress

Page 200. Courtesy of the Library of Congress

Page 209. Courtesy of the National Archives Record Administration, Washington, D.C.

Page 214. Courtesy of the Library of Congress

Page 219. Courtesy of the Massachusetts Historical Society, Boston

Page 235. Courtesy of the Bancroft Library, University of California, Berkeley

Page 255. Courtesy of the Library of Congress

# ACKNOWLEDGMENTS

I first met Clarence King in 1990, in the pages of Patricia O'Toole's fine book *The Five of Hearts*. Of the five friends she focused on, King was for me the most exciting, the most appealing, and the most alive. Because I wanted to know more about him, I did what editors do—I urged his story on some writers I knew. One of them, James Conaway, looked into King seriously enough to satisfy his own curiosity but what he found further whetted mine. Later, as I was writing the book, Jim would be a good person to test my thoughts on. I also talked to Edward Hoagland about King. Hoagland, who had included *Mountaineering in the Sierra Nevada* in a series of nature books he had edited, made King seem more intriguing still by warning that the things he wrote and said about himself were often far from reliable.

By the time I realized that I wanted to write about King myself, I had had the good luck to get to know Patricia O'Toole, who encouraged me to write my own book and later showed her characteristic generosity in sharing materials and advice with me. But I might never have begun without the faith and encouragement of Mary Bahr, a book publisher, editor, and friend. Mary urged me to draft a proposal and then shared it with several of her colleagues at Random House, where she then worked. Their thoughts, and Mary's, helped me begin to think about how I wanted to approach the subject. Soon my friend Adam Goodheart read the proposal and urged it upon his formidable agent, Sarah Chalfant of the Wylie Agency. Sarah offered to represent it, and then launched me on a months-long effort to enlarge and revise it. At one point during this time, another wise friend, Jay Tolson, read the proposal, which had grown to novella length, and offered some good ideas about it. The proposal-writing process was exhausting and at times unnerving, but it forced me to think concretely about King, and made writing the book that much easier.

Eventually Sarah and her assistant Zoe Pagnamenta delivered me into the steady and capable hands of Sarah McGrath of Scribner, who edited my book with a sureness that taught me things as an editor and a writer. While she was away on maternity leave her able assistant, Samantha Martin, kept things moving forward.

When you write your first book in your mid-fifties, too many people you need to acknowledge are no longer around to receive your thanks. First among these are my parents, Helen Hodnett Wilson and Joseph G. Wilson, both of whom died in the last few years. Three of my mentors, who taught me so much about writing and editing, James Boatwright, Peter Taylor, and Noel Perrin, are also out of earshot. Three more people whose memory I carry with me every day are my brother, Joe, my friend Doug Patrick, and my father-in-law, Nelson Ritchie.

One other mentor, Mario Pellicciaro, remains very much alive. His fierce intelligence has poked and prodded me—to what end, as he would probably say. But his friendship has been a refuge. Other friends on whom I have long relied include Russ Powell, Bill Geiger, Steve Goodwin, Tom Gibson, Cheryl Merser, Suzanne Freeman, Malcolm Jones, Ann Hulbert, Anne and Gus Edwards, Jon Wist, Steve Lagerfeld, Ann Beattie, Tom Mallon, Phyllis Rose, and Henry Sloss. Colleagues who have taught and sustained me include Mike Dirda, the late Reid Beddow, Steve Petranek, Craig Wilson, Deirdre Donahue, Ben Brown, Elizabeth Hightower, Brian Miller, David Herbick, Maggie Gamboa, Allen Freeman, Kim Keister, Sudip Bose, Arnold Berke, Sogand Sepassi, Ray Sachs, Richard Moe, Carl Lehmann-Haupt, Richard Nicholls, Jean Stipicevic, and Sandra Costich.

At *Smithsonian* magazine, where an article I wrote about the Great Diamond Hoax appeared in June 2004, Carey Winfrey deserves thanks for assigning it, James Gibney for editing it so deftly, and Brian Noyes, Molly Roberts, and Lyn Garrity for their help in presenting it.

Charles Trueheart, beacon and pal, gave me the title for my book. Anne Matthews and William Howarth showed unrepayable generosity by reading the edited manuscript and offering good advice about it. Doug Stern made the handsome maps. Andrew Starner helped me get photographs. Elyse Graham fact-checked the book, helped write the endnotes, and did photo research. Any errors of fact are of course mine.

For simulating the enthusiasm our mother would have felt for the book, I thank my sister, Laurie Kelly. I'm blessed with wonderful in-laws, too—Dot Ritchie, Susan Barritt, and Charlotte Gatto. My sons, Matt, Cole, Sam, have fueled me with the high-octane energy of paternal pride. Their mother, my wife, Martha Ritchie Wilson, to whom this book and everything I do are dedicated, has given my life its savor and its joy.

I thank you all.

# INDEX

# ABOUT THE AUTHOR

ROBERT WILSON, who was an award-winning editor at *Preservation* and *Civilization* magazines, now edits *The American Scholar*. He writes often for magazines and newspapers, and was on staff at *USA Today* and *The Washington Post*. He lives in Manassas, Virginia.